D0262405

Deliverance

# Deliverance

Everyday investigations into
poltergeists, ghosts and other
supernatural phenomena by
an Anglican priest

Jason Bray

CORONET

First published in Great Britain in 2020 by Coronet
An Imprint of Hodder & Stoughton
An Hachette UK company

4

A CIP catalogue record for this title is available from the British Library

Hardback ISBN 9781529336252
eBook ISBN 9781529336269

Typeset in Electra LH 11.5/16 pt by Palimpsest Book Production Limited,
Falkirk, Stirlingshire

Printed and bound in Great Britain by Clays Ltd, Elcograf S.p.A.

Hodder & Stoughton policy is to use papers that are natural,
renewable and recyclable products and made from wood grown in sustainable
forests. The logging and manufacturing processes are expected to conform to
the environmental regulations of the country of origin.

Hodder & Stoughton Ltd
Carmelite House
50 Victoria Embankment
London EC4Y 0DZ

For Laura, Thomas and Benedict, with love and thanks.

# Chapter 1

## Welcome to my world

When is a cold house more than just a cold house? The fear on my wife's face was the first real clue. After two days on the road, I had returned home to find a bothersome but apparently prosaic problem had twisted into something more puzzling – and a very logical person struggling to come up with logical answers.

'The baby was crying in the night,' said Laura, her voice wavering. 'When I went into his bedroom, it was like walking into a freezer. And it was *icy* by his cot. I was really frightened. I don't know what's going on . . .'

Laura and I had moved into our new home the previous summer, just before my ordination and when she was pregnant with our first child. It was an old council house that the Church felt was ideal for a curate. We first viewed it on a dull January afternoon, when it had been empty for six months, so we thought nothing of the fact that it was so dark and dank. And clergymen and women, especially newly ordained ones, accept the houses they're given.

The house remained cold throughout the long, sticky summer, at the end of which Tom was born and installed in the small bedroom at the front. When winter arrived and the weather took a turn for the worse, the old-fashioned two-bar gas fire in the living room was regularly employed and the heating set to full throttle. But the house refused to thaw. And Tom's room was coldest of all. I borrowed some keys and discovered that the radiator in the room next to Tom's was full of air. But even when every radiator in the house was ferociously hot, the temperature remained stubbornly chilly.

In those days before roving telephones or mobiles, calling family and friends could be an uncomfortable experience for us, owing to the icy draught that seemed to snake down the stairs. This was particularly weird given that the house had new, PVC double-glazed windows. Furthermore, when we tried to locate the source of the draught using a candle, the flame didn't budge. We hung internal curtains throughout the house, but they made no difference. One day, I attempted to drill a hole in the wall, only for the bit to melt because the bricks were so hard. The house was built from solid slag bricks, chilly to the touch, which we decided must be the root cause of our problems. It seemed as good a reason as any.

We considered moving Tom to a different room (the nursery had two external walls and was immediately above the front door), but he didn't seem troubled by the cold and his room had been lovingly decorated especially for him. So there he stayed. It seemed there was nothing else to be done. It was, alas, simply a cold house.

We'd just have to live with it. Then something happened that shook my trust in rational explanations, however thin on the ground they were.

I was reading in bed one night, when I decided that I should go to the bathroom before getting settled. Off I padded down the landing, before doing what I had to do. Having washed my hands, I turned towards the door. It was closed, but I sensed there was something – someone – standing on the other side, staring straight at me. A prickling sensation ran through me, from top to bottom. But it wasn't just a sense, it was a concrete vision. He – and I knew it was a he – was about my height and wearing a wooden mask, roughly twice as wide as his face, with sunrays shooting off in all directions. The mask had holes cut for his eyes which were drilling into mine. It was as if he was on tenterhooks, calculating whether I would react in a hostile manner. I realised instinctively that he was almost certainly a priest like me, although not a Christian priest. After a few seconds, I began to feel his malice towards me. I was absolutely terrified, rooted to the spot and unable to breathe. After what felt like minutes, but must have only been a few seconds, I summoned the courage to raise an arm, place limp fingers on the handle and pull the door towards me. There was nobody there.

I bolted across the landing, ran into the bedroom, threw myself under the covers and tried to tell Laura what I'd seen. I was a gibbering mess, in a state of breathless panic. And I kept insisting that what had happened couldn't have actually happened, because that would be ridiculous. But Laura suspected otherwise. She put a comforting arm around me and said, 'I think it's time we spoke to the vicar.'

I was still only a curate, and the vicar was my boss, so I was a little apprehensive about confiding in him. I worried that he'd think I'd lost my senses or was being melodramatic, and that he would dismiss my story as a figment of an overactive imagination. At the time, *I* suspected it was a figment of my overactive imagination. When I sidled up to the vicar at a cheese and wine party the following evening and said, 'There's some strange stuff going on in the house,' I was prepared to be embarrassed. I expected him to tell me to pull myself together and to recommend a good heating engineer. But, to my surprise and relief, he listened intently to my story and took me seriously. I think the fact that Laura also sensed a presence persuaded him that something other-worldly might be going on. Whatever the reason, his willingness to believe was a lesson I've never forgotten.

At first, the vicar suggested I bless the house myself. Then he paused before adding, 'Actually, maybe not. Given it's your house. I'll do it.'

I didn't know anything about the processes involved, so I was fascinated.

The vicar turned up to the house the following day with a Bible, a bottle of holy water and a sprinkler. Once inside, he walked from room to room while praying silently and blessing the house. When he entered Tom's room, he banished me and muttered prayers that he wouldn't let me see, possibly in Latin. Finally, we all gathered in the living room and said the Lord's Prayer.

The change was almost instant. Balance was restored. The house was light, and it was warm. Suddenly, we were having to turn the thermostat down. Some days we'd turn the heating off completely, in order to avoid melting. The draught on the stairs had gone. But it wasn't just that the house had become lighter and warmer. The atmosphere, which had been almost murky, felt less oppressive. Whatever had been there, with its focus on our baby's cot, was gone. Suddenly, the house was a nice place to be.

Soon after the vicar had done his work, a friend told me that he had never liked being in the house. Whenever he went upstairs to the toilet, he always found it creepy. Other visitors thought we had made alterations. They would look around and say, 'What have you done in here? It feels different.' I didn't tell them what had taken place, but it was nice that they now felt as welcome as we did.

We asked the next-door neighbour about the history of the house, more specifically if anyone had ever died within its walls. As far as she knew nobody had, and she had lived there since the houses were built. Apparently, the first people to live in the house had bought it from the council and sold it to the Church. The subsequent occupants had all been curates, like me, and were all very much alive. A chat with one of the church wardens proved more fruitful. Suddenly and out of the blue he said,

'Do you like the house?'

'Yes. It's quite a nice place to live.'

'Interesting history. When they were digging the foundations for the house, they disturbed a Roman graveyard, next to the main road out of town.'

I affected nonchalance, but the warden's words got me thinking. I didn't know what was going in our house. And I was happy not knowing. But maybe something had attached itself? More specifically, maybe that something had had a particular attraction to our son.

Whatever might have been in our house, it hadn't seemed particularly harmful. But it hadn't been pleasant to live with either, not least the masked 'priest' making unscheduled appearances outside our bathroom. However, because it was my house, my family and my story, I was now determined to find out as much as I could about the possible causes. Perhaps there really were more things in Heaven and on Earth than we already knew about.

## *The deliverance minister*

This all happened over twenty years ago. Since then I have had many more experiences of dealing with what you might call the paranormal, but I am, at heart, your classic Anglican vicar. I am the person at the front of the church on a Sunday dressed in a white robe and a coloured poncho who sings weird chants at you and tells you how much God loves you. And I am the person who then stands at the back by the door, listens to people's problems, shakes their hands and, if I have the chance, sits and drinks coffee with them. I am the priest who will baptise or christen your child, pouring water over their heads, hoping they are not going to scream. I am the vicar who will conduct your wedding for you, who will guide you as gently as possible through the vows, and then invite you to kiss one another for the photos – I'll even get out of the way at this point, so that I'm not in shot! I am also the priest who will come and see you when you have lost your loved one in order to arrange the funeral, and who will then officiate at it. But I do a whole load of other things too. I sit through endless meetings of the church council, where we discuss people, money and buildings, and I go to lots of other meetings too. Some are to do with the church either locally or nationally, and some are to do with charity and community work. I also work extensively with local government departments. Over the course of an average week, in addition to the people who come for church services, I meet all sorts of people: tourists who are wandering round the church, people who have dropped in for a coffee, the church volunteers, the folk who come in for one of the community activities we run, as well as the people who have come to book in for a wedding or a christening. And, yes, we go to cheese and wine evenings, and, yes, the annual church fete is one of the high-lights of the year. That would all be pretty standard for the vicar of a busy parish – and in case you're wondering, 'vicar' is the name we give to Anglican priests who are in charge of parishes, although it does tend to be used as a general term for all Anglican priests.

Most vicars are full time, so almost by tradition we often have specialist areas of interest. Over the years, for example, I have done a lot of teaching, lecturing and training of other priests and of people who are interested in ministry, but don't necessarily want to be priests. I have also trained as a spiritual director, which means people can come to see me to discuss what is going on in their spiritual lives. And I am also a deliverance minister.

Deliverance ministers are experienced priests who are trained and given special permission to deal with the paranormal: in other words, we are exorcists, although we tend not to use the word. Very often it conjures up the wrong image and most of what we do doesn't necessarily fit into the category of exorcism as such – if by that you mean expelling demons from people who are possessed. We call what we do 'deliverance ministry' because we believe that what we are doing is delivering them from whatever it is that is afflicting them, although often the solution is not quite what they were expecting.

Dealing with expectations, to be honest, can be difficult. Despite the fact that I always dress entirely in black (although I also have a sideline in garish waistcoats), that I often wear a long black coat, and I sometimes sport a black trilby – oh and I also have a black bag I take round with me – when I arrive to talk to people about whatever is happening in their lives, I never walk in and say, 'I am the exorcist.' I usually say something along the lines of, 'Hi, I'm Jason, I've been sent to sort out your problem,' more like the gas man than your conventional

Hollywood exorcist. These people will probably already be frightened of what's happening around them, the last thing they need is to be frightened of me too. But they do need to have enough confidence in me to believe that what I do and say will help them deal with the issue.

Each Anglican diocese will have a team of people like me who act as consultants when they are needed, to go out with local vicars to deal with cases that come in, or simply to deal with them and report back to the bishop. We are specifically recruited by the bishop who oversees the diocese, and we conduct this ministry in the bishop's name and with the bishop's permission. This means that we are also covered by his or her insurance. We are never very busy. In fact, months will frequently go by without any cases coming in, and then we will be called out three or four times in as many weeks.

Despite the fact that there is a huge amount of public interest, the whole field of deliverance ministry is veiled in secrecy, to the extent that even well informed people are surprised when they discover that there are exorcists in the Anglican Church.

## The exploding vase

'Hello? Is that the vicar?'
The woman's voice sounded harsh and raspy.

'My house is haunted. I've tried everything. I need you to come round.'

When my phone rings, it could be about dozens of different things. Often it is somebody wanting to book a wedding, christening or funeral. The stuff vicars generally do. Sometimes, it is somebody complaining about the state of the churchyard or telling me that their grandmother has been admitted to hospital.

Some of those comedy vicars you see on TV are incredibly true to life. Indeed, the sitcom *Rev* is so true to life that I mentioned it once – probably at a cheese and wine party or jumble sale – and somebody said, 'You mean that fly on the wall documentary about the vicar in London?' It was hard to convince them it was actually an unerringly accurate satire.

I feel myself going into *Rev* mode occasionally, largely because most of the situations he encounters are genuine. But every now and again, somebody will call to inform me that something supernatural is happening in their home.

The woman on the phone had called me apparently by accident, having used the telephone directory (remember them?) to ring a random Church in Wales parish, but when she began to explain her problem, I realised she might just have called the right person. She explained that she was a single mother with a 17-year-old son, who had lived with her in the house since he was born. The house had held no horrors until about a year earlier, when strange things started happening.

'It started with stupid things,' said Mary. 'My son kept losing his socks. I kept buying them and he kept losing them. It was driving me mad. Sometimes it was one sock, sometimes it was the pair of them. I'd put them out at night, and they'd be gone in the morning. Not always, but often enough to be worrying. Then there were the shoes. Usually, I'd find my shoes at the top of the stairs in the morning, but sometimes his. This really freaked me out, because I knew it wasn't him that moved them. Even he wouldn't be stupid enough to leave my shoes on the stairs at night. One night, I nearly killed myself tripping over them. I was scared. I thought about talking to a medium, but my auntie warned me against it. So, I called in a priest.'

As I listened, I couldn't help thinking that this wasn't particularly interesting. Who hasn't wondered where their socks have disappeared to? And it was hardly beyond the realms of possibility that the son was moving her shoes and simply not telling her. But I have a duty as a deliverance minister not to jump to conclusions – I've heard untold stories about people being told they're making things up – and what she said next certainly got my attention.

'The priest came around,' said Mary, who had been raised a Catholic, 'and he blessed the house, went around the place splashing holy water about.'

'Did that work?' I asked.

'No. It got worse. We were in the kitchen one night, just me and my useless son. I was telling him off for something he'd done and there was suddenly a rattling sound coming from behind us. It felt like a train was making the house shake. Then the cutlery drawer flew open and the knives started moving around. I was terrified, as you can imagine. And my son just sat there with his mouth wide open.'

'Anything else?'

'Yes. We were in the kitchen again the following evening and had been drinking Coke. I hadn't put the top back on the bottle and suddenly it came straight at me. I ducked and it just missed my head and hit the wall behind me. I was screaming my bloody head off.'

'What did you do next?'

'I rang the priest again and told him his blessing hadn't worked. In fact, it had made things worse.'

'And what did he say?'

'He asked if anyone had been playing with a Ouija board. I told him I wouldn't go anywhere near them and my son said he hadn't either. I had no reason not to believe him, because he never has anyone round. But when I mentioned it to my brother, he admitted that he'd used a Ouija board once with his mates, on Halloween. So, the priest thought he had his answer.'

You couldn't blame the priest for thinking he'd solved the mystery. I assume he pictured a bunch of young men huddled around a Ouija board on Halloween, trying to contact the dead on the day that, according to folklore, the dead are said to walk. Mary didn't know what had happened that night – whether the glass had moved around the board of its own accord, conveying a message from the dead to the group; whether the glass had smashed, perhaps because the spirit was angry that one or more of the men were laughing at it. But perhaps the priest thought the spirit had sought revenge and seen an opportunity to cross the divide that separates this world from the next. Perhaps he thought the spirit had attached itself to Mary's brother, and then from him to her son. Thereafter, perhaps, it had spent its time trying to frighten them away.

Mary then banned her brother from her house and begged the priest to try to help her again. The priest returned to the house and said a Requiem Mass, to lay to rest the soul of the unquiet dead. Requiem Masses are common at funerals but are also part of the stock-in-trade of deliverance ministers, Catholic and Anglican. In Mary's living room the priest, fully robed and surrounded by candles, crucifixes, holy water and incense, would have prayed over bread and wine, which would have become the body and blood of Jesus. Jesus' presence should have banished the forces of evil and ushered the dead soul to the next phase of its existence, hopefully forever.

'So, what happened?' I asked, slightly puzzled.

'It got bloody worse,' barked Mary. 'So, I thought I'd try you instead.'

Mary's bluntness had the effect of turning what might have been a solemn conversation into something resembling a comedy sketch.

'Not long after the priest said Mass,' continued Mary, 'I was at the bottom of the stairs and my son was standing at the top. I was giving him hell because he hadn't done his chores, even though he'd been back from college for hours. And then it happened.'

'What happened?'

'Just behind me on a windowsill was my favourite vase. It was this beautiful, big blue vase that my mother gave me, God rest her soul. And suddenly, while I was shouting at my son, it exploded. Shattered into a thousand pieces. It was like a bomb had gone off inside it. I loved that vase. It was all I had left from my mother . . .'

Mary's voice cracked, as bluntness gave way to raw emotion. When she had composed herself, she added,

'Do you think it might have been my mother's ghost?'

'No,' I said, in what I hoped was a reassuring tone. 'The Requiem Mass should probably have dealt with anything like that.'

'Probably?' snapped Mary.

'Yes.'

'Are you sure?'

'Definitely.'

'So it wasn't my mother then?'

'It definitely wasn't your mother.'

The phone went silent for a couple of seconds before Mary added, 'Can you help me?'

'I hope so . . .'

The parish she lived in was between vicars at the time, so I had to get permission from the area dean to do this. To be honest, he was only too delighted not to have to deal with it.

It was a beautiful sunny morning when I visited Mary's house, a couple of days after our phone conversation. As is often, I took a colleague along, in this case a woman. Mary lived in one of those small leafy Monmouthshire towns which have quaint-looking town centres and large villas in their own grounds on the outskirts. But, as so frequently with these places, there were also pockets of significant deprivation. And from her description of her circumstances, I suspected Mary lived in one of the small council estates that had been left behind while the world around them was gentrified.

There was nothing obviously spooky about Mary's house, which was an unremarkable 1950s semi-detached council house set just back from a main road – at least I was right about that. Mary was in her late thirties and you only had to take one look at her to know that life had been tough. Sunk deep into her hard face were two frightened eyes. They also seemed suspicious, as if she felt she was being judged and found wanting in some way.

She showed us into her living room, before explaining that she had been 'on the sick' for years. She also explained, somewhat contemptuously, that her son should have been there to greet us as well but was still in bed.

'Good for nothing little bastard,' she said, 'he's not due in college until this afternoon.'

Even with her son asleep upstairs, I could feel the tension between the two.

For the benefit of my colleague, but also so I could be sure I hadn't missed anything important, I asked Mary to retell her story from the beginning. By the time she had finished, tears were welling in her eyes. The only new revelation was that she and her brother were no longer speaking. She had clearly decided that her brother was wholly to blame for the ghostly happenings.

I suggested that we begin by blessing the house again, just in case there was anything still present (although I privately doubted it as I assumed that whatever my Roman Catholic counterpart had done would have dealt with it). My colleague and I lit candles, blessed some water and added some salt, which I had also blessed. I then began the prayers of the blessing, before inviting Mary to show us around the house. Mary, who had seen this all before – and probably with a bit more of that Catholic razzmatazz – replied that the house wasn't very big and that we were unlikely to get lost. Using a small metal water sprinkler, we splashed tiny amounts of water on the walls and doors of the house, until we reached the front bedroom. I knocked and received no answer, before entering. The curtains were drawn, but despite the murk I could make out naked limbs poking out from under the duvet. There was also the unmistakable whiff of teenage boy. Mary's son was indeed still fast asleep, snoring contentedly like a bear in hibernation. I was grateful that I had a female colleague with me although, being new to all this, she probably didn't share my relief.

Ritual performed, it was time to address what I suspected might be a difficult subject, namely the cause of the problem and its possible solution. Even before blessing the house, I'd had an inkling as to what might be going on but I wasn't quite sure. But it now seemed like an open and shut case.

'Do you mind if I ask you a couple of questions?' I asked, warily.

Mary's jaw tensed and her eyes flashed with suspicion, but she reluctantly agreed.

'These things that happen, do they only happen when your son is in the house?'

'Yes. He doesn't go out much, except to college.'

I carefully explained to Mary what I thought was going on. Being a deliverance minister is a bit like being a doctor in that we look at the symptoms, try to make a diagnosis and hopefully come up with a remedy. And this seemed to me to be a classic case of what we in the deliverance business call 'poltergeist activity'.

Most people have heard of poltergeists, not least because of the film of the same name. Some say poltergeists are ghosts of the unquiet dead, who have somehow retained the power to throw or at least move objects. I had experienced poltergeists myself and heard numerous other people describe their activities.

The really strange aspect of poltergeist activity is that, in as much as we are able to tell, it is always caused by someone alive and physically present. It is also often associated with children, teenagers and sometimes the elderly. It is particularly associated with people who find it difficult to express themselves, because of the environment they find themselves in and/or their character. The theory is that the energy that builds up inside them – which might be described as frustration – is released into the world around them. Think of a lightning strike, which is a release of invisible static energy that can produce visible effects.

Some people refer to this as 'psycho-kinetic energy', which is a scientific-sounding name for something that is actually very weird.

As far as I was concerned, what Mary and her son were experiencing had nothing to do with ghosts or Ouija boards, her poor brother or dead mother.

Instead, whenever Mary yelled at her taciturn son, he felt angry, frustrated and helpless, and these visceral emotions were 'earthed' in the explosion of her vase, just as they had been through the rattling of knives or moving of shoes. No amount of house blessings or Requiem Masses was going to make the slightest difference.

Those kinds of conversations are never easy, because I'm

obliged to explain that what's going on is partly triggered by people's behaviour. Mary and I talked about her son and about their relationship. I explained that he wasn't evil or even aware he was doing anything, including breaking her precious vase. At times like these, I become something akin to a counsellor. I discussed possible ways of living together more harmoniously, how she might be able to make more time for him and show him that she loved him. I suspect that what she really wanted was for me to wave a magic wand and make it all better, but wands aren't part of a deliverance minister's kit.

As we said our goodbyes, she smiled for the first time and her countenance softened. I think – I hope – she understood what needed to be done.

# Chapter 2

## *How on earth did I get here?*

Now you may be wondering how I became a deliverance minister. In fact you may be wondering how on earth I managed to get to be a priest at all.

As is the case with a lot of priests, my family were regular churchgoers, but being good Anglicans (not quite as thin on the ground as you might have thought in the South Wales Valleys I called home), they really didn't believe that religion was compulsory, and they were certainly not 'Bible-bashers'. But they did go regularly. My mother, her mother and occasionally my father went to the 8am early service which took place once a month, and my father's mother went to the main 9.30am Sung Eucharist on a Sunday morning.

Grandma, as we called my paternal grandmother, was one of those sweet old ladies that you can find in and around any Anglican church: she loved her church and it loved her. She also loved talking about it, so I learned a lot just by listening to her. She had spent many years as a Sunday School teacher and, as I grew up, she would share with me some of the material she had used during that time, particularly on a Sunday afternoon when we visited her as a family.

My other grandmother lived at the other end of town, and was a small Argentine lady who encouraged the family to speak Spanish at every available opportunity. Her parents had migrated with their Roman Catholic families to the Argentine (as she always called it) from the British Isles when they were youngsters. Apparently they couldn't remember living anywhere else, although they and their families continued to speak English at home.

My grandmother had very strong views about lots of things and as a girl had refused to go to confession. So, although baptised as a Roman Catholic, she had never received her first Communion and never went to Mass – not that her parents did that often. But her life changed when she met an Englishman whose car had broken down outside her parents' house. He was delighted to find that the *señorita* not only spoke English, but was also very pretty. Not long afterwards, following a whirlwind romance, they were married.

My grandfather had studied engineering and Spanish (which my grandmother said he spoke very well, but with a terrible accent) with a view to travelling to the Argentine, where the railways were owned and run by British companies. In terms of religion, my grandfather was a very devout Anglican, coming from a family of almost hereditary churchwardens in the Leicestershire village they had called home for centuries. Even though there were very few Anglicans in Argentina, his family was brought up staunchly Anglican.

My mother and her siblings were all confirmed by the missionary bishop, and my grandmother was confirmed as an Anglican with them.

Returning to the old country in the late 1950s, they settled in South Wales where they, of course, attended the local Anglican church and probably created quite a stir, but they threw themselves into the life of the church with gusto. At around the same time, their eldest daughter went off with a newly found friend to a dance where she met a dashing young man from a family famous locally for making sweets. He had just finished his national service in the Navy, and had entered the family business. They too were married not long afterwards, at the same church which most people in both families now seemed to attend. They would, in the course of time, have three children, of which I am the youngest. It was also there at church that my grandfather had begun to explore the possibility of being ordained as a priest, despite vehement opposition from his wife. After he died, my sisters and I would spend Saturday nights with his fiery Argentine widow and she would always make sure we went to Sunday School every week at 11am. Then when I joined the church choir and went to big church at 9.30am, she'd make sure I got there too. And I've never really looked back. There was just something that captivated me about the whole thing. For a start, I discovered a love of choral music through singing some big set piece Anglican anthems with the choir, and the priest was an excellent preacher and teacher. But there was something else too: a sense that there was some-thing beyond what I could actually hear and see. About a month after joining the choir I was confirmed by the bishop, which meant I was able to receive the Holy Communion (the bread and the wine that so many Christians believe to be the Body and Blood of Jesus), and that became a mystical experience for me. It really was the high point of my week. In fact, it still is one of the high points of my life.

It is difficult to describe that sense of closeness with the Other that I feel, but it seems to put life into perspective for me.

One particular experience, however, stands out. When I was around sixteen, I went on pilgrimage to the Shrine of Our Lady of Walsingham in Norfolk with some friends from school. The story of Walsingham is that, during the reign of Edward the Confessor, the Lady Richeldis, who was lady of the manor had a vision of the Blessed Virgin Mary instructing her to build a replica of the house in which Jesus was brought up in Nazareth. Walsingham, with its Holy House and statue of Our Lady, then became one of the greatest pilgrimage shrines in the Middle Ages. It was famously visited by the pious King Henry VIII, who walked barefoot to the shrine and pleaded to be granted a son with Catherine of Aragon. The lack of a male heir, of course, led pretty much directly to the break with Rome and the subsequent destruction of places of pilgrimage such as Walsingham, whose statue of Our Lady was destroyed in the 1530s. The shrine was revived by the Roman Catholic Church in the 1890s, and then in the 1920s an Anglican shrine was created, complete with a recreation of the Holy House and a copy of the mediaeval statue. It subsequently became a major place of pilgrimage, where pilgrims of all ages could pray all day, and then quench their thirst with large quantities of gin and tonic. Traditionally this was known as 'mother's ruin' but, because of the large quantity of very High Church Anglican priests at Walsingham, in this instance 'father's ruin' might have been more accurate!

One evening during the pilgrimage I found myself in the Holy House itself. It was fairly dark, illuminated only by subdued lights and hundreds of flickering candles that had been lit during the day.

There was only one other person there, so I sat quietly at the back. I wasn't actively praying, in fact, I wasn't consciously doing anything at all. I don't know how long I sat there, but strangely it felt as if someone was standing right behind me, and slightly to my left. I didn't hear a voice. I didn't see anything at all. But I did have the sensation of being held in love. I cannot tell you how long I was there, or how long it lasted. I do know that I sobbed quietly for a long time, and I also know that somehow my life has never quite been the same since.

It's difficult to put all this into words. Although I felt that, somehow, I had been touched by God, it didn't seem like a miracle at all, certainly not if you think that by miracle I mean something that alters the material world. It was more like a sense that I was being called to change the world myself in some way.

I realised that the possibility of being a priest was something I needed to explore, and was delighted to learn that my grandfather had felt some sense of calling too. My own vocation was also fostered by a teacher at school, who was a priest as well, and who encouraged me in my pursuit of academic theology. It was under his tutelage that I fell in love with the Old Testament. So when I went off to Durham to study theology, that was where my main interest lay and, not being able to get enough, I stayed to do a master's degree in Old Testament. I then found myself in Cambridge doing a doctorate, where not only was someone paying me to write a book on the Old Testament full time, but I was also able to indulge my love of studying ancient languages.

I had studied Greek, Latin, Hebrew, Syriac and Aramaic in Durham. Now I did courses in Akkadian (Assyrian and Babylonian), Ancient Egyptian, an intensive course in Hurrian, some Sumerian and threw in a bit of Spanish, German and Italian too!

My life had changed personally as well. I had met Laura years before in the church choir in South Wales and now, to my delight, she agreed to marry me. Halfway through my three-year PhD study time, we tied the knot. By this stage, I had also been accepted to train for the priesthood for the Church in Wales, but instead I stayed in Cambridge to study at Westcott House, a 'liberal catholic' theological college. 'Liberal catholic' by the way means that part of the Anglican Church that enjoys dressing up, is happy with gay priests and women bishops, but tends to be much closer to Roman Catholics on other aspects of theology such as the theology of the sacraments.

And the paranormal? Well, as a boy I used to enjoy watching *Scooby Doo*, and later graduated on to other spooky stories, but despite living in an old house where things might occasionally go bump, I didn't really give it very much thought. As a student I discovered M.R. James by accident. I was looking for a short story to read one night when I couldn't get to sleep, and picked up an anthology of twentieth century short stories which began with 'Casting the Runes' – needless to say, sleep was a long time coming! But despite feeling that James was in some ways a kindred spirit, that was about as far as my interest went.

M.R. James is now best known for his ghost stories, but in his time he was Provost of King's College, Cambridge, and then Provost of Eton, and also left a considerable body of scholarly work. Most famous is his *The Apocryphal New Testament*, a 1924 edition of the 'lost' works of early Christian groups now deemed heretical by the mainstream Church. Occasionally there is a flurry of new interest in such works, most of which exist in only one copy (which may tell you all you need to know), but very often, if you try to research them, you will find that James got there before you.

Most of his ghost stories feature a solitary scholar of antiquity discovering something in a lost library, and I have to admit that I once terrified the wits out of myself in the stacks of Cambridge University Library's North Front one January afternoon as a result of one of James's stories.

It was getting dark, and the upper floors of the North Front are among the darkest and least visited parts of the Library, because they contain the sorts of books not very many people are interested in. These books are in long shelves with a passage at both ends, but are basically in darkness unless you turn the light on using the sort of light fitting you find in a bathroom, complete with pull cord. I was searching through the stacks for a nineteenth century edition of an ancient Jewish text which, I hoped, would shed light on my chosen field of study, or at least give me another entry for my bibliography. Unfortunately, as I looked for it, James's short story 'The Tractate Middoth' came drifting through my mind. In the story, a young librarian is looking for the Talmudic Tractate Middoth in what James calls a famous library, and although he doesn't say it's Cambridge, given the fact that he spent most of his life in Cambridge, there is no reason to suppose it was anywhere else. When the librarian finds the right place, he notices that someone else has got there before him, someone who appears to be a priest, dressed in a dusty black, but as the priest turns to him, he realises that he is facing a reanimated corpse. Despite the fact that I've only ever read the story once, it is etched on my memory. Many things that have had a powerful effect can come back to haunt you when you least need them, and this was happening to me there. I told myself that the University Library I was standing in was not the same building and began to relax, until I looked around to realise that I was surrounded by editions of Talmudic

Tractates, and that a (or was it *the?*) copy of the Tractate Middoth was just in front of me. The sudden thought that in James's story it is not so much the building that is haunted as the books sent me scurrying for the exit, light cords flying out behind me. Once I was into the better lit parts of the building, I started to feel very stupid, but maybe that lesson in how easy it is to be spooked has served me in good stead.

At Westcott House where I trained to be a priest there was supposed to be a session on the ministry of deliverance, but for some reason it never happened: 'Not a lot of call for it' was the excuse. I did, however, spend eight weeks on an intensive mental health placement at the local psychiatric hospital, which has proved immensely useful over the years, so at least I came out of college with probably more than a basic knowledge of mental illness and some preparation for encountering people in extreme distress.

However, finding myself newly ordained and in a haunted house was quite a shock but, as I have already said, I was intrigued and wanted to know more. The opportunity came when I moved to the Cathedral in Newport, South Wales. Now, when you think of a cathedral, you immediately have images of Winchester or Salisbury in your mind. Newport Cathedral is not like that at all. It's an ancient, relatively small but rather beautiful parish church, which happened to be in the largest town of the newly created Diocese of Monmouth when the Church in Wales was cut loose from England in 1920, and after various vanity schemes (putting a roof on Tintern Abbey among them), it found itself as the cathedral.

When Laura and I moved to Newport, we moved with Thomas, our older son who had been born in Abergavenny, and while we were there, our second son Benedict was born. His claim to fame was that one of the first people to see him after he was born was Archbishop Rowan Williams, who was based in Newport at the time. Benedict was born late in the evening, and, although I was there at the time, I didn't get there the following morning until about 10am, only to discover that Archbishop Rowan had beaten me to it. The staff had told Laura that there was a priest to see her and whether she was up to visitors, and she said, 'That's fine, it'll just be my husband. But, of course, it wasn't. I explained that I had bumped into the Archbishop outside the cathedral, and when he asked me if there was any news about the baby, he'd gone straight to the hospital which was only a couple of hundred yards away, whereas I'd gone home first to change.

My job at the cathedral carried the title of 'minor canon' and, although I did see the Archbishop regularly, it basically meant that I was the cathedral curate. With my fellow minor canon, I helped the dean administer his cathedral with all its run of daily services, but we also ran a large inner-city parish with a massive council housing estate at the edge. So life was busy. An average day might consist of morning prayer at the cathedral, a funeral, visiting parishioners in the hospital, a meeting about a special service at the cathedral or a visit to see a churchgoer at home, followed by choral evensong, and as often as not, there might be an evening meeting after that too. If you were lucky, you might get to eat with the family, but that wasn't a given either. To be honest, this is a pattern that most clergy will recognise in some way or other, all as part of being a jobbing parish priest. It's what we do. Sometimes life will be very busy, but on other occasions it will be quite quiet – there will be nobody you need to visit in hospital, and no funerals or weddings. Many of us priests also have our own specialities. In my case, it was the fact that I used my academic training and lectured on the Old Testament: so for ten weeks every autumn I'd excuse myself from choral evensong on a Wednesday, and take myself off to Cardiff to St Michael's the Church in Wales's then theological college.

But, just occasionally, we would get a call out for a deliverance case, which, in those days, was just something that came with the job. If you were happy to do it yourself, off you went; if you weren't then there was someone else who would do it for you. In my experience, most Anglican priests are not really very interested in dealing with the paranormal, so they are usually delighted if someone else does. But at the cathedral, it was usually my colleague, the senior minor canon, who did the deliverance cases. In fact, at first, I was never aware that any of this went on, the administrator just handed them straight to him. But one day they were having a chat about a case that had come in, and my ears pricked up. My colleague was more than happy to share experiences and knowledge with me, and recommended a series of books (including an excellent one by Bishop Dominic Walker – more about him later), and some basic equipment. Realising that he would shortly be moving on, I knew that one day soon I would be called on to go into the field on my own, armed with my own special deliverance bag, although I wasn't quite sure what to expect. Other than the fact that I had lived in a house which was the subject of deliverance ministry, I had no knowledge or experience, and I wasn't even sure what I believed about the paranormal. In the case of my own house, it looked like something there was causing a problem, an entity that shouldn't have been there. My vicar asked God to deal with it, and it went. As simple as that. And now, as my colleague in Newport thought about moving on, I knew that the chances were that sometime soon I would be called on, so I needed to be prepared.

In case you're wondering, all deliverance ministers worth their salt have a bag where they know (or at least hope) they have everything they need. In addition to prayer books and service sheets from a variety of sources, it will usually contain vessels and containers for Holy Communion: a small chalice or cup for the wine, and a small paten or plate for the bread, as well as bottles for wine and water, and a small box for communion wafers, plus linen cloths to act as an altar cloth and for cleansing hands and the vessels, and very often some anti-bacterial hand-gel too. I usually also carry some tealight candles with me and a cigarette lighter as well as a crucifix to act as a focus. Most churches and very many clergy will have such a bag, but for the deliverance minister, as well as acting as a way of taking communion to the housebound, we also may need to use all this to celebrate a requiem for the souls of the departed – or in our case, those who are not as departed as they should be! But most of us will also carry another bottle of water which can be blessed to provide holy water and a small supply of salt that is traditionally added to this. You can never guarantee that people will have salt at home, especially in these low-sodium days. Salt, by the way, has been used by Christians for many centuries as a sign of purification, although the Bible barely mentions it, and its use is optional. In addition, my bag came with a small silver spoon, technically for Holy Communion, but it comes in very handy for holding a couple of grains of salt. A holy water sprinkler is also very useful too! As well as all this, I usually carry a small pot containing oil that the bishop blesses once a year for the healing of the sick.

In the New Testament the letter of James says that if any member of the Christian community is sick, they are to call the elders who will pray for them, and anoint them with oil, so that is what we still do. It is also quite useful to have a stock of crosses that can be left as a focus for people after a visit, and I have my own crucifix which I often hang around my neck when I'm out on a case – it makes me feel a whole lot better! As well as this, we usually take a stole – a sort of holy scarf and if I know I am likely to celebrate a Eucharist, I might take additional vestments – an alb (long white robe) and the poncho-like chasuble. They are not strictly necessary but, again, they make me feel much more confident. I know that one of my colleagues likes to use scented candles, and I'm sure there are all sorts of other adaptations deliverance ministers might feel they need.

But as well as that, I also needed a set of words to use, because to some extent all these things are props. There are two basic forms of service deliverance ministers use: one is that for the blessing of a house, and the other for the Eucharist for the dead. There are numerous forms of words that we could use, but they do the same thing: a house blessing is a formal invitation for God to be present in a particular place, and a Requiem Mass, at least according to traditional doctrine, actually allows God to be present, and we'll look at this idea a little later.

The basic service for the blessing of a house is one that I have used from the beginning of my ministry, and begins with a sort of formal greeting, *Peace to this house and to all who live here.* I then say the opening prayer: *Almighty and everlasting God, grant to this house the grace of your presence, that you may be known as the inhabitant of this dwelling, and defender of this household. Through Jesus Christ our Lord, who lives and reigns with you and the Holy Spirit, one God, for ever and ever. Amen.* This is followed by the blessing of holy water and then the blessing of salt which reads: *Almighty God, we ask you to bless this salt as once you blessed the salt scattered over the water by the prophet Elisha. Wherever this salt and water are sprinkled, drive away the power of evil, and protect us always by the presence of your Holy Spirit. Grant this through Christ our Lord. Amen.* Once I have the water-sprinkler full of the newly blessed holy water, the blessing itself begins: *Visit, O blessed Lord, this house with the gladness of your presence. Bless all who live here with the gift of your love; and grant that we may manifest your love to all whose lives we touch. May we grow in grace and in the knowledge of you; guide, comfort, and strengthen us, and preserve us in peace, O Jesus, now and for ever. Amen.*

I then usually invite the family to show me around the house, and will bless it with the water in silence, although I will pray silently throughout. I then invite the family to say the Lord's Prayer with me, and there will be a final blessing of all those present.

So, there I was all kitted up with my order of service printed and laminated (in case of holy water ingress!) and ready to go, when I had my first call while my colleague was on holiday. The cathedral administrator rang and asked me to get in touch with a council housing officer who was working with a family experiencing some sort of paranormal activity. The administrator sounded dubious about whether this was something worth bothering about, but I had no doubts, my theoretical ghost-busting skills were going to be put into practice! And so, I made the phone call and arranged to drop round to the house on the council estate where I would meet the housing officer.

## My first case

The first thing that struck me was how matter of fact it all was. The housing officer seemed bored and on the phone the family didn't seem very interested either: 'Yeah, we saw this shadowy figure over there, and we were, like, really frightened. So, we called the council, and they called you.' All right, I thought, this isn't at all what I was expecting, especially as, despite what they said, the family didn't seem frightened. But, drawing on my reading, and my conversations with my colleague about his experiences, I explained, as much for my benefit as for theirs, what I was going to do. 'I'm going to bless some holy water, and then if you can lead me round the house, I'll splash some water at the walls, and then we can say the Lord's Prayer together.'

They didn't quite shrug and say, 'Whatever,' but they got pretty close to it. But this was my first time, so I lit my candles and carefully placed the crucifix on the linen cloth. I made sure I got all the words right, and managed to get most of the salt into the water, and then the water into the sprinkler without any significant spillages; I proclaimed with my best 'proclamation' voice that we were about to drive from this house the forces of evil and darkness. And they looked on, completely indifferent. They did lead me round the house, and we did splash holy water at all the walls, and we did manage to get through the Lord's Prayer, but that was that, although they seemed strangely bored by the whole thing. I gave them the blessing in my best 'blessing' voice, reassured them as best I could (although I think it was I who needed reassurances), and told them to get in touch with me if they needed to. I then made my excuses, and left.

'Thanks, father,' said the housing officer as he showed me out, 'they should be all right now.'

'How did it go?' my colleague asked me, excitedly. I shrugged and explained what had happened, and he started laughing. 'Yes, I get loads of those,' he explained. 'They basically don't like the house they are living in, and if they manage to persuade the council it's haunted, they get moved somewhere else.'

'So that explains why they were all so matter-of-fact about it,' I ventured.

'Yes,' he said, 'you can tell if there's something real going on because if there is, they'll be frightened.' Makes sense, I thought, and he was right.

Over the next couple of years, I had the occasional call-out, but there was one that stuck in my mind and pointed me in the direction of specialising in this ministry.

## Are you the priest?

It was a lovely summer Saturday in Newport, and we had gone out for the day as a family, returning fairly late in the afternoon. As we were getting the boys out of the car, a nervous-looking young man approached me. 'Are you the priest?' he demanded abruptly.

OK, we lived opposite the cathedral but after a day on the beach with the family, I barely looked like a priest, was certainly not dressed like a priest, and was in fact looking forward to a quiet evening at home. 'Why are you asking?' I enquired, not really feeling comfortable with the situation.

'Just answer,' he asked again, becoming slightly agitated, 'are you the priest?'

'Yes, I am. Can I help you?' Now, 'help' at the cathedral came in various forms but most often, if someone approaches on the street or at the door, it is because they want something: often food, sometimes someone to talk to, almost always money. So I was wary.

'Great,' he said, gesturing towards a car, 'can you come with me?'

'Wait a minute, can you just explain?' I played for time, looking over anxiously at the family.

'It's my baby daughter,' he said, 'she's not "thriving", and we feel some presence has attached itself to her. My partner's auntie is a psychic, and she told us to come here, to this church, and to talk to the priest who would be standing on the pavement, because you'd be able to help. Can you?' He looked desperate. I looked at my wife, and she looked at me.

'Yes, I can help,' I said, 'but I need a couple of minutes to get some things together, and then I'll meet you at your house. Where do you live?' And he gave me an address, not that far away, but still a good twenty minutes' drive even on a quiet Saturday evening. But I had agreed so I said, 'Give me about half an hour, and I'll see you there.'

'Promise?'

'Promise,' I nodded. So I went inside, quickly explained to Laura who had taken the boys inside while I was talking to the young man what I was doing (which was a huge risk on all sorts of levels), ran upstairs, and, because it was my day off and I hadn't already shaved, I decided I needed to do that too. I changed into my priestly black, grabbed my trusty bag, and drove off. As I was driving, I reflected on my curious encounter with the young man. Part of me felt special – they had somehow known they would find a priest there. Part of me felt a fraud – it was probably someone else they were looking for. Dismissing these thoughts, it occurred to me that I ought to have called the local vicar to meet me there, because even though it was still in the same diocese, this was not my patch. I then remembered who the local vicar was and felt even more guilty because this was someone who would never have taken this seriously.

And so, I arrived. It was about 6.30 and a classic barbecue evening, and quite clearly this family were about to have one. The young man I had encountered earlier met me at the door, now a little more relaxed, and introduced me to the family. Crammed into a small living room were his partner, his partner's psychic aunt, and their baby.

'Yes, he's the one,' the aunt declared as I walked in and, after thanking me, she began to explain. Baby Bethan had been born at around the time her grandmother had died, and the family felt that somehow the soul of the grandmother had attached itself to the baby. 'She's just not thriving,' those words again. 'She gets infection after infection, and she seems to look at you with eyes that are too old, and sometimes she will look at something or someone that isn't there. We know you can help.' She had more confidence in me than I had, to be honest.

'Is anyone else in the house affected?' I asked.

'No.'

'Have you seen anything or felt anything untoward?'

They shook their heads. 'It's just her,' said the aunt again, 'it's not the house. I'd know.'

Being a deliverance minister is a bit like being a doctor sometimes. People come to you with a self-diagnosed problem. But this time, I believed her.

'Has she been baptised or christened?' I asked, not because

this offers any sort of special protection, but being baptised meant that I could offer to anoint her with oil.

'Yes,' said the mother, speaking for the first time, 'we had her christened when she was a couple of months old.'

'How old is she now?'

'Just coming up for a year.'

I thought for a moment, 'OK, what I'm going to do is to bless her, to say prayers of protection for her, and then I'm going to anoint her with the special oil for healing. Is that all right?'

They nodded quietly, and so we began. I knelt on the floor, with her father kneeling next to me, and as gently as I could I said the prayers, and anointed her with the oil for healing, and also said quiet prayers for the repose of the soul of her grandmother. The whole little service could not have taken more than five minutes, but I can still remember the moments to this day, the anxiety of Bethan's father in particular, her mother tense and worried, and the quiet confidence of the aunt.

We were silent then for what felt like an age, but couldn't have been more than a minute, and in that time the tension and the fear quietly dissipated. Despite the strangeness of the little group, everything felt normal.

'That's it,' breathed the aunt, 'that's it,' she nodded, 'yes, she's gone.' I made to get up, but before I could she said, 'I've bought a cross for Bethan, she's my god-daughter you see, so I was wondering if you could bless it for her, father.'

'Of course,' I said, fumbling in my bag for a bottle of pre-blessed holy water from my last case, and slowly went through the quiet prayers for blessing a cross.

Bethan's father left the room for a moment, but came back brandishing a pair of tongs, 'We're having a barbecue,' he announced, smiling properly for the first time, 'do you fancy a burger, father?'

Actually, I did fancy one, but I knew that food was going to be ready at home, so I declined full of regret – the bitter regret of a meat-eater living in a house of vegetarians!

'Can we give you some petrol money?' he asked and, as always, I told him to keep the money, but if he wanted to give it to his local church he could do that. And so, I took my leave, giving them my contact details if they needed me again. The aunt smiled and nodded again.

## A *new ministry*

It was a strange experience in many ways, and I still really don't know what was happening with this particular family, whether there was an entity that had attached itself to the little girl, or whether they were worried effectively about nothing, but the idea of being called to the ministry of deliverance was beginning to crystallise in my mind. However, I soon had other things to think about, including the fact that, as a family, we were on the move to a new parish, Blaenavon in the upper reaches of the South Wales Valleys. I would be responsible for the two churches in the town, as well as for the training of curates across the diocese, in what the church describes as dual-role ministry (I was still lecturing as well, but the church doesn't recognise more than two jobs at the same time).

Blaenavon is a small place. There were occasional call-outs there for a house-blessing or something like that, but most of my work focused on the churches, the schools and the community. However, I was able to use my position as a training officer to enhance my own knowledge and skills as a priest as well as those of my newly-ordained colleagues.

One of the first people I invited to talk to my colleagues was a retired priest who I knew was interested in the deliverance ministry, although he was more interested in the Bermuda Triangle than anything else! I was given another opportunity, however, when we had a change of bishop as Rowan Williams went from being Archbishop of Wales and Bishop of Monmouth to Archbishop of Canterbury. A new Bishop of Monmouth was elected to replace him – none other than Dominic Walker, who had written the book on the ministry of deliverance. I took the opportunity to invite him to address the curates, and the results were fascinating as Bishop Dominic took us through the theory and practice in his very thorough and disarmingly frank way. I spoke to him afterwards about my own experiences, and found myself being appointed as a proper diocesan deliverance minister. I was packed off on the training course.

The officially sanctioned training course for Anglican deliverance ministers is run by an organisation called the Christian Deliverance Study Group. It was set up in the wake of the notorious 'Barnsley Case'. And the Barnsley Case really has affected the way in which this ministry is conducted, at least in the Anglican Church.

In a nutshell, late one Saturday evening in 1974 a man called Michael Taylor went to see his local vicar, who had claimed to have had some success in exorcisms and the ministry of healing, and told him that he was possessed. The vicar then called his colleague from the Methodist Church and, together with their wives and some others from the church, they exorcised Taylor. They named the demons they were casting out and, apparently, they pushed crosses into his mouth. Taylor went off telling them that he was cured. On arriving home, Taylor murdered his wife in the most gruesome of manners and was found naked in the street, covered in her blood, declaring, 'It is the blood of Satan.'

At his trial for murder, despite the fact that he was acquitted on grounds of insanity, his counsel blamed the clergy and 'religion' in general. Barely surprisingly, there was a good deal of media interest and soul-searching from the Church. Some suggested that all such practices were outdated and should be banned, whereas others tried to professionalise them.

To some extent, that is still where we are today. Some in the Church are very wary of deliverance ministry, whereas others have tried to make it a normal part of church life and practice. The Christian Deliverance Study Group is part of the latter movement, but with a strongly professional and medical emphasis.

You will probably want to know what we did on the course. The Harry Potter fans among you may be wondering if we stood in rows and practised our holy water flinging skills with our right hands whilst holding a crucifix steady in the left ('swish and flick'), all the time uttering Latin incantations to banish the forces of evil. Please remove these thoughts from your mind, despite the fact that doing something like that might have been fun (clergy sometimes do have fun, by the way). The course was not fun, believe me, and focused almost exclusively on psychiatry and psychology. We had talks on the basis of human personalities. We talked about the different categories of mental illness. We were shown films of people who claimed to be possessed and were asked which of them was in fact possessed – the answer was none of them. We had brief sessions on ghosts and poltergeists, but they were brief, and we also talked about religious cults and even a little bit about paganism and satanism. But the most important thing we learned was that real demonic possession is so vanishingly rare that, although the staff admitted there was a theoretical possibility it might exist, you would almost certainly never come across a case where you might say, hand on heart, that someone was possessed (or was suffering from 'possession syndrome' as the medics preferred). The basic message was that you will almost certainly never have to conduct the exorcism of a person who is demonically possessed, so we were invited to put that out of our minds.

And it's true, I have never encountered one of these. I've come across loads of people who tell me that they think they might be possessed, or that a family member (usually their mother-in-law – not a joke!) is possessed, but these cases are probably the result of cultural pressures or overactive imaginations, or maybe just wishful thinking.

At the other end of the scale, I've encountered people who I strongly believe are in the grip of evil and whose very presence makes my flesh crawl and my hair stand on end, and I worry about them more, but possessed? Probably not, I hope!

## An anatomy of the paranormal

Rather than having a haphazard approach to their work, as exemplified by the poor priest caught up in the Barnsley Case, deliverance ministers are encouraged to have a basic framework through which to approach their work. A lot of this comes not so much through what we learn during the Christian Deliverance Study Group course as from the massive amount of reading we are expected to do before and after attending it.

We are encouraged to think about how to 'diagnose' each incident, and to deal with them accordingly. As is the case with medicine, whose language we have borrowed, we don't always get it right – or at least not first time, as you will see. But in general terms, we tend to divide paranormal phenomena broadly into things that affect homes and things that affect people, although there is often a grey area between the two.

Things that we tend to regard as affecting homes include poltergeist activity, 'place memories' and what we call 'true hauntings' (for want of a better phrase), although I suspect the phenomena are lumped together more for historical reasons than anything else. This is especially the case with poltergeist activity which, in the past, was usually assumed to be caused by the restless spirit of someone who had died; however, this does not seem to be the case.

We have already encountered **poltergeist activity** in the case of the exploding vase. As we have seen, it is caused by someone *alive and present* who may be undergoing significant trauma or stress and is unable to communicate their distress. This will result in things moving round. Frequently this will include kitchen utensils and, for reasons I've never fathomed, shoes.

Sometimes this activity happens when there are people present and occasionally it has been captured on film, although it makes for less interesting viewing than you might imagine. On other occasions it happens when there is no one there to see it, and can be manifested in things going missing and reappearing in a different place. What often makes it difficult to diagnose is that very often other forms of paranormal activity can trigger a poltergeist response. In other words, if you are living in a haunted house it will freak you out on some level, and that may well mean that things start moving around all on their own. The job of the deliverance minister is to work out why this is happening, and to deal with it.

We call the most common form of haunting the **place memory**. In theory this describes a building or a piece of ground somehow replaying something that has happened there in the past, but where there is no attempt to communicate with the living. Classically it could be something like the fox hunt that comes through the pub wall from time to time, to the terror of late-night drinkers. There is no attempt to communicate with the living, it is almost like watching a film – the ghost is not really there in any real sense, despite being distressingly visible.

Sometimes, however, it may be of a different order. It could be a memory of a traumatic event such as, for example, a previous homeowner falling down the cellar stairs and breaking his neck, so that the modern-day occupants feel they have to step over him. Place memories can sometimes be triggered by building work being carried out, but can also occur seemingly at random. Although from experience, if this is a new thing, something will almost certainly have caused it, maybe a change in family circumstances such as the birth of a new child.

Even though there is no attempt at communication, place memories can be very unpleasant to live with. However, all types of place memory are dealt with through blessing the building or by celebrating a Requiem.

Much rarer is the phenomenon we usually refer to as a **true haunting** although, to be honest, the differentiation between the place memory and the true haunting is not always very clear. True hauntings are, however, characterised by the fact that there is an attempt to communicate with the living in some way, often, but not always, by someone you knew. This may be quite comforting but can also, of course, be very frightening indeed, depending on what they are trying to communicate and who it is. As in the case of the place memory, this may well be accompanied by poltergeist activity, which can be quite violent. Deciding which category you are dealing with is not very easy, but is also basically unnecessary because true hauntings are dealt with in the same way as place memories.

I am a priest and a theologian, so what do I think is going on with these phenomena?

Sometimes it would appear that people have an attachment either to a place or to a person that seems to suggest that death is not quite as final as you might have thought.

Christianity is, of course, founded on the idea that Jesus of Nazareth, a historical human being who lived and died in the first century AD, did not remain dead but was resurrected and revealed as God. In the stories his followers wrote after his departure from the world, he is described as bringing the dead back to life. In two cases these are the recently dead, but one instance concerns his friend Lazarus, who had been dead and in the grave for four days. This case is described in St John's Gospel chapter eleven.

In that story and in other parts of the Bible, as well as in some later Christian thought, the idea is that death is not the end of human existence. And in my ministry I encounter people who have had very similar experiences of the paranormal and whose stories seem to be broadly consistent with one another, so I am convinced that sometimes the dividing line between life and death is not final. But as a Christian priest, I am also equally convinced that God has the power to deal with these anomalies, and that he responds to prayer.

41

As C.S. Lewis once put it, 'I've a sort of idea he likes to be asked.'

When we move on to things that are deemed to affect people rather than places, we tend to place them into two categories: oppression and possession.

*Oppression* is something of a nebulous concept, but is when someone feels that they are oppressed by some malign external force. The case of Bethan earlier in this chapter would be a good example. Sometimes it can manifest itself in the form of repeated and inexplicable bad luck. In such cases, rather than concentrating on the building, we bless the people concerned, and offer prayers for their protection.

*Possession*, on the other hand, is a very specific phenomenon where someone's entire being is taken over by an external evil spirit – a demon, for want of a better word. Possession is exceedingly rare, even though I frequently encounter people who *claim* that they are possessed. However, once a deliverance minister is certain (and I mean certain) that a person is possessed by an external form of evil, we can then proceed with an exorcism.

Very few deliverance ministers have encountered anyone they believe to be possessed, but I am open to the possibility that there may be spiritual entities which, although subject ultimately to God, seem able to take over the wills and bodies of those who are already inclined to evil.

It is particularly with regard to things that affect people that a sound knowledge of mental health issues is crucially important. Which is why the training courses home in on this. Exorcism is always the last resort, and conducting an exorcism on someone who is not possessed is highly dangerous.

On a more practical level, it won't solve the problem; in fact it will almost certainly make it a whole lot worse.

This is the basic framework that I was given, and years of experience in the field have made me appreciate it as a working model. There are always anomalies and, hand on heart, telling the difference between a place memory and a true haunting is not always easy, or indeed helpful. Sometimes it can take several conversations to work out what is going on, especially where there is poltergeist activity involved, but as I tell my story, I will use the basic framework as a guide. So firstly, we'll look at the things that affect places, roughly in the order set out above, and then the things that afflict people.

So, going back to the story – I did all the reading, I went on the Christian Deliverance Study Group course, and came out anointed as a deliverance minister, knowing more about the human condition than I did before and, even though my holy water flicking skills were not honed on the course, they have come in really handy over the years as I have encountered the supernatural, the paranormal, the weird, the bizarre – and the occasional hoax.

# Chapter 3

## *Things that go bump in the night*

Having dispelled the idea that deliverance ministers spend all their time exorcising demons, what do they spend their time doing? Well, most of us are jobbing parish priests, although some deliverance ministers work in specialist ministries, such as being hospital chaplains. And, to be honest, the number of times we get called out is very small, so if the team deals with a dozen cases a year, we are doing well. Nearly all the call-outs we get are related to ghosts and other visitations in houses, rather than to people who feel they might be possessed or oppressed.

The activity we deal with in houses falls usually into one of the three groups I described in chapter 2 – poltergeist activity, place memories and true hauntings.

We have already seen poltergeist activity in the story about Mary and her exploding vase, but over the years I have encountered the phenomenon over and over again. Sometimes it can be very obvious what is happening, and on other occasions completely baffling.

## The rattling bracelet

A really straightforward case that I dealt with over the phone concerned a young woman who had been given my number by the local funeral director (who else do you call if you think one of your loved ones won't stay in the grave?).

But after the traditional, 'Is that the vicar?' the conversation continued with the classic, 'I think I might be possessed.'

It was going to be one of those days. I had already dealt with the drug addict who had taken up semi-permanent residence in the church looking for enough money to buy his next fix, and had only just staggered into the office to deal with the stream of emails which inevitably mount up overnight. So, I admit that I had a sinking feeling as I reassured her, and got her to explain the situation from the beginning.

'It was the other night. Me and my friend had been watching horror films,' I felt another inward sigh coming on, 'and then the bracelet I had from my dead nan started moving on its own. That's a sign that I'm possessed, isn't it?' Further reassurance was obviously needed.

'I don't think you'd be telling me this if you were really possessed, I think there might be something else going on. Has something happened that might have upset you recently?'

'I'd just had a massive row with my boyfriend and had gone round to my friend's house.'

'Were you able to talk to your friend about it?'

'No, because I was just too angry.'

'How did you feel after the bracelet moved?' I enquired.

45

She stopped before replying, 'I just felt really tired.'

'Did you feel less angry?'

Another pause for thought. 'Yes, I suppose I did.'

'I think this was just all that energy letting itself go through your bracelet. It's like when there's a big thunderstorm, and all that built up energy releases itself in the lightning.'

'OK,' she said, 'my friend told me I needed to talk to a priest in case I was possessed. But she also said it might be my nan trying to communicate with me.'

'No, I'm sorry, it's probably not your nan either.'

'That's OK,' she said, sounding relieved.

'If it happens again, you know where I am.'

She laughed. 'Thanks, you've really helped.'

'Oh, and do you know the Lord's Prayer?'

'Yes,' she sounded surprised, 'I went to a church school, we used to say it all the time.'

'Great,' I said. 'Well, if you ever feel frightened, just say the Lord's Prayer, and that's about the best thing you can do.'

'Really?'

'Yeah, really.'

'OK, I'll do that,' she said brightly. 'And thanks again.'

'Any time,' I said, and went back to another email that had pinged through during our brief encounter.

It's rare for me not to meet the people face to face, but this one seemed so clear-cut based on previous experience and easily dealt with that we left it at that. Poltergeist activity, however, comes in many different forms. Sometimes it's simple and easy to spot, but on other occasions, it can be so bizarre that nobody quite knows what's happening, and that was true of another case I dealt with relatively early on in my ministry.

## Rats

'Is that the vicar?'

It was a quiet time of year in the parish – they do happen sometimes – and this one was after Easter when the evenings are getting lighter, and the promise of summer is on the way.

But clearly someone was not quite as full of the joys of spring as I was!

'Is that the vicar?' she asked again, sounding panicked, what appeared to be the natural huskiness of her voice beginning to rise.

'Yes, hello, can I help?'

'It's these rats, they are eating my mother alive!'

Now you have to admit that, as a conversation starter, that's a good one. In fact, for most people it's a sentence they will never hear, but there it was coming straight at me.

'I'm sorry,' I said, playing for time, 'did you say rats were eating your mother alive?'

'Yes, that's right.' The panic was beginning to subside, to be replaced by something else – doubt. 'I was told you could help me.'

'I'll do my best,' I said as confidently as I could, although this was bizarre even for the sort of conversations I usually have.

Most people take quite a long time to tell me that there is some sort of paranormal problem, but not in this case – assuming that it was paranormal, and she hadn't confused me with environmental health.

'Can you tell me what's happening exactly?'

'Well me and my mam live together. My dad died a few years ago and I've never married, so it's just the two of us.' I grunted encouragingly. 'But then a couple of weeks ago, mam had gone to bed, and I heard her scream really loudly.

'So, I ran in to see what was happening. And she was just sitting there, holding her stomach, saying, "Get them off me, get them off me." So, I asked her what the problem was, and she said it had felt like her insides were being eaten away by something, but when she'd turned the light on, there was nothing there at all – everything was like normal. She was really frightened, and I told her it must have been some sort of nightmare. But she didn't want to go back to sleep. I stayed with her until she was completely asleep, and then I went to bed myself. Two o'clock in the morning she was screaming again. "Mam," I told her, "you'll wake up the neighbours". But she said it had come back, only this time it was like rats eating away at her insides. Again, I stayed with her until she went back to sleep. And she seemed all right the following morning, although I felt like death warmed up, and dragged myself into work. My boss asked me if I was all right, and I just said my mam had been up in the night.'

Once the story had started to flow it was difficult to get a word in, so I just let her talk.

'Next night it happened again. Just after she had turned the light off, they came again. Of course, I went running, and saw that the bedclothes had been disturbed, but there was nothing to see, other than my mam who was absolutely bloody terrified.'

She paused for breath, so I took my chance. 'How long has this been going on?'

'A couple of weeks.' She sounded terrified and exhausted, barely surprisingly.

'But it got worse,' she continued.

'Worse?'

'Yeah. Because I saw them!'

'You actually saw these rats?'

'Well,' she said, 'I've been sleeping in the room with her, and it always happens as she's going to sleep with the light off. But I talked her into sleeping with one of those plug-in night lights. She wasn't happy about it, mind, but I told her I wasn't going to stay with her unless she did. So, the same thing happened. She turned the main light off and, after complaining that it was too light sleep, I could tell she was nodding off. And then,' and I heard her choke.

'Oh God, it was terrifying. I *saw* them. It was like this seething mass of bodies under her bedclothes! It was . . . sorry, vicar,' and she started sobbing, 'it was like I could hear them too, chattering to one another, as they were eating her alive.'

The narrative dried up. 'Are you OK?' I asked gently.

'Yeah, oh God . . . Yeah . . .' and she began to compose herself.

'So, you saw the rats?'

'No, I didn't see them, because when I pulled back the bedclothes they had gone. Anyway,' she continued, 'they've been really worried about me in work, they keep telling me I'm not myself, so I told them a bit about what was happening. One of my friends said that you had helped his mother-in-law,' and she mentioned the neighbouring town where she lived, 'so she told me to get hold of you. Have you ever come across anything like this before?'

'No, I haven't,' I admitted.

'But can you help?' she asked with trepidation.

'I'll see what I can do.'

'Thank God for that – oh, sorry, vicar,' the relief was palpable as well as the embarrassment of casual blasphemy – we get used to it, and to the embarrassment!

'So, you'll come around.'

'Yes, of course.'

'OK. Half an hour?' she said eagerly, giving me her address.

And, despite the fact that I was looking forward to a quiet glass of wine with my wife that evening, what else could I do? In fact, unusually in this instance, there seemed to be so great an urgency that I didn't have time to contact anyone to come along – in most instances, we go out at least in pairs.

I had barely had time to think this one through, and despite the fact that you now know this one is going to be another example of poltergeist activity, at this stage, I had no idea. My mind was running towards some sort of weird manifestation of a place memory (we'll come on to place memories soon).

Before I go out on a case, I will usually spend some time praying for protection and guidance, but in this instance, there was only time to get my kit together and to say a hasty St Patrick's Breastplate, which I hoped would work.

This, by the way, is a traditional prayer for protection from evil that is said to go back to St Patrick himself, and has been regarded as a sort of spiritual armour, hence breastplate. It is quite a long poem, and in the translation we usually use it begins, 'I bind unto myself this day the strong name of the Trinity . . .' However, the best-known part of it is:

> *Christ be with me; Christ within me;*
> *Christ behind me; Christ before me;*
> *Christ beside me; Christ to win me;*
> *Christ to comfort and restore me.*
> *Christ beneath me; Christ above me;*
> *Christ in quiet; Christ in danger;*
> *Christ in hearts of all that love me;*
> *Christ in mouth of friend and stranger.*

These are the words that we would pray before a deliverance case, and for us it feels like being surrounded with a sort of protective force field, although those of a certain age may also remember advertisements on television for cereals said to provide children with a golden glow!

I found the house easily enough and sat outside for a few moments. It was a late 1960s building set high off the road, with large windows that would have had an amazingly good view of open moors in daylight.

I tried to focus on what I was about to encounter. You really never know what you are going to find when you walk through the door, so there is usually that sense of trepidation.

In this instance, however, that sense of fear was completely lacking, as if it was perfectly normal for the vicar to come round at 8 o'clock on a weekday evening.

Mother and daughter both seemed remarkably composed, especially given the high degree of urgency that had been suggested. I asked them to tell me again what they had experienced, and although there was a degree of heightened tension about this, it all seemed so matter of fact. The mother didn't seem to show as much fear as I thought she might, and the daughter was considerably more composed than she had been on the phone.

I asked them the usual questions about the house – they were the first family to live there, and there had been nothing in the way of structural alterations since. I enquired about their family: the father had died many years ago and had never lived in the building, so he could probably be discounted because this seemed to be something new.

I asked about their health and they both told me they were very well, all things considered. I was puzzled. These people were experiencing a high degree of some sort of paranormal activity, but nothing I could find out about seemed to have triggered it.

In my experience, such activity rarely comes out of a clear blue sky, and is almost always caused by a change, whether physical or psychological. There are, however, exceptions and maybe this was one.

'OK,' I said, 'we'll start off by blessing the house. In nine out of ten cases this works.' This is true but in this instance, because I couldn't work out what was going on, I needed to *do* something – one of the golden rules is that the deliverance minister never leaves the house without doing at least something, and a simple house blessing seemed the best option.

By tradition, house blessings begin and end in the main room of the house, and despite the fact that I was in a large and comfortable living room that looked over the moors, they told me that they spent most of their time in the kitchen at the back of the house. This proved to be a very modern room looking out over the back garden, and in the far corner had a sitting area and a TV. They turned the spotlights on for me, and suggested I use the amazingly well-lit granite island work surface as my base.

So I laid out my equipment: a square linen corporal (an altar cloth we usually use for the Eucharist), some tealights, a crucifix, a bottle of clean water and my sprinkler, and asked them for some salt while I found the right words on a prayer card and lit the candles. The salt was duly procured, and I began the prayers for blessing a house with holy water.

As I was holding my hands in blessing over the water, much to my horror the spotlights in the ceiling started to go out one by one. I have to admit that I was not at my best: I had had little time to prepare, I was alone and there was something not quite right here. This does not really excuse the mounting sense of panic that came over me like a dizzying wave as I fumbled the prayers and stammered myself to a halt, clutching the work surface as I began to lurch forwards and downwards.

'It's OK,' said the daughter, who was standing next to me, 'we've just had them put in, and the wiring's faulty. Look, they're coming back on now.'

I managed to right myself, and somehow got through the prayers. 'Pull yourself together, Bray,' I thought to myself. 'These people are relying on you.' And so, we began, the daughter leading me around the house.

Traditionally, holy water is sprinkled at each of the walls of a room, at the windows and at the doors, particularly the external doors, which traditionally are where evil enters the house. This is the reason why so many old houses will have a piece of iron, often in the form of a horseshoe somewhere near the front door, since iron was thought to repel supernatural evil.

And I tend to try to make two splashes notionally in the sign of the cross as I go. There is something deeply comforting about this, at least for me, and I hope for the people who live in the house.

Some deliverance ministers will use a series of different prayers for each room with a Bible verse that reflects the use of the room (although some are more obvious than others – bathrooms and toilets do not feature hugely in the Bible!). I prefer to use a general prayer of blessing for the whole house, and then to move round the house in silence, or as close to silence as we can get. Often people will point out features of the house that they are proud of, or the exact place where Uncle Albert fell when he died of a heart attack on Christmas Day 1976, or most often, people apologise for the fact that they haven't cleaned or tidied up. I am usually so busy concentrating that when I tell them I won't notice, it's true.

I will, however, stop and pray silently in a room where there has been a particular manifestation of the paranormal, and this was the case with the old lady's bedroom, which looked over the front of the house.

So, I stopped there, looked down at the bed that had been the focus of so much paranormal activity, and prayed for the old lady, for her daughter, and for the repose of the souls of the dead. We then moved back to the kitchen, where I blessed one of my wooden holding crosses for them and said the Lord's Prayer with them. And that was it, nothing dramatic, no changes in temperature or atmosphere. As always, I told them that if there were any more problems to get in touch with me, and so I took my leave of the old lady.

The daughter showed me to the front door, closing the living room door behind her as she did. And as we stood on the doorstep, she once again became the anxious and agitated woman I had spoken to on the phone: 'Thank you very much for coming to see mam – it means a lot that you were prepared to come out at short notice. I've been so worried about her, you see, but I have been trying to put a brave face on it for her, and I think she's really embarrassed that we have had to call you out.'

'You're very welcome,' I said, puzzled.

'She's all right is she, your mam?' I tried to probe.

And she began to break down. 'She won't talk about it to anyone, and she'd be furious if she knew I was telling you about it now.'

'The rats?' I asked, confused.

'No, the *cancer.*'

'Cancer?'

'Yes, but she won't talk about it – it's her age,' she said.

Just to explain, when I was first ordained in the late 1990s, cancer was one of those things that people didn't like talking about. It was almost as if it was a shameful disease that you had somehow brought on yourself, and you would be at pains not to tell anyone about it. I would frequently go to see families to arrange a funeral, and they would go out of their way to tell me that, although their loved one had died of cancer, I was not to mention this during the service. Although very often they would ask me to mention that donations in lieu of flowers were to go to Cancer Research, which I always felt was giving the game away. But there are many things that as a priest you think but don't say, and that is one of them! I'm pleased to say that things have since changed, and that people feel they can talk about cancer and other illnesses without stigma and shame. But just occasionally, old attitudes persist, and they certainly did in this old lady.

'Can I ask, what sort of cancer?'

The daughter looked nervous, and glanced over her shoulder just in case her mother was listening in. 'Bowel cancer,' she whispered.

'Oh, I'm sorry, how long has she had it?'

'Oh, it's not been confirmed, she's waiting to have the test results back.'

'Well, I hope it goes well.'

'Please don't tell anyone. She'd kill me if she knew I'd told you. In fact, I shouldn't have told you,' she gulped.

'No, that's fine, you've done the right thing. I won't tell anyone else, and I'll remember her in my prayers.'

'You sure?'

'Yes, of course.'

'Thanks again for coming out.'

'Call me if you need me again.'

'Will do,' she said, scuttling back inside.

I walked back to the car, feeling more tired than usual after a deliverance case. It had been hard work, but then at the end all had been revealed: somehow the mother had externalised the cancer she couldn't talk about so that the rats eating away at her insides represented the cancer she thought was eating her bowels. But in this case the fear had been so great that it had almost given substance to the hated rodents, to the extent that the daughter could actually see something moving under her bedclothes.

It was an extreme case, I have to admit, but just occasionally I have encountered others like it. They include an old lady who was suffering from bladder cancer and whose 'poltergeist' seemed to be gently stroking her back every evening until she went to sleep.

I know which sort of poltergeist activity I'd prefer!

Priestly ministry can be very intense and personal, so it may come as a surprise to know that it is not uncommon for us to spend a huge amount of time and effort with people and never to see them again. This often happens with weddings – once they are down that aisle and out of the church, that's it for good, and the same applies to people who come to bring their children to be baptised (or 'christened' as they will usually call it). It also applies to deliverance ministry: I rarely see them again.

But in this instance, I did. In the supermarket a couple of months later, I nearly collided with the daughter, who looked terrified at seeing me.

'How's your mother?' I asked.

'She's fine,' she said quickly, looking round to see if anyone could see us talking to one another.

'Did she have . . . ?'

'No, false alarm. See you.' And she fled.

## The Muslims and the ghostly monk

Poltergeist activity comes in all sorts of different forms, but sometimes there is so much going on, it can be difficult to see. This was the case with the incident that brought me to public attention.

It was the Wednesday of the week before Christmas, which in the world of the clergy means almost wall-to-wall carol services, even in the village where I was the vicar at the time. But sometimes, depending on when the school term runs, there can be gaps in the diary, which was just as well in this instance.

'Is that the Reverend Doctor Jason Bray?' asked the voice on the phone, sounding as if he was reading my title.

'Yes, can I help you?'

'I've been given your number by the Bishop's Office because they said you would be able to help me.'

'I'll do my best,' I said, slightly intrigued.

'I'm a social worker, and I have a really strange case that I'm hoping you might be able to help with.'

'OK,' I said, my interest piqued.

'One of the families I deal with has had a whole load of really strange things happen. There have been all sorts of things flying round the house, and then the other night one of the sons saw what he thinks is the ghost of a monk. Now they are Muslims,' he continued.

'OK,' I said, in more than my usual bafflement. 'Muslims?'

'Yes, so I spoke to the local imam – not that they go to the mosque very regularly, but they had some sort of connection with one. And he refused to help them. He said that if all this was being caused by the ghost of a monk, it was a Christian monk, and so we needed a Christian priest to come and deal with it. Do you think you can help?'

'I don't see why not, but is the family happy to have a Christian priest come and deal with it?'

'As long as it goes away, I don't think they care very much. Will you come?'

'Yes, of course, when?' I fished out my diary.

'There's something else you need to know. The father passed away recently, so they are very frightened.'

'Do they think he's going to come back and haunt them?'

He sighed. 'In a nutshell, yes. So, the sooner you come the better. Can you make it tomorrow?'

'Tomorrow!' I choked – this was after all the Wednesday before Christmas!

But I looked down, and there was a gap in the diary. 'Actually, I can get to you for 11am. Where am I coming?'

And he gave me an address adding, 'I'll meet you there.'

'I'll need to at least tell the local vicar I'm doing it, and he may want to come along. Is that OK?'

'As long as someone comes, I don't think they will care much.'

Contacting the local vicar is, as I have suggested, always a bit worrying. The Anglican Church in Wales is really small, and we tend to know everyone else reasonably well, and vicars come in all shapes and sizes. Some vicars will run a mile before going anywhere near a deliverance case. Others are sceptical about the whole enterprise. And at the other extreme, others are just that little bit too keen to be involved. But most of the time, I encounter two reactions – 'Thanks for letting me know, you don't need me, do you?' or, 'Thanks for letting me know, can I come along?'

This local vicar was one of the latter, who also happened to be miraculously free on the Thursday before Christmas, and I arranged to collect him so he could direct me to the house. This also gave me the opportunity to put in some parameters: basically, I do the talking, you shut up and pray – I had had bitter experience of this going wrong!

So, pep talk duly delivered, we arrived at the house – a large, anonymous council house at the end of a row of similar houses, and we rang the doorbell. As I have said, you never know what to expect when you arrive. Sometimes people can be welcoming and friendly, but often they are nervous and need a huge amount of reassurance – actually, they *always* need a huge amount of reassurance, but sometimes they hide the nervousness better.

In this case the door was opened by a lady in her fifties, with hair that had clearly been dyed not too recently, and as she looked at us, she looked anxious and tired.

'Come in,' she said, opening the door wide. 'Dave's already here.'

Dave was her social worker, and he welcomed us with virtually open arms and a broad smile. 'Great to see you,' he said confidently as we were ushered into the living room. I said you never know what to expect, but a huge, fashionably black Christmas tree was not quite what I thought I would find in a Muslim household, nor was I necessarily expecting a huge pile of half-opened presents strewn around the floor, which the lady half-heartedly kicked out of the way as she introduced me to her large family, made up of girls and boys aged between about eight and seventeen. There were also other young people in the house, judging by the noise coming from the kitchen. In fact it sounded like a whole party was taking place in there.

After the introductions, Dave began. 'So, would you like to explain to Father Jason what's been happening?' The lady looked frightened and then, as she told her tale, she began to relax a little.

She and her husband, she explained, had both been born in

a small village in Pakistan, and had had an arranged marriage. 'I learned to love him,' she said, with not a huge amount of conviction. Once married, they moved to Wales to begin a new life together. Her husband worked in a local factory, and she got a job working in a supermarket.

'His heart was in Pakistan, always in Pakistan. And his English was never good' – her English, although accented, was excellent. 'He longed to go back before he died, but,' she sniffed, 'it never happened.' And she burst into tears, to the horror of her children, who looked at her helplessly.

My colleague, however, came up trumps and went over to her, holding her hand until she had quietened down.

'I'm really sorry to hear about your husband. When did he die?' She looked at Dave in some confusion, so he answered for her.

'He died on Monday,' he said quietly.

I gasped slightly in shock. 'This Monday?'

He nodded.

'Four days ago?'

And he nodded again.

'I am so sorry,' I said to the lady, who acknowledged my sympathy.

'That's why they're so frightened,' Dave explained after a few moments, almost as if the family wasn't there. 'They are worried that it's going to get worse.'

I decided to backtrack slightly, so I asked her to tell me about her husband. 'He had cancer, real bad cancer, and he was in a lot of pain, but he didn't like hospital.'

I nodded sympathetically.

'So, I cared for him here in his house,' she said proudly, 'and he died here too.'

'I'm sure that's a great comfort to you,' I said – which was obviously not the right thing to say, because she suddenly looked terrified again and muttered something about a ghost. I could sense this wasn't going well. In most deliverance cases, you don't usually have to deal with the recently bereaved. In fact, in many cases, if someone has died it may be many years in the past! Priests, of course, deal with the bereaved all the time, but the sorts of questions we have to ask are very open about their (hopefully) happy memories of their loved ones, and what sorts of hymns of music they might like at the funeral.

Dealing with a recently bereaved lady who was terrified of being haunted by her dead husband was totally unexpected. But still, to be able to help her, I did need to ask a series of questions that I hoped would not be too painful.

'I'm really sorry,' I ventured, 'but can you describe what sorts of things have been happening?'

She looked nervously at Dave, who nodded back in reassurance. 'Last week, we were sitting having breakfast, and the things from the table started to fly across the room.'

'Do you mind if I ask, what things?'

She thought for a moment. 'My husband's bowl and his spoon.'

'Thank you. Any other sorts of things?'

Another pause. 'Another day, a pair of slippers flew across the room and hit the wall.'

'Nearly hit me!' interjected the oldest son.

'But they didn't?'

'No, just missed. Scary, though!' It's unusual for things which are the subject of poltergeist activity to hit anyone, or at least not with any force.

'Do you know what might have been causing it?' my colleague, the local vicar, asked, and received a brief, but surreptitious glare.

'It was the monk!' wailed the lady, and burst once again into floods of distraught tears, comforted again by my colleague. This really wasn't going well at all!

After a suitable pause, I asked, as gently as I could, 'Can you tell me about the monk?'

The lady looked as if she was going to start weeping again, but pointed at her eldest son. 'He saw it.' I turned to look at the son, who in turned looked at her.

He gulped and began. 'It was, like, the other evening. I'd just walked my girlfriend home, and then I was coming back. And there it was.' I nodded reassuringly. 'It was, like, a hooded figure, just standing there in the mists.'

'Why did you think it was a monk?' I asked.

'Er, it just looked like one.'

'Can you describe it a bit better?'

He paused. 'Well, like a monk, a hooded figure in the mist at the bottom of the lane just by the house.'

'How long was it there for?'

'Not very long. I saw it, and, like, didn't hang around – know what I mean. But when I turned around, it wasn't there any more.'

'OK, thanks,' I said. 'Did it try to communicate with you?'

He thought for a moment. 'No, it just stood there.'

'And you think it *was* a monk?'

'Yeah, well someone told me there were monks here once, and something's causing all this stuff here at home.' He started to look very uncomfortable.

'Thanks for telling me,' I smiled.

'Can I go now? My girlfriend's come round to see me, like.'

'Yes, of course. Thank you again.' And as he went, the middle child went off to join his friends in the kitchen.

So, there you have it: the story of the ghostly monk. And, yes, he was right that there had been Cistercian monks in the area certainly at some stage in the dim and distant past. So, entirely plausible.

The question was, however, whether the monk and the poltergeist were related to one another.

As I've said, poltergeist activity is always caused by someone alive and present at the time, but it can be triggered by a range of factors: emotions that can't be expressed is one of the most common, but it can sometimes be a reaction to other forms of paranormal activity. Hauntings are often accompanied by poltergeist activity not caused by the ghost itself, but by the reaction of the living to their fear of the paranormal.

But what was this? When we go to see people, we tend to assume that they are telling the truth, but very often there is a gap between what they are reporting and what is actually there. In this case, it was entirely possible that what the boy had seen wasn't a monk. It might have been a swirl of the mist in the lane, or someone wearing a hoodie and, of course, the poltergeist activity was manifesting itself in the house, not in the lane. But then again, it might have been the ghost of a monk.

I needed to do more investigation.

'I'm really sorry to ask this, because I know you are all very frightened, but since your husband passed away, has any of the activity got worse?' She shook her head, so I pressed on hesitantly. 'May I just ask, did the activity stop when your husband died?'

The question brought her up short. She sat up and looked at me with a sense of understanding. 'Yes,' she said simply.

I smiled gently at her, and nodded. 'Thank you.' And she looked at me directly for the first time, and nodded back.

'OK. So, what we'll do is bless some holy water, and if it's all right with you, we'll bless all the rooms in the house, and I think that should do it. Are you happy with that?' She had gone back into anxious mode, but she gave her assent. 'Are you sure you're OK with that?' I asked again.

'Yes, please,' she said.

So, we blessed the house, and as we did so the youngest child followed us around with a degree of curiosity. We began as always in what they considered to be the main room of the house, in this case the living room, where I was careful to avoid the presents still strewn on the floor, and then asked the lady to guide us round, so off we went, the local vicar and the youngest child.

Dave the social worker stayed in the living room. In the kitchen we found about half a dozen young people who were watching TV, and had been joined by the rest of the kids, but they didn't seem very interested. We splashed holy water at the walls and left them to it. She led us around the house, to her own room, and that of the other children, and then stopped at a closed door. 'My son's room,' she said.

'Can we go in?'

'Of course,' she said.

But something stopped me. I knocked gently on the door. There was a rustling sound coming from the other side and muffled voices. So, I knocked again, a bit louder, as the lady of the house reached across and opened the door. This time, it was my turn to be horrified: it was clear than her eldest son had been entertaining his girlfriend, and when we burst in they were hastily readjusting their clothing and moving quickly away from one another. There was a snigger from behind us as the youngest child took in the situation. 'I'm really sorry,' I muttered, dying of embarrassment, 'I'll just be a moment.' And, careful not to look too closely, I blessed the room in record time, ushered the others out, and hastily closed the door. I looked at the lady, who just shrugged. Obviously whatever her eldest and his girlfriend had been doing was a regular occurrence.

Safely back in the living room, I gave a final blessing, and noted a now noticeably more relaxed lady sketching the sign of the cross on herself, her youngest still watching with fascination. 'I think that's it,' I said smiling, 'but if there are any more problems, please get in touch.'

Dave nodded and showed us to the door. After a few moments, the vicar and I found ourselves sitting in the car. 'That was amazing,' he said, his eyes sparkling with excitement. 'So we exorcised the ghost of the monk!'

'What monk?' I shot back – having spent over an hour being extra nice to the family had made me feel really tired, and maybe less inclined to be diplomatic.

He looked crestfallen and puzzled. 'The monk the boy was talking about,' he stammered.

Feeling thoroughly guilty, I moderated my tone considerably. 'I'm not convinced there was ever a ghostly monk,' I explained, 'in fact, I suspect he was never convinced either.'

'But what did he see?' he asked, flummoxed.

'Could be anything, really, but that wasn't what caused all the disturbance.'

'Really?' He now sounded shocked. 'So, what was it?'

'I think it was the old man.'

'What, he's in there haunting the house?!'

'Do you remember I asked the lady whether the activity had stopped since he'd died?'

'Yeah, sort of.'

'OK. Well the reason I was asking was because if it had continued after he'd died, that might have been the explanation, or the monk if it ever existed.'

He nodded sagely.

'But it stopped when he died.'

'How come?'

'Poltergeist activity as we call it is always caused by someone alive and present, so it was someone in the house, and because it stopped when he died, it must have been him.'

'So, no ghosts?' my colleague now sounded disappointed.

'No ghosts,' I agreed.

He was silent for a few moments, and then he turned to me, eyes sparkling once again with excitement. 'That was amazing!' he gasped again.

I have often thought about that case and to this day I feel so sorry for the father. When he was young, his life was full of hope: his arranged marriage to a girl who had quite clearly once been beautiful, and then their promise of a new life. But on a grey day in December few places are at their best, and I suspect that his housing estate wasn't lovely at any time of year. He must have missed the sun and the light so much!

But his life was never the same. The fact that his English wasn't good would have cut him off from his neighbours, and then his delight in his family must have been diminished by the fact that they truly had gone native! I can imagine him sitting there, in pain from his cancer, in a turbulent house full of fornicating teenagers, far from home and cut off from everyone.

And then that moment, when one morning he can't cope any longer, and the tension earths itself in the slipper that flies across the room, striking just a few inches from the son, his eldest boy whom he no doubt loved, but who was so different from anything he might even have been able to imagine when he was a boy. Poor guy.

## 'Minimum of publicity'

It was, as I've said, this case that brought me to public attention, which is a little embarrassing because one of the usually observed protocols is that the ministry of deliverance should be conducted with the minimum of publicity – being splashed across the pages of the nation's newspapers barely counts as 'minimum of publicity'. So, you may be wondering why I'm telling this story, rather than any of my colleagues. A friend of mine is both a priest and a law lecturer, and as such is interested in the ways in which the two worlds she inhabits collide. In particular she is interested in human rights legislation, and approached me with a proposal. The Law School in Nottingham Trent University where she works was hosting a workshop for academics and practitioners on how changes in human rights laws may affect the work of deliverance ministers.

You may think that there is no link between them but, given the fact that a 'major exorcism' – the exorcism of a person who genuinely is possessed by a demon – is likely to take place without the consent of the unfortunate person (the theory being that demons do not readily submit to being exorcised), the question arises, are their human rights being violated? The workshop sought to explore some of these issues and others, including changes in rules about the insurance of deliverance ministers.

It may surprise you to learn that deliverance ministers need insurance of some description and, at least in Anglican circles, cover is provided by the Ecclesiastical Insurance Group (EIG), which also insures the majority of church buildings. In recent clarification, the only practitioners who are actually covered by the EIG are those who are commissioned by their bishop. If a vicar who is not a commissioned deliverance minister is approached, they are covered only if they consult one of the commissioned ministers and are acting on their advice.

At this stage you may be wondering what might go wrong. But if it is generally known that a house has been 'exorcised' then the price of the house may drop, which would mean that the minister might be sued for the difference. In a world of litigation, it's best to be safe than sorry, so there have been wholesale changes in the Church's practice on these matters.

Now, I am not an expert on human rights, but I am up to date on the insurance position, and I was drafted in to talk about it and to give some context to the whole day. So, I duly gave my little presentation, complete with cheeky 'Gothic' graphics, and then questions were asked.

A hand went up at the back. 'I'm a pagan exorcist,' said the man, 'have you ever had any interfaith involvement?'

I thought for a moment and said, 'I was once called in by Social Services to see a Muslim family who claimed one of them had seen the ghost of a monk, and because it was a Christian ghost, they were told they needed a Christian priest. I'm pretty much convinced it was poltergeist activity, and not a ghost.' I paused to think. 'That's about it, really.'

The mania of Christmas came and went, and then one Wednesday afternoon my parish administrator had a phone call from *The Sunday Times*: one of their journalists wanted to speak to me urgently.

When I got through to them, they told me that they were about to publish a story about me being asked to conduct the exorcism of a Muslim woman, but I had refused because I was worried about ritual sexual abuse! Wow! To be fair, at the day in Nottingham someone had brought up the subject of exorcism and sexual abuse, but that had been much later in the day. Nevertheless, this had been added to my story, which now had everything: paranormal activity, immigrants, Muslims and sex!

When I spluttered that this wasn't what had happened, the answer was that they were going to publish anyway, so I might as well get the story right. I found myself giving a damage limitation interview.

As soon as I got home, I spoke to the Church in Wales press officer, who was very supportive, as was my bishop when the story hit the press – and not just *The Sunday Times*, but the *Sun*, the *Daily Mail*, the *Daily Express*, the *Mirror*, and the *Daily Telegraph*. It was also featured on Radio 4's Sunday press review, and was on the front page of the *Daily Star* the following day. In fact, pretty much the only UK national newspaper that didn't pick it up was *The Guardian* which, of course, meant that almost none of my clergy friends were aware of this at all, being *Guardian* readers to a woman, man and probably child!

Various branches of the BBC were interested, and the parish administrator was rushed off her feet, dealing with the BBC Asian Service ('nothing to see here' was our reply), and BBC 3, which wanted to film me doing a real case (no chance!), as well as an American talk radio station called *Midnight in the Desert* (which we ignored). I was asked my views on the Loch Ness Monster (Nessie and I have a non-disclosure agreement, so please, no further questions), and we were inundated with requests for deliverance cases, most of which were re-routed to local vicars.

The most high profile request came from Radio 5 Live. This proved to be one of the most frightening experiences of my life – dealing with terrifying paranormal occurrences is nothing compared with being interviewed live.

Much more gentle was an interview with BBC local radio – they even gave me the questions in advance, although I was faintly discomfited to realise it was being broadcast on Halloween, much to the amusement of a new colleague who couldn't believe how naive I was when I had an interview request on 30th October, and failed to see the significance of, 'It'll be going out tomorrow!' Clergy really do live in a parallel universe, or perhaps it's just me.

And the reaction? From my clergy colleagues, a lot of sympathy and support: for most clergy this would be their worst nightmare, and I have to admit I lost quite a bit of sleep over it. The reaction of the Church's media officers was more nuanced.

There was a lot of support, but also a feeling that maybe this is something the Church needs to talk about a bit more. They knew that these things should be done with the minimum of publicity, but the suggestion was that this referred to individual cases, and not to this ministry as a whole. It was an interesting perspective, and once my name had been put firmly into the public domain, explaining what we do seemed like a better option than pretending it didn't exist. Hence this book.

The reaction of people outside the Church has been fascinating. There has been a whole load of people who are surprised that the Anglican Church has deliverance ministers, and had assumed that this was something that only Roman Catholics did.

And then, there has been the hostility. As you may have guessed, I live in a bit of a bubble. I rarely encounter people who are hostile to the Church, because they would probably avoid me. Occasionally at weddings or christenings I encounter boredom or indifference ('Can we get the God bit over, so we can get to the party?'), but I usually manage to win over at least some of them by the bouncy, genial persona I present for these occasions. So, it came as a surprise when I encountered the full force of the listening public as BBC Radio 5 Live's Emma Barnett read out a series of hostile tweets, and asked me to counter them!

So, just to get the record straight: No, we don't charge for the service! No, we don't collude with people's delusions, and yes, we do encourage them to see their doctors or other medical professionals! And, yes, we do believe in God, but we respect your right not to, thanks!

# Chapter 4

# Is there such a thing as the supernatural?

The ordinary life of a priest seems exactly that – so ordinary that we seldom stop to think about the supernatural aspects of the whole thing. If you read pretty much any novel written before the angry young men of the 1960s, you will discover that stories are peppered with references to the vicar – or more likely in country parishes the rector – who is seen as part of the establishment, just like the squire or the village postmistress. Think of all those whodunnits by Dorothy L. Sayers or Agatha Christie – they are there, just as they are in Jane Austen's work. In fact, they are so much a part of the fabric of life in Britain (as in many other parts of the Western world), that we forget they are there to represent the supernatural aspects of life.

In fact, it is possible to be a priest in today's world and to forget this too. Often the clergy themselves see their role as being to represent 'the Church' which acts as some sort of benevolent (well, usually benevolent) NGO, doing good works, organising food banks, sitting on endless community and charity committees, and generally being benign. Indeed, the Church is so often seen as an essential part of society that the supernatural aspects of the job are sometimes forgotten. Yes, we state in church that we believe in God – who is surely a supernatural entity if ever there were one – but out in the world, we barely mention God at all. He's still there, lurking at the back of people's minds, but definitely not there in the foreground. And maybe for many people (priests included) that's where *he* needs to stay – safe and out of the way.

In church, things are theoretically different, but sometimes the whole thing can become so much of a performance that we forget about God. I was deeply touched by some feedback I received about the informal church service that has developed in my church in the last few years. It runs alongside the very formal services and, other than the fact that it was attracting people and that we had hit on a formula that seemed to work, I hadn't really thought about it very much.

The textbooks on how to grow your church will tell you not to run things for families on a Sunday, and especially not on a Sunday morning because families prefer afternoons or weekday evenings. But this service is at 9.30 on a Sunday morning which seems to suit our families very well indeed. A lot of kids are up at 8am, watching TV or playing computer games, and most parents are up with them. Church at 9.30 probably comes as a relief. The service is a combination of relatively modern worship songs and some traditional hymns. There is a Bible reading, some prayers, often a short film on the theme for the Sunday, a very short talk from the clergy, and an activity prayer that will require everyone to stand up and move around. It lasts only 35 minutes, theoretically because people have places to go, but most of the time those people are still there drinking coffee at 10.50am, when another group is coming in for the next service at 11am. Also, and again slightly unusually, it attracts a genuinely cross-generational congregation. Yes there are families with young children, and there are also teenagers (a rare sighting in most churches), but there are also people in late middle age and even old age too. Once a month there is a Eucharist for which I wear the full traditional robes and talk through what I'm doing and why I'm doing it, and at which (thanks to a Church in Wales change of rules) everyone who has been baptised or christened may receive Communion, whereas it is still the case in the Church of England, for example, that people have to be confirmed before Communion. In Wales this ruling applies across the board, although under-fives aren't allowed any of the wine for legal reasons.

Obviously, I was aware that this was working, and growing, but I had never really stopped to think why, until one day a man arrived from a free evangelical church that he had attended for many years, liked what he saw, and came back.

'What I like about it,' he explained, 'is that everything is focused on God.'

'Isn't that what worship is about?' I answered.

'Yes,' he said, 'but it so rarely is. Most of the time it's going through the motions, or it's about the minister, or some big guest preacher you have. I like the way this is all about God.' I was taken aback and humbled, because I'm not sure I am very good at all this, despite twenty-odd years' experience of doing it.

But just occasionally the 'supernatural' for want of a better expression seems to break through. Sometimes I'm sort of expecting it, and sometimes not. Now, you may be wondering what I mean by 'supernatural'. There are numerous definitions, but maybe for me what I mean is something that is outside normal experience or that modern science cannot satisfactorily explain.

The most usual place for an awareness of the supernatural to break through is when I am at the altar in church, celebrating the Eucharist, the central act of Christian worship where we bless bread and wine, which many Christians believe become somehow the Body and Blood of Jesus. There are all sorts of theological explanations of this (transubstantiation being just one of them), but I just know that sometimes when I am elevating the host (holding up the communion wafer so people can see it) I am somehow gazing into eternity or at least somehow standing on the edge of a sphere of being that is beyond what I can normally see and perceive, and when this happens I am aware that what I am holding is the most precious thing in the world.

It can also happen to me when I am baptising new Christians (usually, but not always, babies), and when I stand over the font. The years seem to fall away as I stand where so many priests before me have stood, but also in the place Jesus himself is standing. I know it sounds weird, but this is the supernatural aspect of being a vicar.

But it happens on other occasions too. As well as offering ministry of deliverance, we also offer what we call a ministry of healing. It is one of the traditional seven sacraments of the Church, and one that has become fashionable in some evangelical and charismatic churches particularly since the 1960s – although they would probably deny it is a real 'sacrament', but then religious professionals of any description are very good at disagreeing with one another. For more traditional

Anglicans like me it takes something of a back seat, although when I visit people in hospital I will always offer to pray for them. Sometimes I will use the healing oil like I did all those years ago with baby Bethan, but most of the time I just touch them and pray for them to be healed. Just occasionally the results are extraordinary. Take the story of Brenda.

Brenda was one of my parishioners, and a regular church-goer, and I was told one Sunday afternoon that she had had a very bad stroke and was in the local hospital, where she was not expected to pull through. I scrambled my things together, and went to see her as soon as I could. There she was in a side ward. There was no one there with her, although the nurse told me her husband had just popped home for a few things.

I was quite shocked when I saw Brenda. The previous week, she had been a confident lady in her 70s, but now she could barely speak and just about managed to hold my hand. So I held her hand, and prayed for her and with her.

As I did, I was aware that my hands were very warm, but thought nothing much of it. I made the sign of the cross on her forehead as I said a blessing for her, and then I left the room. As I walked sadly down the corridor I bumped into her husband, and we stopped to have a chat before he went back to sit with his wife. 'If there's anything I can do, please let me know,' I said. I expected the next call, if there was one, to tell me that she had passed away.

Yet during the week, I was delighted to learn that Brenda had been well enough to leave hospital and was back at home. It was one of those weeks where I barely had time to think, but the following week I was surprised to see her in church.

After the service we had a chat and she said, 'Thank you very much for coming to see me, Father. I felt so much better after you'd gone.' Brenda had a very dry sense of humour, so I was not sure whether this was supposed to be a compliment or not. I smirked, and she gave me a stern look. 'No, I mean it, because after you'd gone, I felt like my face had come back to normal, and when my husband came in I could speak to him clearly.'

And then she fixed me with a twinkling eye. 'Do you have healing powers?' Utterly taken aback, I muttered that as far as I knew I didn't.

Again, she gave me an appraising look with a thoughtful, 'Hmm.'

This isn't the only time something like this has happened. Another parishioner I went to see came out of hospital unexpectedly after a similar incident and, although he died not long afterwards, used the time to make his peace with his family.

Is this an instance of the supernatural, a placebo effect, or the body's amazing ability to heal itself? Are my feelings of closeness to the supernatural at the Eucharist and at baptisms generated by my unconscious mind, or are they genuine? As a deliverance minister, I am expected to deal with the supernatural, as well as with things that people think are supernatural but turn out to be very ordinary indeed. In fact, so far, we haven't met anything that you could say was definitely paranormal, other than borderline cases of poltergeist activity. So it's time to meet our first proper ghost.

## The phantom organist

'I know it sounds really corny, but we can sometimes hear organ music.' The woman speaking was Lucy, a close friend who knew I had recently been on a training course for the deliverance ministry.

'Organ music?' I enquired – imagining something out of the Phantom of the Opera.

'Yes,' she said, obviously hearing my thoughts, 'not like big thunderous Bach, like you hear in the Phantom of the Opera, it's a sort of jolly Yamaha-like music, more like the sort of thing you'd hear at a fairground.'

'Was it loud?' I asked.

'Not really. In fact, we thought it was coming from next door, but it wasn't loud at all. It's always difficult with neighbours, in case they think you're complaining, but I did get the chance to say how impressed we were with the organist, because sometimes we could hear them playing. Anyway, the neighbour gave me a really strange look, and said that they didn't have an organ, but that the lady who lived in our house before us did have a sort of Yamaha organ, and was really good.' Lucy paused for breath. 'The other odd thing is that there have been all sorts of things going missing . . .'

'OK, tell me some more.'

'Well, my son keeps losing his shoes. Now, he's really meticulous and tidy about his stuff, and he always puts things in the right place, but he'll get there and, say, one of his football boots will be missing, and we'll find it on top of the kitchen cupboard. It's all really weird.'

'It sounds it,' I said. 'This organ music, how long have you been hearing it?'

'Since as long as we've lived in the house.'

I did a quick mental calculation – their teenage son had been born in the house so this had been going on for a long time. 'How long has your son been losing things?'

'Oh, forever. Stuff always goes missing round here. In fact,

I blame my great-grandmother. I've always felt close to her, and sometimes it's like I've felt her standing just behind me, watching me do things. I don't really mind. We were really close when she was alive and now she's gone, well, she's not going to do me any harm is she?'

'No,' I agreed – my friend doesn't need very much encouragement to open up.

'But I'm beginning to wonder whether it *is* actually her or someone else,' Lucy admitted.

'Was it the organ music?' I suggested.

'No,' she sounded puzzled, 'it's only recently I've had the conversation with next door. They're moving, and I was just chatting to them about how I'd miss them, and the music came up in conversation.'

'Oh, I see. So, you think it might be the lady who lived in the house before you?'

'I'm pretty much convinced it must be because they said that she used to be a fantastic organist in her time – she'd played at the local cinema as a girl apparently, and she was very attached to the house.'

'Right,' I said.

'In fact, I think I've seen her.'

'The lady?'

'Yes. It was a couple of nights ago. I was doing some housework, and was standing in the living room, and for some reason I looked towards the stairs, and there she was, walking down the stairs. I was absolutely terrified, I can tell you.'

'Did you see her face?'

'No, thank God, I didn't. Because of the angle of the staircase, all I saw was the bottom couple of feet of her nightie – it was an old-fashioned pink nylon nightie like old people used to wear.'

'What was she like?'

'Er, it was like she was actually there. Like there was some creepy old lady who had been asleep upstairs and was now coming down the stairs to see me.'

'What did you do?'

'I screamed, and then I told her to go away because she was frightening me.'

'And did she?'

'She did, thank goodness. At least when I looked again, she wasn't there.'

'Are you sure you didn't imagine it?'

'Yes, of course I'm sure. If I'd imagined a ghost coming down my stairs it would not have been wearing a pink nylon nightie!'

'Just asking.' I felt suitably abashed. Lucy paused for breath.

'Has there been anything else weird going on?' I asked.

'Yes,' she said. 'For years now, we've been able to hear the sound of someone running their hand along the wall on the stairs you know, going up and down. And we've always assumed, a bit like the organ music, that it was coming from next door. But I've been thinking about this for a while, and I asked my father-in-law when he was here the other day what he thought. "Solid as a rock," was what he said. "You'd never hear people moving round next door with walls as thick as this." So we were wondering if that sort of rubbing sound might be part of it. What do you think?'

What I thought was that this seemed to be a fairly clear-cut example of what we call a place memory. Place memories appear in all sorts of different situations, and sometimes they become famous. One of the best known examples is the house by the Minster in York where people have seen Roman legionaries moving through the cellar at a little below ground level, which is where the Praetorium (military headquarters) was in Roman times. The Roman soldiers are not *there* in any real sense. You can't communicate with them, and they make no attempt to communicate. It is as if they are somehow recorded by the building and played back. The famous Borley Rectory stories that I – like generations of children before and since – terrified myself with when I was a child ('the most haunted house in Britain') are probably also examples of the same sort of phenomena. Closer to where I grew up, there are stories of hauntings at Llancaiach, an old farmhouse owned by the local authority where they hold twice nightly ghost tours in the season.

Then there are the stories about haunted moors, haunted pubs and all those sorts of things, all of which (if they are not a figment of people's imaginations) may reflect place memories, effectively a sort of ghost that does not try to communicate.

The textbooks tell you that if a deliverance minister is dealing with a place memory, they should celebrate the Eucharist for the repose of the dead spirit, a ritual also called a Requiem Mass. This is a mildly controversial subject, because there are whole branches of the Christian Church which at least in theory refuse to pray for the dead. They work on the principle that, once you're dead, you're in the hands of God and there's nothing anyone can do about it: in the Anglican Church most evangelicals will hold to this view. On the other hand, the majority of Christians (including Roman Catholics, Eastern Orthodox Christians and many mainstream Anglicans) are perfectly happy with the idea of praying for the dead.

From the point of view of the deliverance minister, the whole thing raises interesting questions about life and death. You could argue that place memories are simply not there at all. But at the same time, even though there is often no direct attempt at communication, they can still be evidence of people whose attachment to life has not been completely broken by death. When there is evidence of attempts at communication, we appear to need a much more flexible approach to the whole life-death divide, which is what Christians have often insisted with their talk of the 'Church militant' (still alive) and the 'Church triumphant' (the dead), although they would rarely apply this language to the paranormal.

Belief in ghosts is common in most human societies, and is certainly found in the Bible, the foundation document of Christianity, as we shall see when we come to look at what I have called 'true hauntings'. Nevertheless, belief in ghosts plays a negligible part in Christian theology. Christian theology is, however, based on the experience of the Church, and the fact that the Church continues to appoint people to be deliverance ministers (or exorcists) suggests that there is some wriggle room.

In this case of this particular ghost, I had no reason to believe that my friend was not of sound mind: she does not suffer from any psychiatric illnesses, and the fact that quite a few people heard the organ music and the noises on the stairs would lead me to believe that what she experienced was true. It certainly fits the type of place memory found in the textbooks. These same textbooks tell you that you deal with them by celebrating a Requiem Mass, so that is what I offered, and that is what happened. Just as a caveat, this was an early case for me. These days, even if I think it is a place memory, I would usually start with a simple house blessing, and then offer a Requiem Mass at a later stage. This is partly because many deliverance ministers treat the Requiem as a last resort and also because, from experience, a simple house blessing almost always works. House blessings include prayers for protection, a prayer that God might be 'known as the inhabitant of this dwelling and defender of this household', and the Lord's Prayer, which contains the words, 'Deliver us from evil.'

We call any service of Mass or Eucharist a 'celebration' because Christians regard it as a celebration of the death and subsequent resurrection of Jesus. This is the central fact on which Christianity seems to stand or fall – that on the first Easter day Jesus, who had been crucified the Friday before, rose again. In the service, traditional Christians believe that Jesus the Son of God becomes really present in the bread and the wine, as they somehow become his body and blood. So the Requiem Mass as used in a haunted house is, to put it very crudely, a way of bringing the physical reality of God into contact with the soul of a dead person or whatever entity is there that really should not be there: it's quite powerful stuff, and not something to be taken lightly.

For this reason, as well as the usual prayers that deliverance ministers always say before going on duty (St Patrick's Breastplate is one we often use, in conjunction with the Lord's Prayer), when I am celebrating a Requiem Mass, I wear the traditional vestments. To be honest, I will wear these even when I am celebrating a very informal Eucharist at the All Age Service, too – never let it be said that I miss an occasion to dress up! But at the same time, vestments are strange and in some ways comforting: it is almost as if, when we put them on, we are like actors who put on costumes to 'become' someone different. And the similarity between priests and actors is not coincidental: the very first plays in the West were performed at religious ceremonies.

Occasionally priests in non-Western cultures have worn masks, a bit like the ghostly priest I sensed when I was a curate.

So, in this case, I donned a long white robe called an alb, which I then half-tied with a piece of white cotton rope which we call a girdle (yes, priests find that funny too!). There is then a coloured scarf, the stole, which is traditionally crossed over at the front and is held in place by the girdle.

Finally, over the top, is the poncho-like chasuble.

Occasionally in films (such as *Robin Hood Prince of Thieves*) and in TV dramas you will see priests wearing the stole over the chasuble – this is almost always wrong. Also in these things you might see priests or bishops wearing such vestments outside a church service. Again this is not something we do: vestments are only worn in church when we are conducting services in church and on no other occasion. They come in several basic colours depending on the time of year or the reason for the celebration of the Eucharist: funerals and commemorations of the dead are usually celebrated either in black, or more often in purple.

On this occasion I went for purple, and was just about to put the chasuble over my head when the doorbell rang. Lucy looked at her watch. 'It's just my parents. I told them to come at 11.30,' she said, 'but they knew you were coming, so they've come a bit early.' Pat and Frank were people I knew, yet I was slightly nonplussed at having an audience. But, I thought, maybe it's just as well to have some backup. So, I greeted them, composed myself, and then placed the chasuble over my head: we were ready to begin.

At the centre of the living room, we had set up some candles and placed the vessels with the bread and wine on the linen 'corporal' which I carry in my bag as an altar cloth. I went to it and began the Requiem Mass, which is a pared down version of the service you will find in parish churches across the world every Sunday: obviously there were no hymns, and only a short reading from one of the Gospels, and then the rite of the blessing of holy water with the sprinkling of the house.

'My son asks if you can give the back bedroom a good go, because he says it's always been a bit creepy in there,' whispered Lucy.

When I conduct a rite of deliverance, or when I am taking a service in church, I am usually so 'into' what I am doing that it's almost like entering a different zone. And despite the fact that I felt rather self-conscious to begin with, this case was no different. Eventually we arrived back at the living room where we had begun, and the Eucharist continued, again just like church on a Sunday morning, except with an explicit intention of the repose of the souls of the dead.

As part of the central Eucharistic prayer, after I said the words of Jesus over the bread – 'Take, eat, this is my body which is given for you: do this to remember me' – as always, I lifted the 'host' (communion wafer) high so that they could all see it, and placed it carefully back down, kneeling in front of it for a few moments, before taking up the chalice of wine, and continuing with the prayer.

We then said the Lord's Prayer together, and we all received the Communion of the bread and wine (I knew that they had all been confirmed like good Anglicans, even if only one of them went to church with any regularity), and then there was a final blessing.

'It feels different,' said Lucy, 'lighter, somehow.'

I shrugged – I was unaware of this, but didn't disbelieve her.

Later on, she rang me to say that her son was thrilled as the creepiness had gone, and since then she has never reported any untoward happenings.

That wasn't, however, quite the end of the story. I found myself talking to Lucy's mother Pat a week or so later, and she said, 'As you know, Frank sometimes *sees* things.'

I was aware that he might be what you could call a psychic, and we had had the occasional chat about it.

'Well,' she continued, 'when you were doing that house blessing, Frank says he saw something. Maybe you might have a chat with him about it.'

It was all a bit mysterious, so I tracked Frank down and asked him about it. 'It was really strange,' he said. 'I didn't see a ghost or anything, but while you were doing the service, I was aware that there was a mist that was gathering just in front of you in the living room. It was like swirling mist, and seemed to be getting darker, and then it suddenly vanished like it had been sucked up the chimney while you were doing that long prayer.'

'The Eucharistic prayer?' I asked.

He looked thoughtful for a moment. 'Is that the one with the bread and the wine?'

'Yes, that's the one.'

Frank nodded.

'Just as a matter of interest, can you remember exactly when the mist left?'

'Oh yes,' he said, 'it was when you picked up the bread.'

'At the beginning, the middle or the end?'

'You said something about it being Jesus' body, and then you lifted it up high, and that was when the mist disappeared.'

I was stunned. It's one thing learning about the semi-supernatural parts of Christian practice, things like the traditional belief that Jesus becomes present when the words are said over the bread and when it is lifted up, but it is something completely different having these ideas confirmed.

If there was any moment when a mediaeval theologian might have said that a spirit of the dead might be freed from the earth, it would be this one! I was, as I said, stunned, but also just a little disappointed, not that the ritual seemed to have worked, but that I had missed it.

## The light-dark house

St Giles' Church in Wrexham has, as I've suggested, a significant ministry to children and young people, so the appearance of a young couple with a toddler in a pushchair is not as unexpected as it is in many churches. They were both in their early twenties and they looked deeply uncomfortable, even more than most people do in a church when speaking to a priest they don't know! The most likely explanations for the appearance of a young family in church are that they either want to get married, or they want to have the baby christened. I assumed that it was one or the other or indeed both of those possibilities, although because they were clearly very uncomfortable I instinctively invited them to join me in a quiet corner while my colleague dealt with another couple with a baby.

The young man cleared his throat, looked nervously at his other half. 'We were wondering if you could help us, please?' he began. 'We've got . . . er . . .'

'What he means is, we think we've got a ghost,' the woman's voice sounded slightly exasperated, as if they had rehearsed how this was going to go, and he'd agreed that he would do the talking, but had bottled it at the last minute.

'All right,' I said as gently as I could, 'why do you think that?'

They looked at one another again. 'We keep seeing these shadows around the place,' the young man had found his voice, 'and then stuff seems to go missing all the time.'

'What sort of stuff?' I asked, gesturing towards one of the pews at the back of the church, where they sat down.

'Thanks,' said the woman. 'The stuff that goes missing is usually to do with the baby – her shoes and socks and things like that.'

'Is there anything else? These shadows, do you tend to see them anywhere in particular?'

'Yes,' continued the woman, 'we tend to see them around the baby's cot, and we're terrified. We spoke to my husband's mother about it, because she's a Catholic, and she told us that it was a ghost, and not to do anything about it in case it becomes destructive. But we can't live there any longer. We don't like leaving one another alone, and the house is just horrible: it's dark and cold.'

'We're on the verge of selling it,' continued her husband, 'but even though my mother told us not to, we thought we'd come to you first. Because,' he reasoned, 'even if we do annoy the ghost, it won't follow us to another house. Will it?'

I wasn't sure whether that was a genuine question or not, but decided to treat it as such. 'If it's a ghost, it won't follow you, because from my experience if it's a ghost it will be sort of attached to the house.' I had a hunch it was probably a place memory because it sounded a little bit like the house we had lived in when I was a curate.

And then it occurred to me. 'The house – you said it was dark and cold. Is it an old house?'

They thought about it for a moment. 'Oldish,' said the woman, 'built after the war, I think.'

'OK. But it's cold and dark?'

'It shouldn't be, but it is,' she answered. 'It looks over the park, and the whole of the front of the house is south-facing, so it should be light. And we've had new heating installed, so it shouldn't be cold, but it is.'

'All right, thanks for telling me. Can I just ask, how long have you lived there?'

'We've been there about four years, now,' she said.

'And has it always been cold and dark like this?'

Again they thought about it. 'No,' said the man slowly, 'it was like that when the baby was born.'

'Before or after?'

They looked puzzled.

'Before, I think,' he said.

'But then I was pregnant, so the ghost might have attached itself to the baby in the womb.' The woman looked slightly sheepish. 'At least that's what my mother-in-law thinks.'

I nodded sympathetically. 'Can I ask one more weird question?' They suddenly looked very anxious, so I continued quickly. 'Did you have any major structural work done to the house before you had the baby?'

The man looked dumbfounded. 'How did you know? We had the house knocked through so we could put the baby in the back of the living room while we were in the front.'

'Thanks,' I smiled and nodded.

'So can you help us?' asked the woman, almost as if she sensed this was some sort of trick.

'Oh, yes,' I said.

'Really?' she asked.

'Yes. Because I lived in a house like that, and the local vicar came and blessed it, and that was it.'

'Will you come around and bless our house too?'

'Let's have a look,' I said, flicked through my online diary and, after a snatched conversation with my colleague at the other side of the church, came back and asked, 'Is Tuesday morning any good?'

They looked at one another. The man, they told me, was self-employed and the woman a stay at home mother. 'So, Tuesday's good,' said the husband.

Place memories seem to be somehow attached to places or buildings, but they seem to be triggered by a range of things. One of the most common causes is major structural work: pulling down internal walls or adding extensions seem to release something, as very often does the arrival of children in the house. It is useless to speculate on whether it is the house that is the problem or the people who live there but, from twenty years' experience, when I ask if they have had any major structural work done, nine times out of ten they will behave like this unfortunate young couple and treat me as if I'm either psychic (which I'm most assuredly not), or as if I am a latter-day Sherlock Holmes (more flattering, but closer to the mark more by default than anything else).

Tuesday proved to be a sparklingly bright day, and there was not a cloud in the sky. My colleague and I hadn't had very much chance to talk about it since the Sunday morning service, so we travelled together, which gave me the chance to fill in the details. The house when we arrived was truly lovely. It faced south and looked over a large park across a narrow tree-lined road, and although there was a large tree not too far from the front of the house, it should have been filled with light, especially on such a glorious spring day.

But when we walked in, all we felt was gloom, as if the house itself was sad and depressed. The man and woman looked troubled.

'How are you doing?' I asked.

'Once we had spoken to you, it all got worse,' the woman said sadly, 'like it knew that its time had come and that you were coming round. In fact, we haven't been able to sleep here, it's been so cold. And the baby's with my mother.'

I nodded. 'Very sensible,' I said, remembering how icily cold it had been in the house we lived in when I was a curate.

'In fact,' she continued, 'my husband wanted me to ring you and tell you not to come.' He looked a bit shifty under her gaze. 'But I said I had had enough, and I wasn't going to let it hound me out of my own home.' She sounded both proud and tearful.

'That's good,' I said, hoping I sounded reassuring. 'Let's see what we can do.'

One of the great things about having colleagues with you when you are out on a deliverance case is that they can observe all sorts of things that you simply can't, or rather, that I can't. Occasionally they have reported a change in the atmosphere, or an alteration in the way people react and behave, and, although the nature of the incident has never been quite as dramatic as the one Frank reported, it is good to have another pair of eyes and ears.

However, in this case, I didn't need anyone to tell me what was happening. We began, as we always do, in the main room, where we lit candles and blessed water. We then went around the house, with its modern furnishings and decor, and with its pervading sense of clammy gloom. We spent time praying silently in the baby's room, and I made sure that I splashed a decent amount of holy water both at the cot and in the corners of the room. And then we returned to the main room.

For some reason, I decided that the best place to begin

and end was the place where the wall had been removed, and so that's where I was standing when we all said the Lord's Prayer together.

There have been many dramatic moments in my ministry, but this put them all into the shade – in more ways than one.

For a start, as we were praying the words, and as I became aware of the others saying them with me, I felt my body somehow arch backwards, as if it were being stiffened and straightened by forces beyond my control. In fact, it almost felt as if something was travelling through my spine, and contorting it. But that was nothing compared with what happened next.

We all said the final Amen together, and then I heard my colleague's voice. 'Wow!'

This was followed by the woman's 'Oh my God.'

I realised I had my eyes closed, and I opened them.

We were obviously standing in the same room we had been in before. But it was also, at one and the same time, completely different: now, suddenly, in the space of thirty seconds, it was light and bright, as if the clouds had rolled back from the sun, and a gloomy day had suddenly become high summer.

But that was not the only change, because the house was suddenly and unexplainably warm too, as if the temperature had risen by about four or five degrees.

I was utterly astonished. The house that we had lived in when I had been a curate had undergone a similar sort of change but, compared with this, it was almost gradual. This time it was instant. And the change affected the people in the room too, because we all started to laugh spontaneously for joy.

This seemed to me to be another formative experience. For Christians the Lord's Prayer, as well as being the prayer we use most often, is also the most powerful. We call it 'Lord's Prayer' because we believe that it was given to us by the Lord Jesus who, as I've said, Christians believe is the Son of God, or 'God the Son'. So, the Prayer is in some ways God the Son's prayer to God the Father, and when we are saying it, we believe that, somehow, we are sharing in the communi-cation of God himself. I know that's quite a heavy idea, but the more you go into these things, the heavier they get. The Lord's Prayer also contains the line 'but deliver us from evil,' which has been described as a 'minor exorcism' in its own right. We'll come on to exorcisms later.

But going back to this case, it was another example of the way that the bit of the ritual that is supposed to work does actually work! Now, you may think I'm labouring the point, but you have to remember that I'm pretty sceptical, and am disinclined to take anyone's word for anything: my motto might be, 'Don't tell me, prove it to me.' And this, if I needed it, was proof. But whatever the truth, it worked in this particular instance: the place memory was banished; light and warmth and joy had been restored to the house.

## The juggernaut hits

This family had been plagued by some sort of restless spirit which I have categorised as a place memory because there was no attempt at communication. But to some extent, they got off lightly compared with another family. Again, it was a surprisingly similar scenario. Not long after this case, a woman was standing at the back of the church after the main Sunday service, smiling in a very nervous fashion. 'Can I talk to you about something?' she began.

It was one of those amazingly chaotic days – they do happen in church. 'Yes, of course, if you give me a few minutes I'll be with you.' When I had finished what I needed to do, we sat down at the back of the church.

'We've been having a bit of bother at home,' she said. 'Me and my husband and our teenage son and daughter have just moved into our new house, and all sorts of strange things have started happening.' And so she described the classic signs of poltergeist activity: things going missing and shoes (why is it so often shoes?) moving around seemingly on their own. She explained that her son, who was 'sensitive to these things', had seen figures moving around in his bedroom, and was too frightened to stay in the house. 'He used to see stuff in the old house, but it's got worse, much worse in this one.' She told me that things seemed to be going wrong, and the whole family was jumpy and easily upset, and they were having family rows about things that had never bothered them before. 'But we've lived with it,' she said, philosophically.

'OK,' I nodded encouragingly.

'Well, you do don't you? You just live with it, get on with it, and you don't really put these things together.'

'So, what changed?' I asked.

'Well,' she said matter-of-factly, 'we decided to do something about it after the juggernaut hit the front of the house.'

'What?!' I sputtered.

'Sorry,' she apologised, chuckling slightly, 'that's what it felt like.'

'So . . . ?'

'Well, it was about two o'clock in the morning, and we were all in bed and asleep.

'And then there was the most astonishing bang and the whole house felt exactly like a juggernaut had slammed into it. We just couldn't believe it. So my husband ran over to the window in a panic, fully expecting to see the back end of a lorry sticking out from the front window – it was that vivid. And my son did the same. But there was nothing there, nothing there at all. In fact, my husband said that he was being stupid, because the house is up a fifty foot bank, and you're hard-pressed to get a car down our street, let alone a lorry. But that's exactly what it felt like – I'm not making it up! – like some huge articulated lorry slamming at force into our house.' She paused for a few moments to take a breath.

'So, the following morning we looked around, and there was no damage, but then we knew there wouldn't be. And then we spoke to the neighbours, and they hadn't heard anything, not even the people who live in the other half of the semi. They slept through the whole night, and they've got young children.' I nodded sympathetically. 'So, we thought we'd better come to see you, because we'd heard from a friend that you'd been able to help her.' And she outlined what had happened to her friend – someone I had met over the course of my duties.

'A couple of questions, if I may? Do you know anything about the history of the house?'

'Yes, it was built just after the war, and an old couple lived there until they both died last year. They didn't have any children, but their niece was in charge of the sale, and she told me about them. They were devoted to one another, and the house was their little palace.'

'Had anyone else ever lived there?'

'No, they'd had it from new.'

'Just one more question, really,' I said. 'Have you had any work done to the house since you moved in?'

'Oh, yes, lots! It may have been their little palace, but

because they were very elderly, they hadn't really had much done for years. And the layout was inconvenient so my husband, who's a builder, ripped it all back to the shell and completely rebuilt it for us.'

'When you say rebuilt, what do you mean?' I enquired.

'Well, for a start the rooms were in the wrong place, so he took down most of the internal walls, and put in a new staircase. It's completely different now,' she said, enthusiastically. 'In fact, it's lovely, apart from the fact that it's haunted. Do you think you might be able to do something about it?'

'I'll do my best,' I said, and took their number.

In this instance the family lived outside my parish, so instead of asking my colleague from St Giles', I spoke to the local vicar, who sounded faintly shocked when I told him about it.

'I remember the couple, or at least I remember him. When she died, he was in hospital, so I had to go and see him there, and then when he died a couple of months later, I officiated his funeral as well. He was lovely, but the locals tell me she had a bit of a temper about her – well known in the village for all sorts of reasons, apparently,' and he filled in some of the details before stumbling to a halt.

'Will you come with me and see them?' I asked.

'Yes, if I have to,' he sounded doubtful. 'I suppose because I did their funerals, I'd better finish the job.' And between us and the homeowners, we agreed a time and date one afternoon.

When we arrived at the house, my colleague seemed nervous. 'I've never really done anything like this,' he confided. 'What should I do?'

'Just pray with me,' I replied.

'Is that it?'

'Pretty much.'

The lady took us around the house, and pointed out the changes she and her husband had made. Their teenage children, who had just come home from school, explained a little bit about what had been happening.

The son in particular seemed very upset. 'I can almost hear them,' he said, close to tears.

My colleague, who knew the family from the village, was very good with him, calming him down, telling him that the house was now in safe hands. I looked down at my 'safe hands' and wondered. As always, we blessed the house and, as so often, I was unaware of anything happening around me. We stopped and prayed in the children's bedrooms – the boy's room was approximately where the old master bedroom had been, so it's possible that it was there that the old lady had died. Finally, we returned to the living room, where we said the Lord's Prayer together.

'Are you all right?' I asked the family, sensing some sort of change.

'Wow, that was awesome!' gasped the daughter, 'absolutely awesome!'

Her brother just smiled.

'I think that's it,' said my colleague, seeming to take charge of the conversation, 'but get in touch with me and I'll get Jason back in, if we need to.'

As we walked away, I commented on the children's reaction.

'But it *was* awesome,' he said. 'There was an amazing change in the atmosphere: I've never felt anything like it. You didn't notice though, did you?'

'Not really, it's got to be pretty dramatic before I do,' I replied, thinking about the previous case earlier on that year.

'Well,' he said, 'it certainly looked that way to me.'

It helped that the initial contact had been personal, so afterwards my mind kept going back to that elderly couple and some of the details the local vicar had told me.

At some stage, like the Pakistani father in the previous chapter, their lives would have been full of hope. The old man had been in the forces, and when he'd been demobbed, he'd married the woman of his dreams who he'd met during the war. They had moved into quite a large house, hoping no doubt to fill it with children, but that had never happened. According to the gossip relayed by their vicar, the woman had turned to other men for comfort, but still, as the niece said, the house was their little palace.

You often wonder when people die what they might think of what came after them, and whether they would approve. But given their attachment to this house, I wondered whether they might have found a way of holding on, maybe in the fabric itself, which had then been so cruelly ripped out, and, although I was treating this as a place memory, there were aspects of the 'true haunting' about it. But before we turn to these, it is time for a series of encounters where things didn't quite go to plan!

# Chapter 5

## *It shouldn't happen to a priest*

Deliverance ministers are, as I've suggested, just ordinary parish priests who happen to have this as one of a range of specialisms. This may seem a bit strange, but one of the things that clergy are adept at doing is to shape their ministries around themselves.

Priests are unusual people really (and believe me, I have met some unusual priests in my time – at least one of whom will feature in this chapter!), because they are called not so much to do a job as to live a particular lifestyle. In fact, we tend to say that priests are paid a stipend rather than a salary – a salary or a wage is money you are paid for a job you are employed to do, whereas a stipend is money that someone gives you so that you do not have to take on paid employment. In other words, priests are theoretically free to devote their entire lives to God and the Church (not necessarily the same thing) and are paid enough not to have to worry about where the next meal is coming from.

This is all well and good, but of course many Anglican priests have husbands, wives or partners as well as families to take into account. We also often get to live in a nice big house while we are working, but then have to make provision for ourselves when we retire. Occasionally, priests will attempt to supplement their income by writing books or by taking on ministerial jobs that give them a little extra. So I, for example, have been paid a little bit extra for being a training officer, and have also been paid extra for some lecturing work I have done over the years. But, by and large, most priests get by on not an awful lot of money for a highly trained and often eye-wateringly well-qualified group of people.

This ministry, as I said, we tend to shape around us, although we obviously have to do the basics: taking Sunday services, conducting baptisms, weddings and funerals are pretty much part of the territory, although some priests will find ingenious ways to get out of some of these things too! But, by and large, my colleagues are devoted, hard-working and dedicated. What they actually spend their time doing depends as much as anything else on where they find themselves and what needs to be done.

Some clergy spend the whole of their ministries in rural settings. We all have this idea of country parsons spending the whole of their lives as naturalists (not to be confused with naturists, although there are some of those too!), writing learned tomes on the geology of the Cotswolds or the life of butterflies in the Rectory garden. These days – and I take my hat off to them for doing it – they spend their lives running large numbers of churches, all with their own church committees and parish councils, trying to get round all their churches whose service times are governed by the sort of rota you need a PhD in statistics to understand. Then there are the far-flung parishioners to take into account, as well as the fact that many of the church buildings are ancient and in need of attention, or (even worse) are less ancient and therefore in need of even more attention – at least they knew how to build in the Middle Ages! But for those priests who feel they are called to rural ministry, this is what gives them life and keeps them going, even if many urban priests tremble at the very idea of being out in the country.

But then, one urban parish will be very different from another. When I was a vicar in the South Wales Valleys, I felt as if I was there to serve the whole community. In fact one of the churchwardens once said, 'Blaenavon will expect you·to be the vicar of the whole of Blaenavon, and not just the vicar of St Peter's.' I was deeply touched when I left, because he reminded me of this and said that he thought I had fulfilled these expectations.

The question is, of course, how? Part of the way in which clergy shape their ministries around themselves is by taking into account their local communities and working with them in whatever ways they can.

I have known priests who have become heavily involved in local politics, for example, standing for whatever party they feel best fits the needs of their parishioners, whether Conservative, Labour or one of the smaller parties. Despite the fact that both of the main political parties have sidled up to me to ask me if I would join – 'Our party needs you' – by and large I attempt to steer clear of party politics, and have tried to remain non-political. I once mentioned this to someone I was working with on a social justice project and she laughed and said, 'Jason, you are the most political person I know.' One of the problems with being in a political party as a Christian (let alone as a priest) is that, however good they are, no political party will fully align with the teachings of Christ or the Church. I have always, therefore, tried to work outside the system for the good of those caught up in its cogs.

In Blaenavon, as a specific example, my ministry might include work with Communities First. This was the devolved Welsh Government's way of helping the most impoverished parts of Wales (which are shockingly among the most deprived parts of Europe and not just the UK). The idea was that there was a local partnership board which worked with communities on their priorities, and in a place where health was a significant problem we were able to open a fully equipped community gym. I say 'we' because I was the chair of the partnership board, having been nominated and elected probably partly because of my party political neutrality, or you might say that I was the person they distrusted the least!

Another way of being there for the community came when we fought the local authority over the closure of an historic swimming pool, dug out by miners in the 1920s and then mercifully roofed over in the 1960s – it was 1,300 feet above sea level and must have been bracing even in the height of summer. In that campaign, my contribution was to express the feelings of the community in print in an article written in the *Western Mail*, the broadsheet daily newspaper published in Cardiff. I have to admit that, because of the article, I was loathed (probably not too strong a word) by some parts of the political establishment, but I discovered that I was something of a local hero in Blaenavon. That didn't of course mean that more people came to church (God forbid!), but it did mean that the standing of the church in the community was higher than it had been for many years. They knew that the church (or at least I) was there for them.

Respect, then, needs to be earned, although much of the time people will give you the benefit of the doubt – which is just as well because things don't always go according to plan, as this next deliverance case shows.

## The jealous cousin

This particular call came from one of the other priests in the diocese.

'Jason, are you still doing deliverance ministry?' The voice belonged to one of my male colleagues, relatively newly ordained, and quite enthusiastic in his way.

I said I was.

'Because I've got someone living in my parish whose daughter is in the Guides who come on church parade, you know. Anyway, they claim they have some sort of ghost on the landing: they haven't really seen anything, but there's a sort of cold, dark spot, and they also reckon that stuff is moving round the house, so they think it must be a poltergeist.'

'Poltergeist activity,' I muttered under my breath.

'Yes, that's right, a poltergeist,' my colleague insisted brightly. 'Can you come around sometime?'

I looked at my diary and offered him a range of dates. 'I'll get back to you as soon as I can,' he said and, after the usual pleasantries, the phone call ended. A few moments later he rang back. '2.30 on Tuesday suits them really well.' So that was that. I usually try to talk to people before going out on a case, but in this instance I only had my colleague's word to go on. I often have some sort of hunch about what I'm likely to need, so I went off with my trusty bag, ready to bless the house.

On the way I collected my colleague and we travelled through a maze of roads, deep into a North Wales council housing estate, where he directed me to pull up and pointed at a house. 'That's it,' he said brightly. 'Shall we go?'

So, after the usual prayers for protection – St Patrick's Breastplate and the Lord's Prayer – we got out of the car and went up to the house. There is always a sense of trepidation when you approach the door of someone else's house, because you never know what to expect. And in this case what was waiting for us was . . . quite a lot of people!

Clearly, the fact that they had a 'poltergeist' and the vicar was bringing round the exorcist to get rid of it had gone around the extended family and the neighbours, even the daughter's Guide leader (an old family friend) was there.

The atmosphere was more like a party house than a haunted house as they made tea for us and introduced us to everyone, including Max the Yorkshire terrier, and told us what had been happening.

It was pretty much as my colleague had said. They reported a sort of cold spot at the top of the stairs, and although they had lived in the house for quite a few years, it seemed to have got worse recently.

And then there was some poltergeist activity, all fairly low level, but still enough to worry them. There had been cutlery moving of its own accord, and on more than one occasion the lights had turned themselves on and off. One of the friends who was there told me that she was a psychic investigator who was trying to film the poltergeist, but had never quite got there in time with her camera.

At first glance it looked very much like the problem that we had had in our house all those years before, a sort of place memory haunting which had, in this instance, triggered some sort of poltergeist reaction from at least one of the people who lived in the house. Sometimes you can work out who is causing the activity, but on other occasions you can't. Although when you are confronted with a case like this, it doesn't really matter – what does matter is dealing with the place memory.

But for the sake of curiosity more than anything else, I asked, 'How many of you live in the house?' It turned out to be a couple in their late thirties, their teenage daughter Chelsea, who knew my colleague from Guides, and the mother's niece Vicky, also a teenager. Both girls had slipped away and were now in the next room watching television, away from the melee of adults in the kitchen.

'Vicky's my sister's girl,' her aunt explained. 'My sister's been through a really bad time, so she asked me to have her. She's the same age as Chelsea, they're in the same school, and they have always got on really well together. Vicky's no problem at all.'

Now I knew who lived in the house it was obvious, or so I thought as a working hypothesis, that it was probably one of the teenage girls who was picking up some sort of vibe from the place memory haunting on the stairs. Young people do seem to be more sensitive to these things than adults. All that remained to do was to bless the house, and that would be it.

As always, I started with the simple service of blessing, and then moved round the house: two priests, husband, wife and an enthusiastic terrier.

The girls were still sitting in front of the television, but I remember them watching me. Chelsea was a very pretty girl with curly brown hair, but Vicky would best be described as striking – pale with straight dark hair and a faintly elfin look about her. And while her cousin was watching me with a mild degree of curiosity (I was the exorcist after all!), Vicky followed my every move very intently.

The temptation, as I've explained, is always to wonder who is 'causing' the poltergeist activity. My first thought had been that it was one of those girls. Now I asked myself if it was Chelsea, the daughter of a loving family or Vicky, the cousin from a different home? My money was on the cousin, but you never can tell, and before long the procession moved on.

We went up the stairs, the father explaining that they were in the process of decorating, although his wife commented that if he didn't finish it soon, it would be time to start again. And then we stopped at the top of the stairs, and Max the terrier trotted past. 'It's there. That's where the poltergeist is,' said the mother with disgust – how dare this entity inhabit her home?

'Has it always been like this?' I asked.

'How do you mean?'

'Well, it's dark, but then the light's shining on the stairs at the other end of the landing, and maybe it's cold because there's a loft opening up there that isn't quite closed properly,' I pointed out.

Wife glared at husband who muttered something under his breath.

'Does Max react to it?' I asked. 'Because very often animals pick these sorts of things up.'

Animals are, as far as we know, frequently sensitive to paranormal activity, sometimes in the way that young children are. They will react to 'ghosts' very often before humans do. People have suggested that animals may be psychic, but I have also heard people suggest that actually being psychic is simply an animal function. We will look at these issues later.

To get back to Max, apparently he hadn't reacted at all and was quite happy to trot around upstairs.

'Has anything changed at all in the house?' I asked.

'Apart from the decorating, no,' said the husband.

'Has anyone died in the house or the family?'

They both shook their heads. I was puzzled. There was something going on here that I hadn't got to the bottom of, but I trusted that the prayer of blessing would probably work if there was any sort of paranormal presence, and that the poltergeist activity might well stop of its own accord. We made our way slowly back to the kitchen. And there I explained that nine times out of ten the house blessing worked, but that if there were any further problems, they were to contact my colleague who would get in touch with me. After a short debrief in the car on the way back to his house, that was it. Or so I thought.

About a fortnight later my colleague rang me again. 'You remember that family you came to see?'

'Yes . . .' I said.

'Well, whatever you did it didn't work, and it's now back with a vengeance. All sorts of things have been flying round the kitchen, and the lights are getting worse. They've had Coke bottles shooting across the work surface and smashing on the floor, and their friend from the psychical research society has managed to film some of it. It's definitely a poltergeist . . .'

I wondered if he was waiting for me to correct him: I didn't. 'Anyway, they've asked if you'll come and see them again.'

The diary came out again, and a date later that week was fixed. This time, however, I was prepared. I was now pretty sure it wasn't any sort of place memory: not only had the dog not reacted, but the more I thought about it, the more I was convinced that the cold spot was a way of the family explaining the poltergeist activity.

Because that was almost certainly what we were dealing with: pure poltergeist activity. As I say, I thought that one of the girls was at the centre of it, and my money was on Vicky. In fact, so convinced was I that I even printed off a copy of 'Your Poltergeist' – a handout that had been given to me at the Deliverance training sessions all those years before. The handout suggested that you start treating the poltergeist as part of the family and give it a name, presumably working on the principle that normalising it meant that it would stop.

Duly armed we arrived at the house as before, but on the way, I explained to my colleague how poltergeist activity works – that it is caused by someone alive and present.

He nodded. 'Yes, I get it.'

We were greeted at the door by the mother, now noticeably more anxious, and by Max the ghost-hunting terrier, and as we walked into the kitchen-diner, the excited psychical researcher was brandishing her video camera (remember them?), offering to show me real footage of the poltergeist.

Despite what you might want to believe, such footage is never as interesting as you might have thought. I've never seen cutlery fly across the kitchen, so I can't vouch for how dramatic it is, but being forced to watch it on a shaky camera is not illuminating.

'Yes, thanks,' I said after a few scenes.

'But there's more!' wailed the researcher. 'Look! It's real!'

'Yes, thanks, I believe you.'

'You do?'

'Yes, but I'm here to try to see if I can stop it.'

I felt so sorry for the crestfallen researcher. She'd spent

half her life trying to prove that poltergeists 'existed' and some idiot was here to stop the fun.

I got them to explain once again what was happening, and whether they had seen anything other than the flying cutlery. No, they hadn't, but it was still cold on the landing.

'Are the girls in?' I asked.

'Yes, they're in the living room.'

'Do you mind if I ask them what their experience might be?'

'No, they're just watching TV,' said the lady of the household.

A few moments later, I was sitting down chatting to the girls. Vicky didn't seem particularly to want to talk, and seemed now a little sulky. Chelsea – whose house this was – was much more forthcoming. She explained in detail and with a degree of excitement what had been going on: the flying cutlery, the Coke bottle that had shattered on the floor – which hadn't been filmed – the lights that went on and off. And then she asked, 'Can ghosts follow you between different places?'

'In theory, no, because especially this sort of ghost, if that's what it is, is somehow attached to the house.'

She shrugged.

'Why do you ask?' I said.

'It's just that some of these things happen when I'm round my nan's as well.'

'What sort of things?'

'Well, the other night when I was staying with her, the phone started ringing, and there wasn't anyone there. And then the TV just went on and off, but there was no one near it.'

'Were you there with Vicky?'

'No, she was here. It's not her nan, it's my dad's mother.'

And then the penny dropped. I had been stupid because the truth had been staring me in the face. Yes, this was poltergeist activity. And yes, it was caused by a jealous cousin. Just the wrong one! It was the daughter of the household who was totally unconsciously venting her anxiety and frustration at the fact that she was now sharing a house with another teenage girl who was maybe taking the attention away from her.

I now knew what I needed to do. I told the family that there was little point in blessing the house again because we had already done that, but if they wanted me to, I would do it again. Mildly predictably, I found myself walking around the house once again with my holy water, splashing it at the walls, making sure I gave the area at the top of the stairs as good a soaking as my four inch long sprinkler will give.

And then back to the kitchen. I told them that there clearly was not a problem with the house, because we had blessed it twice now, and Max the dog was happy to be there. They nodded.

I explained carefully and gently what poltergeist activity was, and gave them the handout, and talked through it. I carefully avoided naming names or blaming anyone, but told them that whoever was causing it had no idea they were doing it, and I then explained in the simplest possible terms that these things feed on fear and tension.

'Have you seen the Harry Potter films?' I asked.

'Yes,' they all nodded enthusiastically.

'Well, it's like that creature in one of the films that comes out of the wardrobe in the classroom. I think it's called a boggart. Do you remember?'

Again, plenty of assent.

'Well, you'll probably remember that the only way to get rid of it is to laugh at it. It's a bit like that with poltergeist activity. Laughing breaks the tension, and somehow if you laugh at it, it will go away, maybe not straightaway, but just keep laughing.'

This is one of the classic ways of dealing with poltergeist activity especially when it is effectively caused by tension between family members in a large group. In another instance, I suggested that a couple experiencing extreme poltergeist activity needed to go away for a few days together as a way of breaking the tension between them. Or, in the case of Mary, her son and the exploding vase what they needed was to remember they loved one another. All of these are ways of lowering the tension that feeds poltergeist activity.

My suggestion seemed initially to be the correct solution for this family. They looked at me for a few moments, and then began to smile. I took them gently through the handout once more, and suggested they have look at it again sometime. It was hard work especially as, of course, in all probability the causes that had triggered the poltergeist activity would still be there – there would still be two teenage girls living together in the same house. But sometimes normalising the situation makes it easier to deal with, especially with a phenomenon that feeds on tension.

Having what we call 'the poltergeist conversation' with someone is never easy, but I felt the tension ease. They laughed, they smiled, I checked, and both the girls had relaxed. This was about as good as it was going to get: they would cope with it.

I got ready to leave, knowing that I had done a good job.

'OK, call us if you have a problem, but I think we've got this sorted. You know how to deal with it – it's almost certainly poltergeist activity.' I smiled at them, and they smiled back.

And then, just as I was about to leave the room, I heard

a voice behind me say brightly, 'Or maybe it was a ghost.' The effect was instant.

In fact, I have never seen a collective reaction like it. Their faces crumpled.

And as I stood there, the mother started to rock and wail. The two girls looked rigid and hurt. I felt the tension which had disappeared suddenly was back, worse than ever before. If a whole canteen of cutlery had come hurtling across the room, I would not have been surprised. I had lost control of the whole situation.

We didn't speak as we walked back to the car. 'That went well,' said my colleague brightly. I was silent: all I wanted to do was commit an act of violence, either on myself to take the pain away, or on him for the same reason!

I never asked my colleague why he said what he did, but I suspect it was simply because he felt he needed to say something: he was after all the vicar, this was his parish, and maybe he needed to stamp his authority on the situation – he was, as I said, relatively new to ministry.

Whatever the case, the next time I saw him he said, 'That family you came out to see, the one you said had a poltergeist, well, it didn't work. They called me out again, so I blessed the house myself, but they had decided to move to a new house.'

'OK,' I shrugged. I had tried.

I hope that the family was happy in the new home. Poltergeist activity does have a way of simply resolving itself: people grow up, they learn how to express themselves, the factors that caused the initial flare up are either taken away or they become tolerable.

I had learned from this too, and when I was asked to rewrite the local protocols, I did include a clause about respecting the opinion of the deliverance minister, and allowing them to lead. It may or may not have done any good, but it made me feel better, and was easier than a long stretch in prison for grievous bodily harm of another priest!

But it's not the only time I have had problems with the actions of a colleague, as the next case shows.

## The empty flat

B ecause I don't see myself in action (so to speak), I don't know how I come across, but on one occasion a colleague gave me feedback that I've often reflected on: 'Jason, I can't believe how nice you were to those people!' I think I laughed, but I think too that he meant it. Being a deliverance minister means that, whatever your basic personality, you really do have to be the nicest version of yourself. Sometimes, however, this ability to be nice is tested to the limits.

On one occasion in North Wales, a colleague asked me for some help. He'd been approached by a young couple who originated in his parish, but had recently moved to a council flat on an estate on the other side of a dual carriageway, which was a major physical and psychological barrier in that part of the world. The council estate in question, while it was within the same local authority, was in many senses a world away from where his parents lived, even though it was only three or four miles.

'Will you have to contact their vicar?' my colleague asked, with a striking degree of reluctance.

I thought for a moment. 'I think we will.'

'I was afraid you'd say that,' he sighed. 'I'm happy to act as middle-man if you like.'

'That would be good,' I said, mildly relieved. I have to admit that the vicar I was going to have to deal with had a bit of a reputation for being somewhat eccentric, although, because I didn't know her, maybe I was wrong.

As usual, the arrangements were that I would collect the local vicar from her house and that we would drive together, first of all to see the young couple in the young man's parents' house because they had been too frightened to stay in the flat, and then to travel to their flat in her parish if necessary for a house blessing. I duly picked up the vicar, and she seemed fairly normal – for a vicar! Maybe I'd got her wrong. We established that I would take the lead in whatever we needed to do, and that she would basically be there as prayer backup. So far so good.

The parents' house was a standard three-bedroom council house on a mature estate, but when we arrived, as with the previous case, it was packed full of relatives who had all come to see the show. Welsh families can be very clannish, and are notorious for sticking together. Whole families and sometimes their neighbours will frequently make a block booking and head off on holiday together. Many people go away to get away from it all, others take it all with them, and I suspected these were the second sort. In fact, it was mildly overwhelming as people sat on every available item of furniture, on the arms of chairs and on the floor, as the couple outlined for the entertainment of all the story of their ghost.

'We've seen him. He's like an old gentleman who haunts the living room,' said the young man, in response to gentle questions.

'When you say "old gentleman" what do you mean?' I asked.

'Well, he looks like he's always been there: he's got a big

moustache and is smoking a pipe, like something out of Downton Abbey,' he continued, searching for the words, 'or older, like, Victorian, or something.'

'Is there anything else?' I enquired.

'What do you mean?'

'Well, is the room cold or dark?' They looked at me blankly.

'OK, thanks,' I said, trying to think of an intelligent question. 'How old is the building?'

The young man shrugged.

'It's about, oh . . . ten years old,' suggested the young man's mother.

Others in the room nodded. 'Yes, that's about right.'

I looked at the local vicar who nodded. 'Sure to be.'

'Do you know who lived there before you?' It was worth a try.

'No, but the lady from the council said they had been a young family who later moved away,' said the young woman, speaking for the first time.

'Had they lived there since the house was new?'

She shrugged.

'When you spoke to the council, did they say why they'd moved?'

'They had two kids, so the flat wasn't big enough,' she explained.

'OK, thanks, maybe we can go and see the flat, and maybe bless it. Would that be all right?'

They seemed to think it was.

'Because,' I continued, using the familiar line, 'nine times out of ten, that seems to sort the problem out.'

Was it me, or were they less than happy about that? At this point I strongly suspected that this was another case of people who wanted the council to move them out of a place they didn't like into somewhere nicer, or maybe somewhere nearer to their extended family.

'I think we ought to pray,' a plummy voice intruded – that of the local vicar, who sounded different now there was an audience, 'what do you think Father Jason?' What could I say?

'Shall we all stand up to pray?' she continued.

And I can still remember standing in that crowded room, the entire clan standing in silence, waiting for the prayer to begin . . . and begin it did: 'Lord God, heavenly Father, we ask you to be with us now. We ask you to send your innumerable blessings on your servant Jason, as he prepares to go into battle with the Evil One. We ask you to be his shield and defence . . .'

And so it went on, and on. It was like being in a revivalist meeting, and being the person that everyone there is praying for. I was just thankful that I was standing by the window, otherwise I might have ended up kneeling in the middle of the floor, being sort of engulfed in a tide of prayer. I was extraordinarily uncomfortable: not my style, *really* not my style. And most of the time, doing battle against the forces of the Evil One isn't necessarily what I feel I'm doing: bringer of light and peace, yes, I may be; cosmic warrior, no.

Back in the room, the prayer was reaching a great climax, but just before it did, the voice stopped dead.

There was total silence. And then the voice at its most theatrical whispered, 'I sense a presence with us now. Yes, it's here. He's here, with us now! I say begone evil spirit, go back to the place prepared for you before the foundation of the world!'

The voice was now rising in power in an astonishing crescendo.

But I was horrified, not because I thought there might be an evil spirit with us, but because, even if my colleague had felt something, I wasn't sure it was a good idea to draw people's attention to it. The clan, however, seemed oddly comforted by the fact that there was something evil there, and some of them even nodded in assent.

I was rooted to the ground.

But just as suddenly my colleague lowered the temperature: 'He's gone! Thanks be to God, he's gone!' And the assembled throng began to relax.

The prayer began again, and finally wound to a close. 'Amen,' I said in relief.

'And now Father Jason himself will say a prayer for us.'

What?! I thought, but managed to deliver what I hoped was a prayer that came across as sincerely as it was meant, and finished with the Lord's Prayer.

Strangely, after the scene at the parents' house, conversation in the car between my colleague and me was surprisingly easy. Once again, we agreed that I would take the lead when we got to the couple's flat – although I doubted I would be allowed to enjoy all of the limelight.

Post-industrial Wales, North and South, can have a beauty all of its own, and this place was no exception. At one stage it must have been beautiful, and I could imagine the wayside pub nestling at the foot of a range of rounded hills. The old pub was still there, but its surroundings looked blighted by the uniform housing, piled up seemingly randomly around a derelict-looking playground. Even in the sunshine, there was a forbidding air about the place which made me feel uncomfortable.

Would I want to live here? The answer was a simple no. But then I couldn't imagine why anyone would want to live there, and this young couple starting off in life probably wouldn't want to stay either.

However, that was not what I was there to decide.

The young couple got out of their car – their extended family had stayed at home, safely across the dividing road – and took us up to their flat, which was on the second floor of a block that resembled a cardboard box. Clearly all architectural niceties had been spared on this one. And the flat when we got there was just cold, and felt sad and unloved. They showed us round what there was and as we got to the living room, I heard a theatrical gasp. I feared the worst from my colleague.

'Yes,' she spluttered dramatically, 'I see him there. An old gentleman. But, yes, he's smiling. He knows it's time to leave . . .'

I've mentioned the fact that some adults are psychic, and can see things that other people can't, and we'll meet some of these in a later chapter. So was my colleague a psychic of some description? Could she sense something I couldn't? Was there something there? Once she had recovered her composure, I offered to begin the service of blessing, and in the virtually empty flat, it took almost no time, although I was as careful and as reverent as I always try to be. As always, I gave them one of the crosses from my bag that I blessed for them, and a card with some suggested prayers for protection, and we left them to it. There wasn't very much more to be done.

We got back to the car and I broached the subject gently. 'Did you feel anything in the house?'

'No,' she said, quite matter of fact.

'I think it was probably just their imagination,' I suggested tentatively, because the whole thing sounded like a combination of young people being spooked and a whole load of extraneous details.

'Yes, of course it was,' she fired back immediately. 'Nothing there at all. Just wanted to be moved. You can't blame them, can you?'

'No, I suppose not,' I said weakly. And the conversation quickly moved on to safer grounds and away from the perils of religion.

Although I was disturbed by all this at the time, the more I thought about it the more I realized that what she was trying to do was to help them. Their best chance of being rehoused closer to their family was to be able to tell the council that they had had two vicars who had blessed the flat because they thought it was haunted.

And I did feel genuinely sorry for the young couple. It was pretty clear that, either they had made it all up, or their imagination was running riot, but there had never been a Victorian gentleman who had lived on that site, in fact I suspect that no one had ever lived there before the recent past, and most of them probably unwillingly. And, as so often, I never did find out whether the council had moved them, although I rather hoped they had, and with hindsight, I didn't mind being called out. But just occasionally, I feel that people really are wasting my time.


## Shadow on the wall

'No,' said the voice, 'he's far too busy to deal with things like this. He said you were the deliverance minister and that you could deal with it.' I had never met the lady in question, but she was apparently the secretary of one of my colleagues in the area, and she did 'imperious' in a way that even Queen Victoria might have learned from.

I was to ring a young woman whose house was haunted, despite the fact that it was a good forty minutes' drive from me, and it would have been so much easier if the local vicar had dealt with it. I knew he had been trained in these matters, even if he had stepped back from active deliverance ministry.

Life is busy sometimes, and this was one of those times, so I wasn't impressed at being asked to do it, but it was something I had signed up for, so I rang the mobile number I had been given.

'There's, like, this shadow in the corner. We saw it the other night when the girls were round. My friend said it might be a ghost, and I need someone to exorcise it for me.' Her voice was strangely flat and uninterested.

'Have you seen anything else?'

'No, just a shadow.'

'Anything else happening in the house?'

'What sort of things?'

I explained about poltergeist activity, without of course using the P-word – never let it be said that I lead the witness.

She thought for a moment. 'No,' she said decisively.

'Any structural work on the house?'

'No.'

And so it went on. It was a strange conversation. The young woman I was speaking to sounded bored and disengaged, and showed none of the nervousness and certainly none of the fear I usually expect from people describing a paranormal occurrence. She really did sound as if she was having a conversation with a plumber about a leaky tap. In fact, by the time I hung up, I was pretty much convinced that there was nothing to see here (probably not even a shadow), but still, dutiful to the last, I agreed to meet her at her house. Normally, I would take someone with me, but in this instance, I decided not to waste someone else's time as well as my own.

Again, another council flat on another estate, but this one was in one of the prettier parts of Wales, and there were genuinely lovely views out of the back window. We had arranged to meet at 12.30, but she didn't get there until 12.45. But, as always, I tried to be as polite and reassuring as possible, working on the principle that if there is genuine paranormal activity, people will be frightened. She wasn't frightened. In fact, if there was any sense of emotion, it was probably boredom.

'It's over there,' she said, as if she had some sort of problem with the plumbing.

I tried to have a conversation with her, to get some sort of handle on what was going on, but her answers were evasive. So, as always, I began the ritual of blessing the flat.

While I did this, she seemed to be paying no attention at all, and was playing on her phone, or at least she gave the *appearance* that she was playing on her phone. But the longer I was there, the more convinced I was that I was being hoaxed somehow and that she was in fact filming me at work. Blessing a house is usually something that occupies all of my mind, but not this time. I am not proud of the fact that not only did I try to keep my back to her at all times, the whole thing was significantly more cursory than ever before or since. Once that was over, I offered her a cross (noting that her phone had now been put away), but she declined. However, I did leave her my prayer card.

'Get in touch with the vicar if you have any further problems,' I suggested, and took my leave.

When I looked at my watch, I realised that I had only

been there for twenty minutes, for which I felt mildly guilty. As I drove away, however, guilt gave way to anger. I felt increasingly as if I'd been had, and I wondered why she had been filming me. 'Let's get the exorcist round,' might have seemed like an exciting adventure dreamt up during a girls' night in, but in the cold light of day it was much less enticing for me, and for them certainly a lot less exciting than it is in the movies.

To this day, I am still faintly concerned that there might be footage of me blessing the flat somewhere on the web, but if so I've never seen it. However, if anyone out there has, can you let me know?

We have other kinds of call outs that are basically spurious. In the past, many deliverance ministers would go out with a radiator key to sort out those irritating cold spots, or with a recommendation for a good plumber to fix the knocking that comes from the back bedroom, but these days we get very few of that sort of call. Central heating systems are very much more efficient than they were in the past, but at the same time, there seems to have been an increased awareness of the paranormal in modern culture (or post-modern culture if you prefer). Maybe some people just like calling out the vicar.

## The smelly kitchen

'Is that the Reverend Doctor Jason Bray?' asked the voice. 'Yes, speaking,' I said, slightly taken aback as always by the very formal address – but knew somehow what was coming next.

'I've been given your number by the diocesan office, Dr Bray, who told me you might be able to help.'

When you speak to someone on the phone for the first time, your mind and imagination works overtime to create an image of the person on the line. This one was clearly a man in late middle age, with a slight local accent, but he used mainly BBC English and also seemed to know the correct forms of address for clergy.

I almost never get called 'Dr Bray' – in fact I actively discourage it – after an incident when I was a rookie curate being introduced as such. The lady I was meeting had had a freak accident involving a garden gate which had necessitated a series of extensive skin grafts on her upper thighs – I did say it was a freak accident! As I had been introduced as 'Dr Bray, our new curate' she said, 'Oh, doctor, I'm sure you would like to see how my wounds are healing,' and showed me. She wasn't the only person who was scarred for life!

My parishioners, by the way, call me 'Jason' or occasionally 'vicar' unless I can stop them. In the past, some of my parishioners have called me 'Father Jason', which is still my preferred stage name at the primary school – 'Jason' sounds far too informal for them, and anything else far too stuffy for the children.

Anyway, for this man I was Dr Bray – he was obviously a bit of a stickler for these things. 'You see, Dr Bray,' he continued, 'I have a bit of a problem at home that I hope you can help with. I think it may be some sort of ghostly visitation, which is affecting my kitchen.'

'In what way?'

'Well, there's a terrible unexplained smell that fills the entire corner of the room.'

Now, poltergeist activity manifests itself in all sorts of forms, and smell is one of the forms it can take, so that was a possibility. The other thing that fleetingly sprang to mind was that

I was speaking to a schizophrenic who was experiencing an olfactory hallucination. I remembered a long time ago speaking to a patient in the psychiatric hospital where I did my theological college placement who would smell bacon, only to realise that it was such a hallucination.

There was also a third possibility, of course, and that was that there was some sort of problem with his drains. Working on the principle that the simplest solution is probably the answer, I asked if he had ever had any problems with his drains.

'No,' he said, 'I have them checked regularly, and I have poured drain cleaner down them, so I know that's not it.'

I asked gently if he was on any medication. 'Only blood pressure tablets.'

So not a schizophrenic, then – people rarely get to the age I thought he was without being diagnosed.

'So will you come out and do a house blessing?'

I asked where he lived, and discovered that he lived in mid-Wales not too far from another member of the deliverance team, a woman priest with a huge amount of experience, so I suggested he got in touch with her because she was much closer. As it happened, the team-member asked me to go out with her, so I did, although on this occasion she took the lead.

Collecting my colleague meant that we were able to have a conversation on the way to the house, although my colleague had asked the old gentleman the same questions.

When we got to the house, my colleague looked around and said, 'It's really close to the river, I think this part of the world may be prone to flooding. I wonder . . .'

'It's worth asking.'

The old gentleman proved to be more elderly than I had

imagined, but other than that everything was as I had expected. The house was a bungalow on a private estate, and the gentleman's social skills were reflected in a very neat house that also suggested he had travelled extensively. He greeted us warmly and started to explain the problems.

Again, my colleague asked him a series of questions that he was more than happy to answer. One of them was, 'Why did you call us in?'

'Well,' he said, 'I remembered that the last time I had problems with the house twenty years or more ago, it was because there was some sort of creeping damp in the back bedroom. I was really worried that it might be some sort of ghost, like you see in the films. So, I called in one of your predecessors, and he blessed the house for me.'

'Did that solve the problem?' my colleague asked.

'Well, not really – the guttering had slipped in the snow and it made the water run under the eaves, and once I had had that seen to, it all dried up.'

My colleague and I looked at one another. I could tell she was going to ask the question.

'Can I just ask if the house is prone to flooding?

'Oh, no,' came the reply. 'Last year when we had all those floods and the river burst its banks, we were safe here. Most of the rest of the estate was under water, but we're on a bit of a rise here. So, my neighbour two doors down was flooded, and two doors up as well, but these three bungalows were all right.'

My colleague asked, 'Do you think that being on a flood plain might have caused the smell in the kitchen?'

'Oh, I suppose it might have, but I'd still like you to bless the house just in case.'

What can you do? My colleague blessed the house. All

deliverance ministers do things in different ways. This particular colleague's signature flourish was to use scented candles – in this instance when the paranormal phenomenon manifested itself as a smell in the kitchen, I felt this was highly appropriate! And instead of blessing the water there and then, she produced a bottle of holy water that had been pre- blessed. Holy water, by the way, is simply water that is blessed by a priest with the words, 'This water will be used to remind us of our baptism.' It does not come from a special tap, or from the River Jordan – although occasionally when people have been to the Holy Land, they will come back with a bottle of water from the Jordan. Because my colleague had some holy water with her, the ritual took even less time than usual, although we did stand over the sink in the kitchen and pray silently. We also spent longer than usual in the back bedroom, where one of the deliverance ministers of the past had presumably stood and suggested that the old gentleman get his gutters checked, and where in the present day the man described almost fondly the way that he thought the creeping damp had been caused by a ghost. After a final blessing, and some advice to contact a building surveyor, we took our leave.

'What did you make of that?' asked my colleague.

'Maybe he was just lonely and wanted some sort of excitement in his life,' I suggested.

'I think you may well be right. Oh, well, good to see you, and thanks for coming over,' she said.

I smiled. 'Any time.'

# Chapter 6

# *Do you believe in ghosts?*

It seems to be something of a common experience in most human cultures that people believe in ghosts. The very oldest stories in many cultures contain references to the spirits of the dead. Possibly the oldest story we have, the ancient Mesopotamian 'Epic of Gilgamesh', deals with the death of the hero's friend, Enkidu, and his travels as a ghost in the underworld.

The ancient Hebrews who wrote what we tend to call the Old Testament (or the Hebrew Bible as biblical scholars usually refer to it) regarded ghosts as part of their world, most famously when King Saul calls the witch of Endor to call from the grave the ghost of the prophet Samuel in 1 Samuel 28. He was working on the assumption that the now deceased Samuel would have a better idea of the future than anyone else, but not because he's a prophet (he's not that sort of prophet), but because he's a ghost. The practice of getting the dead to predict the future or 'necromancy' was so common in Old Testament times that the law and the prophets constantly condemn it. A passage such as Leviticus 20.27 from the Old Testament law is pretty unequivocal about it: 'A man or a woman who is a medium or a wizard shall be put to death; they shall be stoned to death, their blood is upon them.' In fact, in the story of the witch of Endor, she is terrified of the king because, according to the story, he has had the other mediums put to death. But then consulting the dead is a strange idea to some extent: why would grandma have a better idea of next week's winning lottery numbers now she's dead than when she was alive? Unless, of course, the answer is that she is no longer locked into a world governed by the laws of space and time.

Even in the New Testament, there is a pervasive belief in ghosts. When the risen Jesus appears to his disciples in St Luke's Gospel, they think they are seeing a ghost. He doesn't say, 'Don't be stupid, there's no such things as ghosts' – the great mantra of parents across the world. Instead Jesus says, 'Touch me and see: for a ghost does not have flesh and bones as you see that I have.' Does Jesus believe in ghosts? Not completely clear. Do the hand-picked group of his disciples? You bet they do!

Another great influence on the Western world was, of course, ancient Greece where we also find ghosts. These are almost taken for granted in many of the stories, although there are also those famous tales about travellers in the Underworld. Even in cultures which are very different from our own, ghosts are found. It is recorded, for example, that when the indigenous people of central Papua New Guinea met Westerners for the first time, they assumed they were ghosts.

Belief in ghosts is prevalent in Britain today, to the extent that it is said that more people in the UK believe in ghosts than believe in God! Television programmes such as *Most Haunted* have pervaded the public imagination, ghost tours are increasingly popular and we all like to terrify the wits out of one another by telling ghost stories. And people still make use of necromancers, although we tend to be more polite and call them 'mediums' or 'spiritualists', but it amounts to the same thing.

So, do I believe in ghosts? You would have thought that, given everything I have written, that the answer would be 'yes', but I'm still not quite sure. I am, you will remember, a sceptic about most things, and that's true of ghosts, even when I am talking to people about them who believe they've seen one, and actually dealing with their apparent effects. Maybe the best I can say is I trust God to deal with whatever is it, and that I leave the details to him. I have never seen a ghost. When I had the experience at the bathroom door when I was a curate, I didn't see anything – it may have been a figment of my imagination. And I have only ever once experienced anything like that since.

Being a priest means that we have to deal with all sorts of life events that can be tragic or happy. Conducting a wedding where a very nervous bride says, 'I have never been as happy in my life as I am at this moment,' is an absolute privilege, even if I know I am not actually the cause of that happiness, I've just facilitated it! I have conducted hundreds of weddings, but each one is special, just as I have taken many more baptisms, and each one again is very special.

But the same is also true of funerals. All funerals are special. Sometimes it will be the funeral of a person who has died in extreme old age, with their faculties fully functioning, but there will also be those of people who have died in immense pain. The funeral of a churchgoer can often take on a very different character; often the coffin containing the body will be brought into the church the night before the funeral. Occasionally people will make comments about it being a big lonely place, but for many practising Christians it's home. The following day, the service, even for Anglicans, may involve the celebration of the

Eucharist, a funeral mass, and there is that idea of 'a good send-off' that gives people a huge amount of comfort. But there are also the tragedies: those who have died young or very young, babies, toddlers, children and teenagers, or those who have suffered sudden or violent deaths, or who have died at their own or others' hands. How comforting can a funeral be then?

As with a deliverance case, so with a visit to a family before a funeral, you never quite know how it's going to go. On some occasions, I have spent the whole of a funeral visit laughing, and then there are others where the last thing to happen is laughter. There have been tense visits, and those that have been very relaxed indeed. Sometimes people want to talk endlessly about the deceased, but on other occasions you have to pump them for information. Once the only interesting fact I managed to get out of a family after an hour's visit, was the fact that the deceased had once bred budgies! Sometimes you walk away and wonder whether they actually knew their mother at all (and it is often mothers) – 'She was always there for us' may be a touching thing to say, but if that's literally all you can say, that's just a little bit sad.

## The funeral visit

This particular funeral visit was one of the tensest I have ever carried out. The young man in question had died tragically young. There was a huge amount of raw emotion, as his best friend told me the story of their lives together, and his mother looked on in shocked disbelief. Slowly, during the course of what seemed like a long evening, I learned quite a lot about the young man, possibly more than they intended to tell me, judging from occasional long silences and evasive looks. But eventually I felt able to leave, and as usual I asked whether they would like me to pray with them before I left, or if they would prefer to leave it to the funeral itself. I was not very surprised when they said that it was just too raw at the moment, so, if I didn't mind, the prayers would keep. Part of me felt relieved – guiding people who are not used to the idea of prayer is difficult at the best of times, and this was one of the worst.

By the time I left the house it was dark and quite late, so I arrived home intending to crash out, which meant changing into my pyjamas, sitting down with my wife and kids in front of some mindless television (or a good documentary as the case may be) with a glass of red wine in my hand.

'How did it go?' asked my wife casually.

'As well as you might expect, really. I'm just heading upstairs to get into my pyjamas, and I'll be down in a couple of minutes and I'll tell you then,' I called.

I bounded up the stairs, or at least I began to bound up the stairs, but sensed immediately that there was something horribly wrong. I stopped halfway up. The atmosphere felt suddenly cold, and my skin was clammy. I could feel my heart beating in my chest. Moving up the stairs was an effort, like walking into a dense cloud. My stomach dropped and I felt every cell in my body screaming 'danger'!

After what seemed like an age, but was no doubt only a few seconds, I stood just outside the bedroom door, and I knew that when I walked in, he would be sitting there, smiling in welcome. I had never met the young man, although I had seen photos of him with his tanned complexion and dark brown hair, and I had no connection to him at all, but he seemed to be there and inexplicably so.

I felt utterly helpless, but also violated and angry too: this was my space, my family's space and it had been invaded. So, I stopped where I was, and finally I prayed – prayed that his soul should leave this world, prayed that God would receive him and give him light and peace.

Maybe the whole thing was just the product of an overactive imagination, or a reaction to having spent such an intense evening with his family. But the feeling dissipated, the atmosphere changed, and the house was its usual warm, welcoming place. I walked bravely into the bedroom: there was nothing there, no one there, or maybe just the ghost of a smile.

## The haunted staircase

It's difficult sometimes when you are out on a case, no matter how much experience you have, to tell the difference between different types of ghost sightings. In other words, when is something a place memory and when is it a true haunting, and when does one spill into another?

One winter, a week or so before Christmas, I was called out by one of my colleagues to deal with a case that had arisen from one of his parishioners.

A family had bought a new-build house at the edge of a small rural village in the hills of northern Monmouthshire, and they were worried that they were being visited by the ghost of the husband's father, who had apparently taken his own life when his son was still a child. What they knew about him rested on one or two old photos (his wife had been too distressed to hold on to very much), and the son's haziest memory of his father. The son was now grown up and worked away a lot, and his children were either away at university or had moved out, so his wife was left in the house alone most of the time. She was a sensible lady with a responsible job, and was an occasional churchgoer. But she was convinced that the house was being haunted by her father-in-law's ghost, who had also appeared to her daughter. The story was outlined to me by her vicar, and I agreed to go out and meet him at his church (which, he said, was easy to find). We would then walk to the lady's house a few hundred yards away which, he said, I'd never find on my own.

So, I set off, armed with my trusty satnav, and predictably got horribly, horribly lost. It was a foggy night. I could see signs for the village, but the voice in the car was telling me to go a different way. I was doubly anxious: it was dark, foggy, and I was travelling in rural Wales where the phone signal – and satnav signal – is poor at the best of times. I was also going out on a deliverance case, and that too made me anxious. Eventually, however, I did find the church – it was on the left, but it should have been on the right – so before I knew it I was out of the village, and heading for God knows where, at least I hope He did, because the phone signal was lost completely. Finding somewhere to turn around safely was not easy, so I hoped that nothing was coming either way as I did a three-point turn, although it may have been more like a nine-point turn by the time I had executed it. I went back to the church, where the vicar was waiting patiently.

'Got lost?' he asked cheerfully.

And I explained how I had got there.

He looked at me in puzzlement. 'I didn't realise you could get here that way,' he said. 'Anyway, I've rung Carol, and she's got the kettle on.'

'Great,' I replied, 'is it far?'

'No, just across the road, really.' And he led me out of the churchyard, across the street, down a lane, and into what had obviously once been open land, but now boasted a series of large detached houses. 'This is it,' he pointed to the first one.

The door was answered by an anxious looking lady in her early fifties. 'I'm glad you've come,' she said, as she ushered us in from the billowing fog into a hall which contained a beautiful staircase that rose a few stairs, and then opened into a wide landing before turning ninety degrees and rising to an all round, balustraded landing that allowed access to the rooms above us.

'Lovely house,' I said, impressed.

The lady sniffed slightly. 'I don't like being here on my own. In fact, I've been sleeping at my mother's house for the last week or so, while my husband's away.' She offered us a cup of tea which I wouldn't normally accept – all priests have had bad experiences with hot drinks of varying quality – but sometimes you're just grateful for something warm to hold.

The local vicar asked Carol to tell us her story once we had our drinks. 'I think I've always seen things,' she began and stopped.

'Just to let you know, we are quite used to hearing all sorts of things, so please don't feel embarrassed.' I hoped this was reassuring enough, and she nodded, and began again.

'I suppose people might call me a bit psychic. It's something that has come down through the family. My grandmother used to see things, but my mother doesn't. In my generation, I see all sorts of things, but my sister doesn't. And then in the next generation, it's my youngest who sees things – my daughter, Danielle,' she explained. 'It's something you get used to, and it doesn't happen all the time. You can go for years without seeing the presence of a ghost, and then suddenly you will see someone, usually someone who has died recently. It's been quiet for a while now, until we moved into this house about a year ago.'

She paused for a few moments, so I prompted her. 'Can you tell us about the house?'

She looked slightly relieved. 'The house, yes, it's new as you can see, and we're the only people to have lived here. We bought it from the architect's plan, and we moved here because it was close to my mother, but it's got lovely views across the hills.'

I said I would take her word for it. 'Do you know what was here before?'

'It was just a field belonging to a farmer who had died, John something or other his name was. There was nothing at all here before.'

'Thanks. So, after you moved in . . .' I prompted.

Carol sighed. 'Well, it sounds so weird . . .'

'We do weird quite well,' I encouraged.

'OK. It was relatively all right to start off with, and then I saw him. He was standing on the stairs. I couldn't really see him properly, his face was indistinct, although I could tell he was old, and he was definitely there. I didn't worry about it too much, as I said, I have seen these things before, and they haven't bothered me too much. But I *kept* seeing him. Always in roughly the same place, always dressed the same as if he were going out for a walk. Do you believe me?' she asked, suddenly anxious again.

'Yes, of course,' I responded.

'But then Danielle was home from university and she started to see him too, and that was a little more worrying, because not only did she see him, but he also started to talk to her, and would call her by name at night.'

'What sort of things was he saying?' I asked.

'I don't know,' she answered, 'Danielle didn't want to listen. Like me, she's grown up with this thing, this psychic thing, and because I'm quite open about it with the family, I'm able to offer her support. But that doesn't mean that she likes it. In fact, more often than not she's frightened by it, and this man, whoever he is, calling her name really has been terrifying for her.'

'I'm so sorry,' I murmured. 'Do you have any idea who it is?'

'Yes,' she said, tentatively, 'we think it might be my father-in-law. He hanged himself when my husband was very young, but in the photo we've got he is wearing the same sort of clothes as the man we've seen on the stairs.'

'What does Danielle think?'

'Strangely, she's not completely convinced it is her grand-father, although what she has seen is pretty much the same thing as me.'

'Has anyone else in the house seen anything?'

'No, but then none of them is psychic. But they know there's something there, and it is always cold on the stairs. And I know it's just by the front door, but the bottom of the stairs is quite warm, and the top is as well, but there's a cold spot on the first landing about six stairs up.'

'And that's where you see him?'

She nodded.

'Sorry, stupid question, but when you see him, is he actually standing on the landing as if he were alive?'

She thought for a moment. 'Yes, he is.'

'Just going back a bit,' I queried, 'you said Danielle wasn't convinced it was her grandfather. Is there anyone else it might be?'

Carol shrugged. 'Well, you see, he'd be about the right age,' she said. 'But I suppose it might be the farmer who owned the field before. Someone in the village told me that he was a bit weird, and that the developers had been after this field for years, but that he'd refused to sell it.'

'And that was John?'

She nodded.

'What was your father-in-law called?'

'David,' she said, and then asked, 'Can you help us?'

'Yes, I think so.' I explained that we would bless the house, but also say prayers commending the soul of David to God.

Carol agreed and we began the service.

For a simple house blessing, I don't usually wear any robes other than a stole, and sometimes I don't wear that either. My colleague, however, had brought full sets of robes, and looked slightly upset at not being able to wear them.

As we went up the stairs, it was impossible not to feel a chill in the air, although whether that was because it was the winter or because of any ghostly presence, it was hard to tell. Carol looked worried, but shook her head reassuringly as she looked at the stairs – clearly whoever was haunting the staircase was not visible to her at the moment.

Back in the living room, we said the final prayers and commended the soul of David to God, but quietly I also added, 'and John.' There was a final blessing, and a promise from the vicar to be in touch. Carol seemed relieved, and said she may stay there overnight, and after thanking us, she showed us out in to the night.

'Which one was it?' asked my colleague as we walked away.

'I'm not sure. It was pretty clearly a true haunting, because there was some attempt to communicate with the daughter, but *who* was trying to communicate, I don't know. But,' I mused, 'it wouldn't surprise me to discover that it was the farmer because he was an old man when he died, and the figure they saw was that of an older not a younger man. He also seemed pretty much attached to the land, and wouldn't the father-in-law's ghost be the age he was when he died as a young man, not the age he would be now?'

'I was wondering that too,' he said.

We said our goodbyes, and he explained the easy way to get onto the main road. As I drove off, and looked into the rear view mirror of the darkened car, I fleetingly had the feeling there was someone there in the fog, watching me. But I'm pretty sure that really was just my imagination.

A week or so later I bumped into the same vicar at a training event. 'Carol's been in touch, and she says thanks.'

'Any problems since?'

'No,' he said, 'in fact she says the house is now lovely, and she enjoys being there alone. And one other thing, when they are together, she says the family has stopped arguing.'

'Good,' I said, 'really good.'

## The boyfriend in the shower

It is often said that, in today's world, each generation is more liberal than the previous one, and what was once frowned upon and hushed up is now out in the open. This is certainly the case with marriage and children. I frequently conduct weddings for couples whose children are present in the church as page boys or flower girls, or sometimes as best men or brides-maids, and it is very rare to conduct the wedding of a couple who are not already living with one another. Living 'in sin' as it was known and having children 'out of wedlock', both once scandalous, are now commonplace.

And attitudes are also changing over another great sexual taboo, that of homosexuality. The Church, of course, is involved in a series of tortured debates about it – whether to allow the blessing of same sex marriages in church, or even to allow such marriages to be contracted in church. But most of society seems to have moved on, and is more relaxed about the whole issue. However, in some more traditional parts of the UK, attitudes are slower to change, and being gay for someone of my generation

(I was born in 1969) could be a huge struggle. And so it proved for one of my parishioners, who also became a good friend.

Pete is my age, and gay, but really struggled with the whole idea. He lived for many years with his parents in a Cardiff suburb, and despite the fact that the city centre, with its freer sexual mores, was not too far away, he felt restricted and was unable to form anything other than the most casual of relationships. But he wanted very much more. To this end, he bought a house in Newport and would attend the cathedral occasionally, which is how I got to know him. The new house was closer to work and not too far from his parents, but not too close either, so that he could live his life in greater freedom. But still, the love of his life never came along, and Pete started to despair.

However, his life changed one day when his employer, a large government department, offered him a secondment to London for a year. There was a London weighting to the salary, and with the rental income from his house he realised he could afford to live, if not lavishly, then relatively comfortably. He grasped the opportunity with both hands, and rented a bedsit in a large house.

While he was away, although he wasn't active on the gay scene, he began to make friends who were also gay through one of his housemates, who was Australian and had a wide circle of acquaintances.

One of these was another young Australian man called Craig – tall, not exactly handsome but with a certain vulnerability about him, and Pete, of whom the same might be said, realised he had might well have found his soulmate.

Although they did sleep with one another occasionally, according to Pete, they realised that they were better off as very good friends rather than as boyfriends, and over the months they spent a lot of time together, exploring London's sights and travelling further afield as well.

Towards the end of Pete's secondment however, Craig was taken very seriously ill. As an Australian living in London, he felt completely alone when it came to this sort of thing and he was very frightened. He didn't know what to do, and laid low for a week or so, until Pete dropped round unexpectedly, took one look at him, and realised there was something badly wrong. He then took him along to the local hospital, where Craig was diagnosed with pneumonia, and was kept in for a few days before being sent home to his London bedsit to recover.

For Craig, enough was enough. The damp, cold air of London was, it seemed, quite literally killing him, and he was now very weak, so, as soon as he was able, he made arrangements to move back to his parents' home in Australia. By this stage, Pete's secondment was over and he was back in Newport.

He invited Craig to spend a couple of weeks with him, partly to recover his health, and partly so that he could make the final arrangements. Eventually, after a wonderfully relaxed time together, Craig said goodbye and, promising to keep in touch, flew home, leaving Pete sad but happy that at least the ailing Craig was in safe hands with his parents. And after Craig had emailed to say he'd arrived home, Pete relaxed.

One evening a week or so later Pete was at home watching TV when the house phone rang – not an unusual occurrence as by now Pete had a huge circle of friends. But when he answered it, the phone was dead. There really was no one there. In those days before caller-display, Pete dialled 1471 to find out who had called, and was surprised to discover it was Craig's old number in London. Pete was deeply puzzled. Craig had lived alone, so he rang the number itself, only to be told that the number was not recognised. Even more puzzled, Pete repeated the exercise, but with the same result. Something really odd was going on, but he had no idea what. He sent

Craig an email, but Craig didn't reply, although Pete didn't think very much of it.

In the next couple of weeks, some rather bizarre things started to happen to Pete. Things started to go missing and then reappear in the wrong place, but being a total sceptic, he thought nothing of it. The way in which his friend Annette had been hit in the nose by a flying wine cork one evening was slightly less easy to dismiss, but Pete found it so hilarious he regaled me with the story as soon as he possibly could. Annette, however, had failed to see the funny side of it, and blamed Pete. Protestations of, 'I was nowhere near it, honestly!' fell on deaf ears.

And then, seemingly out of the blue, a month or so after the dead phone call, Pete received a letter from Craig's mother. She had found his address among Craig's things, and had decided that she needed to write. Craig, she wrote, had arrived weak and breathless after the long flight home. He had seemed to recover quite well. But sadly, not long after his arrival, Craig had suffered a massive heart attack which the doctors thought might have been brought on by the pneumonia, and despite all their efforts, he had died.

Pete was devastated. This was not what was supposed to happen. But then he glanced at the date Craig had died: it was the same day he had received the phone call from his old number! As I said, Pete is a friend as well as a parishioner, and so he told me pretty much immediately. 'What do you think?' he asked, anxiously.

'I don't know,' I said, trying to be honest, 'I really don't know.'

'I think it was Craig just letting me know that he'd died.'

'Maybe you're right.' And for the moment, that was that.

Pete and I are friends but lives move on, and while this was going on, my family and I moved on to pastures new. So although Pete and I met up occasionally, and spoke on the phone from time to time, I wasn't picking up on all that was going on. It was only after about six months that Pete decided to call me in. 'You know I told you about that weird phone call after Craig died?' he began. 'Well, it was a little while after that that things started to happen. You remember Annette and the flying cork?'

'Yes, you were killing yourself laughing over that one.'

'Well, not long after that she came round for the evening and, as you do, she went to the toilet, but when she tried to get back into the living room, she couldn't open the door.'

I made a non-committal noise.

'It was like someone was holding it closed from the inside. She was getting so far with it, and then it was slamming shut. I was sitting there watching it, and she just screamed at me to let her in. But I swear it wasn't me.'

Pete explained that he had made quite a few friends in London, and over the months some of them had taken up the offer of coming to stay for a couple of nights. Pete really enjoys showing people round, and having extolled the virtues of South Wales and the Marches to so many people, they were keen to come and see for themselves.

'It didn't happen every time,' he continued, 'but very often people would come down in the morning and report similar sorts of things. When Craig had stayed for those weeks, he had taken over the spare bedroom, and it's almost as if something of him had been left behind. People said they would wake up in the night because it was very cold and they would see, or think they'd see, someone sitting on the bed looking at them. Most of them thought it was a dream, but some of them would come down the stairs and look at the photos on my rogues' gallery, and say, "That's him. That's the guy I saw sitting on my bed last night."'

I was familiar with Pete's 'rogues' gallery': a collection of photos in clip-frames that adorned the wall next to the window in his living room. I was also aware that there was a photo of me there as well.

'Anyway,' he explained, 'the first couple of times I didn't think anything of it, but it does seem to keep happening.' He paused for breath. 'And then, one evening, Craig's photo started to move in the frame.'

'What do you mean?'

'Well, the frame stayed still, and the photo inside just began to move from side to side. I had some friends round that evening, and they saw it too and were horrified. But at least you can tell I'm not making it up.'

Pete seemed to have reached a natural end to the story, so I asked, 'So you'd like me to come out and bless the house for you?'

'Wait a minute. You see I'm now right at the very beginning of a relationship with a guy called Andy,' – I offered my congratulations – 'and Andy has seen him a couple of times as well when he's stayed over. Because I snore and like my own space, he's been using the spare room, and he's seen Craig too.' Pete paused for breath.

'But over the last week or so, it's suddenly got worse. People reported something weird about the bathroom – and again Craig used to spend hours in the shower – but the other day Andy walked in, pulled back the shower curtain, and there was Craig stark naked in the shower! I heard the scream, but of course, there was nothing there when I got there. But it happened again this morning. Andy was staying over again last night, and this time the shower curtain was pulled back, and he could see Craig from the bathroom door. Andy says he's had enough, and would my vicar friend come and sort it out.' Pete was starting to sound mildly hysterical.

'OK. I'm happy to come over and say some prayers, and maybe celebrate a Requiem Mass for Craig if you like.'

'Thanks,' said Pete, 'that would be great.'

'Pete, do you mind if I ask? All these people say that they've seen Craig in the spare room and in the shower. Have you ever seen him?'

'Of course I have.'

'OK, I wasn't quite expecting you to say that.'

'Since it all started happening, I've seen him a couple of times in both places.'

'Were you worried?'

'Not really, although it was a bit of a shock when I saw him in the shower – I wasn't impressed, I can tell you,' he snorted, 'although when he was here he'd quite happily wander round with not much on.' Pete had a bit of a prudish side to him, and it began to occur to me that he was more worried about the nudity than about the ghost.

I felt that I was missing something. 'No, I mean, did seeing Craig frighten you?'

'Good God, no!' Pete sounded mildly shocked. 'He was my friend, he's not going to do anything to hurt me, is he?'

'No, I suppose not,' I replied. 'So why do you want me to come round, is it because you think he's trying to frighten Andy away?'

'No, I don't think he's trying to do that either, although Andy's terrified out of his wits. I just think it's time for him to move on, and to be where he needs to be, rather than being', he paused for the right word, 'earthbound', he settled on. 'Do you think you can help?'

'Yes, I'd be delighted. I'll just get my diary, and we can fix a date.'

Date fixed I put down the phone, and almost immediately

it started ringing, most likely it was someone who had pressed 'dial-back' which you could do in those long-lost days. Much to my surprise it was Pete, sounding deeply anxious. 'Please don't come around!'

'Why ever not? What's happened?' I asked.

'As soon as I put the phone down, that photo I've got of you in my rogues' gallery fell off the wall and shattered. I've just had a look at it. The nail is still there, fixed firmly to the wall, and the picture fell onto the carpet. It shouldn't have fallen off, and it shouldn't have shattered. Please don't come around, I think Craig may be angry that I've spoken to you.'

I agreed that, if it helped, I wouldn't come around any time soon, but that if it got worse, or he got frightened, he could always give me a ring, and I'd come around straightaway.

A month or so later I broached the subject with Pete, and asked him whether anything else had happened.

'It's really strange,' he said, 'but since that thing with the picture, we haven't seen him since, and Andy is much more comfortable being in the house.'

'That's great,' I said.

'I didn't ask this at the time, but why do you think Craig kept appearing?' he asked.

'With this sort of thing, there is usually an element of communication, but from what you've said, he didn't try to communicate with you, did he?'

'Not really,' Pete agreed.

'One of the other reasons this sort of thing might happen is because the dead person may be looking to offer you comfort. Do you think that might be what was going on?'

Pete thought for a few moments. 'Yes, I think it might have been. I know he terrified the wits out of everyone else, but before I met Andy, I was a bit at sea, and I found knowing he was still there a great comfort, yes . . . We're also wondering whether Andy was sort of on approval, and he thinks he may have passed the test.'

'Well that's good news.'

'Actually, I was ringing to ask if you two would like to come round to dinner soon to meet Andy properly.'

I consulted my wife, and we agreed a date. I have to admit that, despite everything, when we went around, using the bathroom was a bizarre experience, knowing that this was one of Craig's favourite places. But even though I walked past the spare room and saw the bed through the open door, and then looked in trepidation in the direction of the shower, whose curtain was pulled back, Craig didn't appear, and hasn't been seen since.


## 'Grandpa!'

It is not that uncommon for people to see a dead relative, especially one who has died recently. Some people see it as a sort of comfort visit, a sort of 'all is well' as the phrase from 'Death is nothing at all' by Henry Scott Holland puts it. On other occasions, I suspect it may simply be a matter of our minds telling us what ought to be there, rather than what is. It happens to us all: we might walk into a room where the picture which has always been above the armchair has been taken away, and we may well never notice. And the same thing sometimes happens with people too. Bert always sat in that armchair, so if we see Bert sitting in his usual place after he's died, is he really there? Is it his ghost? Or is it just the way our brains fill in the gaps to avoid sensory overload from our eyes? But sometimes, it goes a bit further than that.

This referral came via a circuitous route – very often they

do – but one evening I found myself in a traditional Welsh cottage in a village just off the old Roman road that runs parallel to the M4, chatting to a lady about her husband, who had died not long before. They had been together a very long time, and I estimated her age at around the early sixties – she was old enough to have grown up children who had children of their own. But she was relatively active. She explained that her husband had died in a road traffic accident on a notorious stretch of the nearby motorway, and that she had been devastated when it happened, but had managed to rebuild her life. She was now looking after her youngest granddaughter while her mother was in work, and this was a great source of joy, or at least should have been.

'My husband was always very attached to the house. We never really went away, and he did a lot of renovations himself. It's almost as if he put his soul into this place. And since he's gone, it's almost as if I can still feel him around. Just after he died, I actually think I saw him. He was sitting where he usually would in the armchair and, as I walked into the room, I knew he was there, and I could sort of see him out of the corner of my eye. But when I looked directly, he wasn't there any more. I've never told anyone about this, not even my daughter, because she'd be too upset. Do you think I'm going mad?'

As she was speaking, her eyes began to fill with tears, and I could tell that she had loved her husband very much.

Now, as you will have gathered, part of my job is to reassure people, and so I told her that this happens to a lot of people, but that it wasn't something to worry about. Slowly, she dried her tears, and composed herself.

'How long ago did this happen?' I asked.

'About six months ago, about a week after he passed away,' she replied.

There was something else going on here: you don't allow six months to pass before calling in a priest. But the lady was very clearly still upset, so I needed to be very gentle.

'Thank you very much for telling me that. I know it can't be easy for you.'

She smiled a tearful smile, nodded and sniffed decisively. 'The reason I've got in touch is because even though I haven't *seen* him since, I think he's still here.

'As I said, I look after my granddaughter so my daughter can work, and I have done for about a year now. When my husband was alive, I'd spend the day with my granddaughter, and then my husband would come home from work and that was the best bit of the day for her. Even though she's still barely talking, one of the first things that she could say was something that sounded like, 'grandpa', and she was learning to say it when my husband . . .' Her voice trailed off. I sympathised, and allowed her a few moments, and, again, she sniffed. 'I'm so sorry, I miss him so much!' and she broke down properly.

I am not the most tactile of people, and often I simply don't know what to do in situations like this. But I went and knelt in front of her, and held her hand, and slowly the tears abated, and she was able to reach across for a tissue.

'Thanks,' she said in a small voice. 'It sometimes comes over me and I can't help it.'

'It's only been six months, it's really early days,' I said quietly. 'Most people find that they never ever get over these things, but that eventually they get used to them. But that really does take time.' I got up and clambered back across the floor to my seat.

'I think I'm ready to talk about it,' she said, nodding.

'In your own time.'

'My granddaughter used to look forward to my husband coming home from work because he'd always play with her, and he'd got this face that he'd pull which would send her into fits of giggles. She'd laugh, point at him and say, "Grandpa" or something like it. It was something they did every day.' She smiled at the memory. 'And then about a month ago, we were all together here, because it was my husband's birthday, and the family didn't want me to be alone. It wasn't a party,' she made clear, looking at me to see if I disapproved, 'it was just a family gathering.'

'Of course,' I nodded.

'And so, as I said, we were all together, when my grand-daughter sat up in her highchair, pointed past all of us, giggled and said, "Grandpa." We were all so shocked, but we put it down to one of those things that children do. My daughter suggested that maybe she knew that my husband should have been there, and that she'd somehow imagined him. I wasn't convinced, but it was at least an explanation.'

I nodded.

'But then it happened again. It was just the two of us, we were watching children's TV together, and she started giggling again, and then she pointed. "Grandpa," she said, quite clearly. I was really shocked, and looked, but there was nothing there at all.

'But the thing is that it just keeps happening. Not every day, and not at the same time. Sometimes it's when we're here alone, and sometimes when my daughter's here with us. But I've also heard my granddaughter do it when she's on her own, if I've popped out to the kitchen, and then it sounds like they are really playing together like they used to.'

She stopped again for breath, and as the silence grew longer, I stepped in to ask, 'Have you been aware of anything yourself?'

She thought for a few moments. 'I'm afraid,' she said decisively. 'Sometimes when I'm here on my own, it's almost like there's someone in the room with me. Or I'll walk into a room and get that feeling, you know, when someone's just left, and sometimes

I can smell my husband's soap – he always used to use Imperial Leather, but it dries my skin out so I use something else, and when he died I couldn't bear the smell, because it reminded me so much of him, so I threw it all out. But just occasionally I can smell it,' she sniffed slightly, and said in a very small voice, 'just like I can now. Can you smell that too?'

I nodded. 'I think so, but very faintly.'

We both waited with bated breath for a few moments. 'No, thank God, it's gone,' she sighed, and reached for another tissue, and it was true, whether it was my imagination, or whether there really was a scent of Imperial Leather soap in the air, it had now gone.

'Yes, I'm afraid. I was never afraid of him when he was alive, but I *am* afraid of his ghost now. I really don't want to live with a ghost, and I'm worried about my granddaughter growing up. So, he needs to be somewhere else, he needs to move on, and really shouldn't be here. But I wonder sometimes if there is something wrong with me.'

So, I explained that her experiences, although worrying, seemed to be relatively common. Very often small children pick up on things that adults simply don't see, so there was nothing really to be worried about. But also people do sometimes smell things that they associate with loved ones too. Members of a family I know very well occasionally smell the disinfectant TCP in the house or sometimes in the car, and they attribute this to their dead mother.

Like so many people I have been to see, the important thing for this lady to know was that she was not alone, and that these things happen to all sorts of people. I then offered, as a solution, to bless the house as always, but also to say prayers for the repose of her deceased husband. Again, this might have been a case where I could have celebrated a Eucharist or Requiem Mass, but I thought that I would start with a simple house blessing, and work from there.

As I have described before, I feel as if I somehow *enter* the rite, and then I am pretty much oblivious to everything around me. The house felt strangely cold and dark, but then the sun had set while I had been there. There was, however, no sign of her dead husband, and neither of us could smell soap, although I certainly remained alert to the possibility.

There was no incident at all, so we arrived back in her living room, where I usually start and finish the blessing, where we stood and said the Lord's Prayer together. But as we said the final words, the lady staggered towards me as if she had been pushed, and I caught and steadied her.

'Are you all right?' I asked.

'That was so strange, it was almost as if something barged past me,' and she gestured at the chimney.

We both looked at one another. Neither of us said what I suspect we were both thinking: That was him! In fact, I don't think we needed to say it out loud. I continued with the final blessing of the service, and offered to bless one of the crosses I carry with me for her.

'Yes, please,' she said, 'that would be lovely.'

Was it me, or had she changed in the last few moments? The weight seemed to have been lifted from her shoulders, and I realised that she was in fact younger than I had first thought.

I said goodbye, got into the car and drove off, hoping that I would not smell Imperial Leather soap, but naturally I didn't – this ghost had no interest in me.

Not long afterwards I bumped into the lady at a garden centre. It was just before Christmas, and she was pushing a pram with a bouncy looking toddler, but despite looking a little tired after what appeared to have been a hard day looking at Christmas decorations with her granddaughter, she also appeared cheerful and full of joy. She spotted me, smiled and came over. 'Everything all right?' I asked.

'Yes, great. Nothing else has happened since. Thank you.'

And she whispered conspiratorially, 'I'd better go and catch up with my daughter. I never did tell her any of this. I really didn't want her to know her father was haunting me.'

I smiled as she trotted off: 'Maybe that's for the best,' I said.

# Chapter 7

## *Being dogged by evil*

So far, I have been following the classic deliverance framework, and have dealt predominantly with things that affect places rather than people. This is despite the fact that, of course, poltergeist activity is actually person-related rather than related to a building or a house. It's just that when such things happen, they tend to afflict people in a particular place rather than somewhere random, although, as I've also suggested, the framework is probably out of date. But now it is time to turn to the sorts of things that really do affect people and personalities, and this can be much more troubling.

You may remember from when I outlined my training that we spend a huge amount of time dealing with mental illnesses, with how to spot them and how to deal with them. So when it comes to people, we really are on our guard against barking up the wrong tree, although it is remarkably easy to do this. This is basically because human beings are very complex and we are often not very good at seeing what is under our noses.

For the many years I lectured in Biblical studies, I dealt with a whole range of students. As this was a theological college, or seminary if you prefer, they were all training for ministry in one form or other, and most of them were Anglicans, although over the years there were quite a few students from other churches too. But they all arrived with a series of assumptions that they were effectively blind to. So every year, I would try to encourage my group to question these assumptions: I'd give them a blank sheet of paper, and ask them to list personal attributes, experiences and more general things about themselves that they thought might affect the way they interpreted the Bible. (I had to be careful about how I phrased the question. One year I asked for 'things about yourself that might affect the way you read the Bible', only to discover that one of my students wrote things like, 'print size', 'light quality' and 'how thin the paper is' – creative, but frustrating!) And every year I was astonished not so much at what they came up with, but what they didn't come up with. Over the years, very few of them said whether they were male or female, whether or not they were married or had children, or were gay or straight (important when you are looking at some parts of the Bible!). Most surprisingly of all over the course of the years, to the best of my knowledge, not one of them wrote down the fact that they were Christians, even though very often it is our belief system that guides our way of thinking more than anything else.

Now, you might think that we live in a completely rational world where everything is governed by fact and rational analysis. This is a world where the scientist is king, because scientists are perceived to be the most dispassionate of all, but even in the world of science there are still belief systems which, because they are unacknowledged, are more dangerous than if they were overt. This is not a book about science and religion, but from the point of view of a religious believer, there is often no great difference between the way the religious and the scientific belief communities operate, to the extent that in the world of the scientist those who are seen as dissenters are treated to the sort of scorn that would delight mediaeval inquisitors dealing with heretics. Here's just one example.

Just before he died of cancer the great American evolutionary biologist Stephen Jay Gould wrote a book in which he dared to suggest that religion and science both had their place in the modern world in a theory he described as non-overlapping magisteria. The basic idea was that religion should inform things like ethics, while science should inform the natural world. The idea was dismissed by his colleagues.

They said he was dying so he had an irrational eye on the non-existent afterlife. Over the course of his career, Gould had fallen foul of the Darwinian orthodoxy because he had suggested that evolution worked in practice not by the very slow build-up of adaptations, but by what he described as 'punctuated equilibria' – effectively that evolution happens very quickly usually in small isolated populations which leave no trace on the fossil record. This was, however, too much of a departure from the belief system of Darwinian scientists and, despite the fact that his theory was entirely cogent and logical, he was pilloried for that too.

In other words, we all have our blind spots and our own belief systems which carry unargued-for assumptions that colour the way we see the world, however much we pretend that we have none.

Increasingly in the contemporary world, whether we like it or not, what you might call 'spirituality' is playing a significant role. I have put 'spirituality' in inverted commas because it is often different from what Christians have historically meant by that word. For Christians, spirituality has always meant prayer and worship, and mysticism had tended to mean very deep prayer which practitioners believe puts them in direct (and usually silent) contact with God. But in today's world, spirituality and mysticism are words that have become common currency, first of all through the New Age movement that grew out of the experience of hippies in the 1960s and their interest in Eastern religions, and subsequently through the Internet, which is a great trove of treasure and dross in equal measure. These things have permeated society in a way that is quite surprising in many ways.

Take angels for example. In the Old Testament there are spiritual beings which crop up from time to time: sometimes they are seen as members of the heavenly court of Yahweh (God's name in the Old Testament), where they are sent out to do special jobs from time to time. The Hebrew Old Testament described these as 'messengers' which, when it was translated into Greek, came out as *'angeloi'*, which we tend to read as 'angels' rather than 'messengers'. There were also two other types of spiritual being in the Old Testament: there were the cherubim, which were probably depicted as winged sphinxes and which were, in some traditions, the steeds of God, as in Psalm 18.10: 'He rode on a cherub, and flew; he came swiftly upon the wings of the wind.' Then there were the flying snakes that were the personal attendants of God, the seraphim. We see these in action in Isaiah 6, but the same word is used to describe the snakes sent by God to punish the recalcitrant Israelites in Numbers 21. In addition to this, there are numerous images of snakes with multiple sets of wings that have been found often on stones used as personal seals in the Near East.

By the time the New Testament had come to be written, however, the writers lived in a world where God was seen as increasingly distant. The Old Testament God often speaks directly to people, but by the time of Jesus, they believed God acted in the world through a whole series of intermediaries: the system of angelic beings had been invented, and the New Testament reflects this development, especially in the book of Revelation where all sorts of spiritual entities, good and bad, run across the pages. Now, standard Christianity has tended to treat Revelation with a good pinch of salt, which is almost certainly what the author intended (it's best seen as a coded attack on the Roman world in which he lived and not a fore-telling of any future event). But the book found its way into the New Testament, although the fact that it's at the end suggests it's there by way of appendix.

Fast forward to the contemporary world, and angels are everywhere! Lots of people I speak to in the course of my parish ministry tell me that they are 'into angels'. Some of them tell me they believe that angels look after them and somehow guide their lives; a few of them tell me they have read that the souls of their dead loved ones become angels and drop feathers in the bedroom for them to find, and they wonder if I share that belief. In at least one case, I have been asked whether it's true that some birds can sometimes be angels, sent from God to give them messages (scientists, of course, believe that birds are in fact dinosaurs that survived the great Cretaceous mass extinction); some people believe that angels walk among them, and that sometimes you might meet them in the street. There has been a complete explosion on books about angels (cathedral bookshops are full of them – they sell well), people give angel figures as gifts, and you can buy inspirational cards with verses about angelic protec-tion: angels are big business!

But it's not just angels, of course, because if you believe that somehow angels are protecting you and guiding your path, then it's just the next step to start believing that somehow the forces of evil are ranged against you, and that, just occasionally, they can get the upper hand, and that is where people like me come in, to try and banish the forces of evil.

## Sheer bad luck

Relatively early on in my ministry I started coming across people who believed that the things that went wrong in their lives were not the result of sheer back luck, but of something else, some sort of spiritual evil.

One early case is a good example. The house proved to be a typical Valleys terraced house, just like the ones you will have seen in so many clichéd shots – you know, all those rows of identical houses, line after line, coming down the mountainside. Now the thing about clichés is that there is always an element of truth in them. There are urban myths in the Valleys about people moving into a new house, going out in the evening to the pub, and then not being able to remember which house they have just bought.

But at the same time, what the cliché doesn't tell you is that most of the time the houses are immaculately kept: the woodwork will frequently be beautifully painted, often in bright colours (to distinguish them from their neighbours maybe), and when you walk in, you are entering a different world, a world that will often require you to take off your shoes as if you were entering a sacred space. What the cliché masks is that frequently people who live in traditional terraced houses have quite a lot of disposable income. The Valleys may be among the most deprived parts of Europe, but many of the older people will be pensioners on gold-plated final salary schemes, and because the houses will have been bought a long time ago, or will have been inherited, very often people who live in them have never had huge mortgages to pay off. These are people who go on frequent cruises, who travel across America for weeks on end, and who spend their money on the latest gadget for the house or on home decor. Terraced houses in the Valleys are often little pleasure palaces, and that's what this one was: it may have been located in one of the villages I looked after which wind up the Eastern Valley from Pontypool, but this was a slice of paradise.

The door was opened by a small emaciated lady in her early sixties, and standing behind her was a wiry man of around the same age, his neck in one of those soft neck braces you can buy at the pharmacy. They had been expecting me, having asked their daughter to ring and ask me to call round. All I had been told by her was that they had been having a run of bad luck.

Their daughter thought I might be able to help, because they were friends of another family I had helped (I wasn't sure which one), and also because at the end of the day, I was their vicar.

'Come in, vicar,' said the lady, sounding a bit breathless and slightly husky.

'Thank you,' I said, followed by the traditional, 'shall I take my shoes off?'

'You don't have to, love, but you can leave them there,' she answered, giving me the great honour of implying that I might be allowed to enter her house without having taken my shoes off, while at the same time skilfully making it clear that that was exactly what was expected of me. I removed the offending footwear, and examined my socks for holes – none were discernible, thank God. Now suitably prepared the inner door was opened, and I was allowed in.

And, yes, this was a little piece of luxury in the grimness of the Valleys. Not having my shoes on made me appreciate more clearly the fact that my feet were sinking into a very thick carpet with masses of underlay underneath, and I looked round at immaculately papered walls. (Valleys people traditionally put up new paper every year – sometimes they even strip the previous layers before the next layer goes on!) Even now I can remember the shimmer of the light, catching the gold stripes in the afternoon sun that was just allowed in through the half-light above the front door. The other thing that was abundantly clear was that the house smelt really strongly of the fresh ciga-rette smoke that hung in the air, although it also smelt very strongly of floral air freshener, reminding you, maybe, that somewhere outside this enchanted abode, there really was fresh, clean air.

And so, they invited me into their front room. Now, Valleys people have often observed the tradition of reserving the front room for 'best'. In other words, it was a space you could take the minister (or the vicar in my case) for formal occasions, which basically meant when someone had died. It was also the room where the coffin might be brought if the deceased was spending his or her last night before the funeral at home, although that particular tradition had died out (so to speak) by the time I was ordained. But a lot of houses still had a traditional front room. From bitter experience of having been accorded this dubious honour, the rooms are often cold and deeply uncomfortable (what's the point in having heating or comfortable furniture in a room you never use?). And being shown into the front room would usually mean that I will be accorded the honour of being served tea in a china cup and saucer (or indeed *the* china cup and saucer) which was last used when the vicar last called about twenty years ago.

Fortunately, this couple had had both their main downstairs

rooms knocked through, so I was led into a spacious lounge with a very new leather three-piece suite, and the biggest television set I had ever seen. As is usually the case, they didn't turn it off while I was there, but at least they turned the sound down – there is nothing more off-putting than having to have an in-depth conversation about the fact that Auntie Alice has died (or, frequently in my case, that Auntie Alice has died, but is still haunting the landing) and having to compete with *Coronation Street*, or some such delight. The other thing that struck me about the house was that it was full of ornaments. In fact, the more I looked, the more I realised that almost every surface had on it a fish ornament, most of them were goldfish or carp or angelfish, and were brightly coloured, but some of them were quite clearly the sort of fish you eat with your chips.

So, after the usual pleasantries had been exchanged, and I had refused the traditional cup of tea (you would not believe what it is like drinking from a china cup that was last used twenty years ago!), I asked about the fish. 'Oh, don't you know,' explained the lady with mild incredulity, 'they are there to bring good luck. Fish, you see, are very lucky.'

I expressed a degree of surprise – this really was not an idea I had come across before. 'So how many fish do you have?' I asked innocently.

'At least a hundred. Every time anyone goes away, they bring me back a fish,' she said, stroking a ceramic goldfish on the table next to her chair.

'Is it just fish you collect?' I enquired.

'Yes, mainly. Sometimes people get it wrong and bring me other things,' she shuddered.

'Is that a problem?'

'If they are cats it is!' she responded, looking horrified.

'Why?' I was genuinely puzzled, especially as I am a cat lover.

'Cats are really unlucky,' she sounded like she was addressing an imbecile, which maybe I was when it came to these things.

I felt I needed to move the conversation along a bit. 'So, do you buy fish yourself?'

Again, this was clearly the wrong thing to ask. 'The luck only works when it's given as a gift.' Clearly, I was an imbecile of the highest order.

Maybe it was time to move on to safer ground – politics, the death penalty, immigration – but I settled for religion instead. I may be an imbecile, but I am also a priest. 'Thanks for explaining all that, I really didn't know. But your daughter said that you needed a priest to come and talk to you . . .'

The lady began, 'We've had this terrible run of bad luck, haven't we love?' Her husband nodded. 'And we thought we'd ask you to come around to see if you can sort it out, and change our luck for us.'

'Why a priest?'

'Well, we were both brought up going to chapel when we were children, except my husband was Salvation Army, weren't you love?' He nodded again. 'But when we got married, we both stopped going, although we both still believe, don't we love?' Same response. 'Anyway, all the chapels in this part of town have closed because people stopped going, and the ones in town have all gone happy-clappy, and we can't cope with that, so my friend said that you might be able to help. Can you?'

The couple's story was not very unusual (even if they were not quite right about the local chapels). For over a century, the chapels dominated life in these terraced streets. They were the places where you went three times on a Sunday, but they were also the focus of community life. The chapels all had big choirs and a strong network of support. But over the course of the second half of the twentieth century all that dissipated. Maybe it was all part of the permissive society, and the fact that the baby-boomer generation felt that they were now free from the old constraints, and that the chapels were felt often unfairly to be about constraint and nothing else. Society was being remade, and even in traditional places like the South Wales Valleys (actually especially in the South Wales Valleys, where fewer people express a faith than in much of the rest of the UK), there was no room for a religion that began with 'Thou shalt not . . .'.

What actually replaced the prescriptive religion of the chapel is another matter entirely. People in the Valleys certainly embraced the newly permissive society, although not quite in the same overt ways as some other places did, and slowly attitudes changed: the whole stigma attached to unmarried mothers, which would have seen you and your family ostracised in previous generations, had long gone, for example. But in terms of religion, the changes have been towards a sort of nominal Christianity, but with a strong admixture of things such as astrology sometimes filtered through the 'stars' in the tabloids, and in the case of this particular family, towards the idea of lucky charms of all sorts and going along with it, as I have said, this idea of bad luck.

But I needed to know the story. 'Well, I'll do my best to help you, but can you tell me what sorts of things have been happening to you?'

The woman heaved a great breathy sigh. 'Well, we think we've been dogged by bad luck, you see.'

'So, what do you mean?'

The lady looked at me as if she felt she had already given me sufficient information. But I was rescued by her husband, who spoke for the first time in a clear and surprisingly bright voice. Quite clearly she was the smoker and, as if to prove the point, she lit up her first cigarette, grabbing a fish-shaped ashtray from the coffee table, and knocking a couple of asthma inhalers on to the floor, while her husband began telling me about her illnesses. 'She's been in and out of hospital over the last six months. It's her chest,' he explained, as she started coughing. 'She's always enjoyed very good health, and we've always been able to go away, but the last time we were supposed to go – cruise round the Med, it was – she was taken in, and we couldn't go. We nearly didn't get a payout on the insurance, but they coughed up eventually. And other things have happened too . . .' His voice trailed off.

'Tell him about the car,' his wife sputtered, not sure whether to cough or inhale her smoke.

'Oh yes, the car. One day coming back from Cwmbrân, we were driving along, and someone just pulled out at a junction from the side, and slammed right into the side of us. It was a really slow motion thing, and there was almost no damage to the car, but we were really shocked, and since then my neck hasn't been right and I've had to wear this in the evening,' he gestured towards the neck brace. 'My doctor says it's nothing to be worried about, but I'm not sure – you can't be too careful.'

'Thank you for sharing all that,' I said, still mildly puzzled. Clearly being a heavy smoker who is taken into hospital for respiratory complaints isn't an example of being dogged by bad luck, nor is being involved in a minor car crash. 'Was there anything else?' I asked.

They looked at one another, and the wife spoke for them both. 'It's just we were wondering if we'd been cursed.'

'Why would you think that?'

'Well, we were in Cardiff a couple of months ago, and a woman came up to us, trying to sell us some lucky heather. Well, you don't like to turn them down do you, just in case they curse you, so we bought some. But when we got to the bus, I realised we didn't have the lucky heather any more, and since then, our luck has just run out.' At this point, the lady broke down in tears, and needed to use one of her inhalers before she could say, 'Can you help us, please?'

I wasn't quite sure what to say, so I went for the rational approach. 'I'll do my best. To be honest, I don't really believe in the whole good and bad luck thing . . .' My voice trailed off: quite clearly this wasn't the right thing to say as the lady looked incredulously at me – how dare I question it? So I changed tack for something maybe a little less rationalist. 'I mean, I believe that God always wants the best for us, so when we encounter things that look like they might be bad luck, we need to invite God into the process.' I had a peep: this seemed to be going down better, so I kept going. 'So, what I'm going to do is say some prayers for protection, which is a sort of way of just asking God to act.' Another glance suggested that this might be the right approach.

'Can you give us something that will protect us from the curse?' asked the gentleman anxiously while he held his wife's hand.

I thought for a moment. 'I can bless a cross for you if you like, and leave it here,' I suggested. 'Bingo!' I thought. So that's what we did: I said prayers for them, including the Lord's Prayer, and I blessed one of my olivewood holding crosses for them. But through all this, I was feeling mightily guilty, and was desperately trying to think of a way of helping rather than colluding. As we were finishing, the lady began to cough again, this time uncontrollably. 'That sounds really bad,' I commented when she had finished.

'Yes, it's all part of the bad luck I've had,' she answered, reaching for another cigarette.

'Hmm,' I said, gathering up some courage. 'I know we've said some prayers for protection, and I really do believe that God always looks after people, but sometimes I think people also make their own luck, good or bad.'

There was silence for a few moments as they weighed up what I had said. 'Maybe you're right, love,' she said, and probably the only miraculous thing happened that evening, she put the cigarette back in the packet. 'Maybe you're right.'

A few moments later I found myself back in the porch, fumbling inelegantly with my shoes. The lady had said goodbye from the living room, but her husband had followed me. 'I wish she'd give those blooming things up,' he muttered, 'they're not doing her any good.'

'No, I can see that.'

'But thanks, vicar, maybe now our luck will change.'

'I really hope so, I really do,' I said, and meant it utterly sincerely.

With that particular couple I felt that I was in danger of colluding with what they thought was happening to them, but hoped that I managed to salvage the situation. Since that relatively early encounter, I have found it easier to challenge and also to help, as in the next case – where collusion may have proved fatal.


## The electric ghost

Contacts for deliverance ministry tend to come from various different sources. This particular one, I think, came via the Diocesan Office, who sent me an email asking to get in touch with a woman who was afflicted with some sort of ghost. So, I duly rang the number I had been given.

The woman on the phone seemed quite nervous, but then I

had learned from experience that people frequently and quite naturally are nervous when they are living with some sort of paranormal phenomenon. I asked her, as always, just to tell me a little about what was happening to her, and suddenly her nervousness vanished. 'I've been living in this house for many years with my son. He's unemployed at the moment, and he's a bit down to be honest, but my husband's dead, and he's my son so I need to do my best for him, don't I?' I grunted sympathetically. 'Anyway, I've started to see all sorts of things in the house.'

'What sorts of things?'

'Nothing that you could put your finger on, but just shadows and things.'

'Are you sure they are there?'

'Oh, yes, and my son says he's seen them as well, so it must be true.'

'OK,' I responded non-committally, hoping for something a bit more to be going on with. 'Is there anything else?'

'Oh, yes, that's why I got in touch with you. I was in the garden the other day, and there's a really lovely view in two directions. I can see the open hills to one side, and across the water to the Wirral and Liverpool Cathedral beyond it at the front. It's really very special. I sometimes feel that Liverpool Cathedral is out there watching over me and protecting me. I don't like being out the back, though.'

'Isn't it a nice view too?'

'Yes, but it would mean looking at my neighbours' house and garden. They hate us, and don't like us living here. In fact, they sometimes shout at us when we walk past their house, which we have to so that we can get in. They really want to buy the house from us. It's not very big, but it's got a lovely garden, and they want the view, at least we think they do.' She paused for breath.

'So, Mrs Jones, you were out in the garden . . .'

'Oh, yes. Well I was out in the garden, enjoying the view like I said, and then suddenly I felt that my entire body was being taken over by a sort of presence, like a ghost, and I could feel the electricity running up and down through my body, just like I was a pylon or something.'

'Did you say that you felt electricity running through you?' I wanted to make sure that I had got that bit right.

'Oh, yes. I could feel it going through me and then out into the ground again.'

The way she described it, it sounded as if she thought it was a wonderful experience, so I asked her, 'So why do you think it's a ghost?'

'Well, because of the shadows!' she replied, as if only an idiot would fail to make the connection. 'Anyway, I asked my son and he said that he thought the two must be connected, and he's usually right about things. Men often are, I think.'

'Oh, I'm not sure about that.'

'But you're a man, don't you think men are usually right about things?' I was beginning to feel uncomfortable. Many parts of Wales live with traditional values, as I have suggested, so sadly it would not be that unusual among traditional working class folk to find that men make all the decisions, and are usually 'right about things' even when they are quite clearly not. I felt sorry for Mrs Jones, who probably for the whole of her life had been dominated by the men in her life, and now she was a widow she seemed to have devolved the decision-making to her son. I rather wished that I had not been put in this situation, but I realised that whatever I said wasn't likely to be questioned, because I was, after all, a man.

'What I'd like to do, Mrs Jones, is to come around if I may, with one of my colleagues, and we can have a chat, possibly with your son as well if he's there. Would that be all right with you?'

'Yes, when can you come?' And we fixed up a time.

The fact that Mrs Jones had been telling me that her house had a view of Liverpool Cathedral may well tell you immediately that we are now in North Wales. Between North and South there is a large range of mountains, and the two parts of Wales rarely have very much to do with one another. South Wales is centred very much on Cardiff, and has an extended buffer zone consisting mainly of the Forest of Dean separating it from England, whereas North Wales, or at least the parts of North Wales where most people live, is very open to England: Wrexham, the largest town in the North, is only twelve miles from Chester, and less than an hour from Liverpool and Manchester.

Despite all this, Welsh people are remarkably similar in all sorts of ways whether they are from the South or the North. There is an unaffected friendliness about them, and they, by and large, do not stand on ceremony. In all of Wales, there is a strong sense of community, often built on an idea that may be surprising to outsiders – that they live in a conquered nation and need to cling together to retain their identity. Welsh people, for example, when they meet one another in social contexts, will very often try to work out if they have a relative in common, or if they have a common friend or acquaintance, and will keep going until that magic moment when the connection is made, and they are able to say, 'He's a lovely man . . .' or something like that, and then move on to do what people in other parts of the UK do, and talk about the best road between two random points, and where the best service stations are.

Being a vicar in Wales is a bit strange, however. There have always been vicars in Wales, even when the majority of people saw their main affiliation as with the chapel, and each community has a 'vicar-shaped hole' into which you simply put your own personality. It is almost certainly the same with most small communities across Britain, but in Wales there is always the idea lurking at the back of people's minds that you are basically there as the vicar to represent the establishment, and are therefore going to be a bit distant. This is something that I have tried my best to subvert over the years: I do my best to be down to earth and, despite the fact that to most people I simply do not sound Welsh, I usually try to drop the fact that I am Welsh-born into the conversation.

Being a Welsh-born vicar seems to be enough, it seems to make Welsh people feel more comfortable, although the fact that I know Rowan Williams really helps. But in this case, unfortunately, the most important thing wasn't so much being a priest or a vicar, it was having the authority that my gender gave me in Mrs Jones's eyes.

Once I had put down the phone, I thought for a few moments. What she had said began to ring bells. And I was transported back to my initial training as a priest in theological college. As well as all the sorts of things that they think people are likely to expect you to know, they did quite a lot of work on mental health issues with us, and in my case, as I have mentioned, I spent a month on placement in the psychiatric hospital at the edge of Cambridge.

I remember one afternoon being puzzled because a patient whom I knew was suffering from schizophrenia, and who was also quite clearly having a full-blown psychotic episode, started telling the weekly staff and patients' meeting about the fact that she could see the electricity running through the walls, and invited us all to admire it. Some of the other patients were deeply disturbed by this, particularly an elderly patient who took over the television in the common room to play a video tape of Michael Flatley's *Lord of the Dance* every afternoon.

But the whole idea of electricity stuck in my mind, so I asked my clinical supervisor about it afterwards: 'I've no idea why, but that's one of the things about people suffering from schizophrenia. They have a thing about electricity.' So, I wondered, was this the problem with the lady from North Wales? At least it was worth pursuing.

As usual, after a courtesy chat with the local vicar, who was about to go off on holiday, I contacted a trusted colleague. In this case it was someone with some experience of dealing with mental health issues and also happened to be a woman, which I felt was important in this instance. I explained to her what I had been told, and my theory about what might be the cause of the issue. The link between schizophrenia and electricity, she said, was new to her, but wasn't beyond the bounds of credibility.

A few days later, we travelled together to the house, which gave us a better opportunity to have a chat, and to pray together. It was also really useful that she knew where she was going, because once I was off the main road, I was hopelessly lost in the maze of short terraces that seemed to have been placed randomly on the mountainside. Unlike the long rows of terraced houses you find in the South Wales Valleys, post-industrial villages in North Wales (of which this was one) often feature a jumble of short rows. Having abandoned the car in a car park which appeared to mark the site of a demolished non-conformist chapel, we discovered that the lady and her son lived at the end of one of these rows of about five houses. As we approached, the view to our right, which had been obscured by the houses opposite, suddenly opened up to give a breathtaking view across the sea towards the green swathe of the Wirral and, yes, if you squinted, you could in fact make out Liverpool Cathedral in the far distance. Stunned, we stood for a few moments in silence before turning and knocking on the door. It was soon opened by a lady who looked like she was in her mid-seventies, was neatly dressed, but had sad blue eyes. She introduced herself as Mrs Jones. Then she looked anxiously down the path to her right. 'The neighbours didn't give you any trouble, did they?' she asked, concerned.

'No, we didn't see them.'

'I bet they saw you, though. They are always causing trouble for us, my son and me.' I nodded to acknowledge her pain and anxiety, and she let us in.

The house was very sparsely furnished. At one end there was a dining area, with a Formica-topped table and just two battered chairs, and at the other end the front door opened directly onto the living area, where there was an old style television, and a three-piece suite that had seen better decades. The carpet under our feet was threadbare, the curtains old and faded, and there seemed very little in the way of comfort. There was none of the almost palatial luxury of the house in the Valleys in the previous case.

The lady seemed quite nervous. 'I'm very sorry,' she explained, 'my son's not feeling very well today, and I'm afraid he's still in bed.'

'That's not a problem,' I reassured her. People in these situations always need a huge amount of reassurance, but for whatever reason Mrs Jones needed more than most. As always, I asked her to describe again what she felt the problem was for the sake of my female colleague, I explained. She smiled at my colleague, and then ignored her for the rest of the conversation. Quite clearly in her world this could only be solved by a man! And so, she told us (well, me) about her sense of unease in the house, and the way in which she had seen shadows. Once again, it was striking the extent to which she relied on her son's acquiescence to all this. Even though he was not physically in the room, his opinions counted more than hers: Mr Jones always trumped Mrs Jones.

But, of course, I was most interested in her visitation by the electric ghost, so I asked her to describe it again. Mrs Jones herself seemed less interested in this experience, but she began to open up. 'As I may have told you on the phone, it was an amazing thing to happen. It was like being taken over, with the electricity running up and down through my body. My friend says that your nerves run on a sort of electricity, so it might have been that, but it felt more as if it was coming from outside of me, like I'd been plugged into the National Grid or something like that.'

'That's really amazing,' I said, 'but has anything like this ever happened to you before?'

Mrs Jones stopped and thought for a moment. 'Not quite like that,' she answered eventually, 'but sometimes I can feel something a little bit like electricity in me.' She sounded both unconvinced and somehow pleading, as if she was concerned to say the right thing, and was worried that she had got it all wrong.

'I'm really sorry about this, Mrs Jones, but do you mind if I ask you if you take medication for anything at all?'

'Oh, yes,' she responded enthusiastically – this was something that she could tell me about that would please me.

'Do you mind if I ask what for?'

'Oh, for my schizophrenia, of course,' she replied, as if it was the most obvious thing in the world.

I didn't do a victory dance, I didn't react. I could, however, tell my colleague was looking at me with an 'I hate it when he's right' look on her face. 'Do you mind if I ask when you last had a medical review?' I asked.

'Quite a while ago now. I've been on the same dose for years. Why?'

'Well, I was wondering whether you might need to have your medication reviewed.'

'Do you really think so?'

'Yes, I do. Do you have a community psychiatric nurse who looks after you?'

'Not at the moment. The last one left, and I haven't got one. Is it important?'

'Yes, I think it is, but you will need to make an appointment with your doctor, pretty much as soon as we've gone. It's only 2.30 now, I'm sure they'll be open for a while.'

'You really think so?' she was back to unconvinced pleading.

'Yes, I do,' I said with authority, 'and you'll need to tell the doctor what you've told me, especially about the electricity.'

'I'll do that,' she said. And then she paused. 'So, it's me isn't it, and not the house?'

I was impressed by the fact that she had caught on quite so quickly. 'I'm pretty sure it isn't the house, but would you like me to bless it for you anyway?'

'Yes, please, just to give me the reassurance.'

'OK, we can do that.' I didn't want to take up too much time, because the most important thing was that she got her medication sorted, but also, I didn't want to rush. The house, however, was very small. There was a basic kitchen in a lean-to at the back, and as we went upstairs, I was aware again of the fact that her son was still in bed.

'Will your son mind if we go into his bedroom?' I whispered.

'Not at all. I did tell him you were coming.'

'That's OK, then.' In fact the son, if he had been listening, would have heard. His bedroom was at the top of the stairs, overlooking the kitchen and the back garden, and other than a computer on the desk, there was little indication that it was someone's bedroom except that he was in residence. He was in fact sprawled face down on the bed, with various limbs poking out from under the duvet, but unlike Mary's son in a previous story, this troublesome son was corpulent, bald and looked from the angle I was at to be in his fifties. I was as fast as possible there, and then moved into Mrs Jones's almost equally bare room, although I did stop to admire the stunning view for a moment or two, hoping that she would feel safe, protected by the distant cathedral.

Not long afterwards, we were back in the front room, where once again I took advantage of my God-given gender, and reminded her that she really did need to phone her doctor immediately with a view to a medical review. As we walked down the path and the amazing vista of the Wirral and distant Liverpool disappeared to our left, we made sure we didn't upset the neighbours. Safely at the end of the row, we turned back. Mrs Jones was standing on the doorstep, phone thankfully in her hand, looking happy and relaxed.

The idea of oppression as something that deliverance ministers deal with can be fairly nebulous. Sometimes, it takes the form of a general sense of bad luck, sometimes it looks like it has other causes – as in the case we have just looked at, where it was clear from the outset that the cause was a psychiatric illness. Although to be honest I also was concerned that the son appeared to be oppressing his mother. However, if that was the case I suspect that there was nothing anyone other than Mrs Jones herself would have been able to do about it, and even then, if she had been aware that she was in a toxic relationship with him, she probably wouldn't have done anything about it anyway. But occasionally I come across cases where problems have a much more clear cause.

## 'Do you think I let something through?'

Back in South Wales, there was an occasion where one of the other priests in the diocese got in touch to say that he had had a call from the family of a teenage boy called Jake. They said he had terrified himself out of his wits playing with a Ouija board, and was now starting to experience all sorts of strange things. The priest said he didn't really feel qualified to go out himself, but was happy to give me the details if I thought it worth following up. It seemed a bit cavalier, really, but I said I'd be more than happy to at least to talk with them. So, I rang the number, and spoke briefly to the boy's mother, and arranged a time to go for an exploratory chat, if nothing else.

The address proved to be another of those on the modern housing estates that are common in the Valleys, where a group of houses is perched high above the valley floor, except that this wasn't just a group of houses, but a vast estate of virtually identical houses whose only saving grace was that they were so high up you could see the distant Bristol Channel and the Mendip Hills beyond. It was late afternoon, a time that we had organised so that Jake would be back from school. The house, when I found it, like Mrs Jones's home in the previous story, really did have an amazing view and was clearly positioned to take advantage of it in a way that the North Wales house hadn't been. The garden was very well kept, and the front door had the air of belonging to a family that takes care about appearances. The door was opened by a mother with an anxious smile, and I was ushered into a gloriously light-filled interior as the afternoon sun poured in though the French windows at the back of the house. I sat down on a very comfortable sofa and looked round a very clean-lined and modern room while his mother called Jake, who was apparently doing his homework upstairs.

There was a clatter on the open-plan staircase, and Jake walked in, took one look at me and blanched. We stared at one another with open mouths for a few moments, before I recovered first and said, 'Hi, Jake. I hadn't realised it was you.'

Jake looked like he was going to die of embarrassment while his mother looked more than mildly puzzled.

'He's in the same class as my son Benedict,' I explained. The school in question took pupils from a very wide geographical area, and although I had seen Jake at various school events, and he was in the same broad friendship circle as my son, I had no idea where he lived and had never met his parents. Once this was explained, Jake's mother recognised my son's name, and appeared a lot happier. The same could not be said of Jake, who continued to appear horrified. So, I found myself reassuring him that he was perfectly within his rights to tell my son or indeed anyone else about this, but that I was not, and that whatever he said was bound by confidentiality rules. His mother nodded, and he began to relax, at least a little.

'So, Jake, can you just tell me a bit about your problem?' I asked.

Jake glanced nervously at his mother. Clearly having to explain to a friend's father was bad enough, but in front of your own mother made it a whole lot worse. 'It all happened a couple of weeks ago, really. One of my friends found a Ouija board up in the attic, and brought it in to school so we could see how it worked.' He looked at me and added, 'Benedict wasn't there.' Clearly, he felt I needed some sort of reassurance that my son wasn't involved.

'Thanks,' I nodded, relieved.

'Anyway, we played with the board, and it was really strange, because we felt like there was something there that was directing us, moving our hands to spell out the letters. I was really, really frightened. I thought it would be just a piece of fun, but suddenly it all felt a bit too serious, and I was worried. So, I took my hand away. My friend who'd brought it in yelled at me, and told me that I might have let something in.

'He said something about the board containing the spirit, but now it was free.' Once he had begun to explain what had happened, his nervousness about telling me the story with his mother listening in evaporated, to be replaced by a much stronger emotion – sheer terror. 'Do you think I let something through?' he asked, fighting back the tears.

'I don't know, to be honest. I don't know very much about Ouija boards,' I said, which is in fact true. Some Christian groups have apparently insisted that they are very dangerous and can allow demons entry into the world, although I have discovered recently this is an idea that almost certainly originated with the 1973 film *The Exorcist*, before which Ouija boards were regarded as an old-fashioned parlour game. I don't have strong views about them, for me they are akin to consulting a medium – it's not something that I would approve of, but I have yet to be convinced of its absolute harm.

On this occasion, while I was formulating an answer to Jake's question, his mother interjected. 'Of course you might have let something through! What on earth did you think you were doing?'

I didn't feel this was necessarily helpful, so I sought a way of defusing the situation. 'As I said, I just don't know enough about Ouija boards, but what makes you think you might have, as you say, let something through?'

Jake gulped. 'All sorts of strange things have been going on since then. I've felt uneasy, as if there's something looking over my shoulder. I keep thinking I see shadows, and,' he gulped again as he struggled to keep the tears in, 'I think I saw my shoes move on their own! I'm so frightened!'

At this point, while Jake sniffed, we were disturbed by the sound of his father arriving home from work. 'I'm sorry I'm late,' he said as we shook hands, 'I've been really worried about Jake, and I wanted to be here when you came. How are you, mate?' he said, turning to him.

He looked up. 'I'm OK, dad. I've just been explaining to Mr Bray what's been happening to me.'

He turned to me. 'What do you think?'

I turned back to his son. 'Thanks, Jake, for telling me all this, I know it hasn't been easy. I don't think you allowed anything to come through, as you said, but I do think you've had a really frightening experience.' I paused for a moment. 'I think that basically you've completely spooked yourself out, and sometimes when this happens people do see things like shoes move round, and they do imagine people standing behind them, but I'm pretty sure it's nothing to worry about.' Jake started to look relieved. 'Does that make sense?' I asked. 'Yes,' he said, 'yes, it does.'

'As I said, I'm pretty much convinced there's nothing to be worried about, but if you like I can say some prayers to ask God to protect you. But before I do, can I ask if you've been baptised or christened?' As I've explained before, if someone is baptised, it provides more options.

Jake looked at his mother, who replied for him. 'Yes, he has, in fact he's been confirmed as well, and he used to be in the church choir too.'

'Good,' I said, faintly surprised. 'In that case as well as that I'll anoint you with the holy oil, that the bishop blesses once a year, and I'll leave you one of my holding crosses too. Would that be all right?'

The family assented, and so that's what we did. After the blessings, and the Lord's Prayer, I began to take my leave. 'Thank you for coming,' said Jake's mother.

His father nodded. 'Yeah, thanks. I think that's the last time Jake's going near a Ouija board,' he said, and looked across at a newly stricken-looking Jake. I smiled at him and saw him nod very faintly. I suspect his lesson had been learnt. Ouija boards may or may not provide a link with the beyond, but the fact that this boy felt that he might have let something through from the other side meant that I suspected that might be the last time he'd dabble in the paranormal.

## 'Can you come around again?'

There are various ways in which people manage to get themselves into difficult situations where they feel like they are being oppressed by some form of evil. Jake's encounter with the Ouija board was one example, but there are other more damaging ways of doing it too.

Janet is a young woman who got in touch with the Diocesan Office to say that her house was haunted. The new receptionist at the office was a bit concerned, so I found myself offering her reassurance as well: yes, she was talking to the right person, and yes, this was a 'normal' part of what I do, and yes, I would ring Janet and arrange to get out to see her.

Speaking to Janet on the phone a few moments later, I got the impression that I was speaking to someone who was highly professional, organised and confident. She explained that she had recently moved into a new home in a town about half an hour's drive from me, and was experiencing all sorts of paranormal problems. She had filmed her necklace moving, and there were shadows in the corners, and she was also worried that she had seen a ghostly figure in her bedroom. She explained that she had a connection with a free evangelical church, but that they had advised her that she needed to contact the Anglican deliverance team.

A quick initial diagnosis suggested that there might be some sort of place memory there, but, as always, I wasn't convinced until I had spoken to her face to face, and then, of course, there is always an element of trial and error about these things. So, I arranged a time to go around. She had just started a new job at a school she said, but could I come at about 4.30? I told her that I'd be bringing another member of the team with me, so I'd have to check. Fortunately he was also her local vicar, so at least I didn't have to worry about contacting someone else as well, and after consultation with him, I confirmed the time and date with her, and agreed to collect him on the way.

As I have suggested before, one of the unforeseen problems of being a parish priest, let alone a deliverance minister, is the fact that you spend a lot of your time driving round at slow speed up and down suburban roads, looking for the right house. This particular road was classic suburbia with the emphasis on classic: large houses set back from the road with occasional groups of semis. This may not be quite your image of what urban North Wales looks like, but this part of the world could have been almost any well-heeled neighbourhood in any prosperous part of Britain. Nothing, however, corresponded to the house number we were looking for, and despite the fact that this was in his parish, my colleague was none the wiser. Eventually we drove to the very end, pulled into the car park of a low-rise block of flats, and rang her. 'Hi, Janet, it's Jason from the church. I'm really sorry I can't find you.'

'Are you driving a gold Berlingo?'

'Yes, we are,' I said, looking round.

'Well, I think you're just outside my front door. I'll come down and open it for you.'

I looked up at the block of council flats: not quite what I had expected in that rather upmarket area, and Janet when she came to the door was also not quite what I had imagined: small, with shoulder length dark hair, but wreathed in smiles that somehow didn't quite get to her eyes. 'Thank you for coming,' she said as she led the way upstairs.

The flat had obviously been newly decorated, its white paint relieved by the sorts of home decor including cushions and wall-hangers that have 'Welcome to our home' written all over them in various different ways. The living room at the back of the flat had a large window that faced south over some houses, and then over to trees and distant hills beyond, but I noticed that in the corner there was what appeared to be a sort of shrine: a table with a white leather Bible, an unlit scented candle, a praying hands ornament, and an elaborate standing cross.

'Did you say you'd just moved in?' I asked.

'Yes, do you like it?'

I looked around. 'Yes, it's really light and airy.'

She nodded, and then looked sad. 'I really like it, but, like I said on the phone, I think it must be haunted,' and she launched breathlessly straight into the story. 'I split up from my partner not long ago, and I've been living with my mother for the last year with my little boy, but I decided it's time to move on, so the council found this flat for me, and it's not far to walk to work.

'But as soon as I moved in, things started to go wrong. There were, like, these shadows on the walls that kept moving when there was no one there. My little boy was so frightened, he went back to living with my mother across town. And then my necklace started to move one night, like it was trying to strangle me. I filmed it. Would you like to see?'

My colleague and I looked at one another as Janet fumbled for a few moments with her phone.

'There, you can see, it's moving!'

What we were looking at was basically a slightly shaky shot of a necklace that was moving fractionally.

'Can you see?' Janet asked excitedly.

'Yes, I think so,' offered my colleague. 'I've never seen anything like that,' he continued, and I believed him.

People assume that seeing footage of poltergeist activity must be exciting: believe me, it isn't! The footage lasted around two minutes, but it seemed quite a lot longer. During this time, her necklace did move a little, but not nearly as dramatically as you might expect for a full-scale paranormal phenomenon. It was time to move the conversation on. 'Did you say you'd seen something? A figure, or something like that?' I asked.

'Yes, that's right, you have a good memory,' she said. 'One night I was lying in bed, and I felt like a weight on my chest. I couldn't breathe, and I think I saw a face looking down at me.'

'That must have been terrifying,' I said.

'Yes, it was,' she replied after a moment, 'yes, it was terrifying.' We sat in silence for a few moments.

'Is there anything else that has happened to you?'

'No,' she said, 'after that I contacted my friend at the church, and she advised me to get out and go and stay with my mother, and to call you guys.'

'Janet, do you mind if I ask if you're on any medication at the moment?' I asked, as always trying to work out what was causing all this.

'I'm on a low dose anti-depressant because I split up from my partner, but other than that no,' she replied.

'Thanks for telling me that. Has anything like this happened to you before?'

'No, this is all new,' Janet said. There seemed to be something here that wasn't quite right about what she was saying, but I couldn't put my finger on it. I asked my colleague if he had anything he wanted to add, and he shook his head.

'OK, Janet, I'm not quite sure what's causing all this, but what we're going to do is to bless the flat for you, if that's all right, and we can also bless a cross for you too. If you like, we can bless the cross you have here,' I said, gesturing to the table in the corner.

'That would be lovely,' she cooed, 'thanks.'

While I got ready for the house blessing, Janet chatted happily to my colleague about where he came from, his family and his church, as if nothing particularly untoward was happening in her home, and I wondered about the effects of the anti-depressants. However, a few moments later, we were moving round her flat, splashing holy water at the walls. Like the living room the kitchen was simply furnished, as was her bedroom, although I did notice a large rosary hanging next to the bed. The final room was her 'little boy's' room, but a bit like the rest of the house, really, it didn't seem to be have been personalised, although I was not at all very clear how old the son was. Once we had finished, we returned to the living room, blessed the cross for her, and then offered to bless her too, and, after asking if she had been baptised (she had been christened as a baby, apparently), we offered to anoint her with the oil, just as I had done with Jake.

'Thank you,' she purred afterwards, 'I feel so much better already, and I feel strong enough to spend the night here on my own.'

'Well,' I said, 'with any luck we have dealt with whatever it was that was bothering you, but if you need us again, you know how to get hold of us.'

'Yes,' she said, 'I'll save your mobile number from when you called me just now, so I'll get in touch if I need you.'

'That's not a problem,' I smiled, knowing that I try not to give out my mobile number when I am out on a deliverance case, but that people rarely ever call back.

As we walked away, my colleague and I had a short debrief. 'I was worried that it was going to be one of those poltergeist things where you have to explain that it's them causing it,' he commented, 'but let's hope a house blessing will sort it out for her.'

'I know what you mean,' I said, 'I hate having the "poltergeist conversation" with people, because you never know how they are going to take it.'

'Well,' he replied, 'with any luck we won't have to.'

About a week later, while I was walking down the street to the bank, my mobile phone rang. Now, I'm not from the mobile phone generation, but I do have one, and usually carry it around with me. The parishioners all have my number, but they regard it as a sort of last resort: if they need to get in touch with me, they contact Ann the administrator at the Parish Office, so my phone ringing is something of an event.

'Hello, Jason, it's Janet.' She could clearly tell from my confused silence that I didn't know who she was. 'You came around the other day to bless my house, remember?' she continued.

'Oh, of course. Hi Janet, are you all right?' I tried to sound as pastorally concerned as I could on a busy shopping day in Wrexham.

'Oh yes,' she answered enthusiastically. 'I just wanted to let you know that everything's OK at the flat, and I wanted to make a donation to your church.'

As I always do when someone offers money, I tried to deflect her – I really don't want anyone to think that this is something we charge for. 'I think you need to give it to your local church if you can. Would that be all right?'

'Yes, of course, I just felt so grateful and so happy, I wanted to show my appreciation.'

After a few closing pleasantries, we concluded the call. Janet had seemed very happy indeed, but, if this is possible, almost too happy.

My suspicions were to prove correct, unfortunately. Not long afterwards, Janet was back on the phone. 'I'm really sorry about this, Jason,' she said, sounding about as down as I had ever heard her, 'it's all come back – it tried to strangle me with my necklace again last night, and I saw the shadows flitting round. Can you come around again?'

So, after the usual arrangements with my amiable colleague, we fixed up when we would be there, but this time we both knew we would have to have the 'poltergeist conversation'. We, of course, found the flat first time tucked away in its bucolic corner of North Wales's answer to Surrey, and Janet was there to meet us.

Again she explained, and once again we had to endure even more extended footage of poltergeist activity, knowing of course that from our point of view this was just delaying the evil hour!

'I'm really sorry about this, Janet, but has anything changed in your life since we last met?'

Janet thought for a moment or two and said, 'My little boy has decided that he now wants to go and live with his dad.'

'And you don't get on with his dad?' I tried to probe as gently as I could.

'Things aren't good between us, and my ex-partner now lives in Liverpool,' she said with a huge sigh.

'So, does that mean you won't see him very often?' She just sobbed in reply.

'I'm really sorry,' said my sympathetic colleague.

'I'm so sad,' Janet whimpered.

'Is everything else the same?' I asked after a suitable pause.

'Work's not going quite as well – they don't seem to understand what I'm going through, and I've been suspended,' she replied, 'and my mother's not speaking to me at the moment. It's all going wrong.'

I suppose any one of these things might be enough to send someone over the edge, but Janet's life seemed to be in free fall at the moment.

'Do you think all these things might be related to what's going on in the house?' she asked after a few moments.

'Yes, we think they might be,' my colleague nodded at her when she looked in his direction.

'Sometimes,' I explained, 'people seem to react to different types of stress in different ways, and we think you might be the sort of person who internalises all these things, because even when you're going through a really rough time, you manage to seem cheerful.'

She nodded. 'Yes, I tend to bottle all these things up.'

'Yes,' I continued, 'but they have to find their release some-where, and we think that a lot of what's been going on in your house and around you is this energy being released in the objects around you.'

'Does this happen to other people as well?' she asked.

'Yes, it does. In fact, most of what we do when we go about this sort of work is to deal with things like this.'

Again, an affirmative nod from my supportive colleague.

'Is there any way you can help?' she asked.

'We could bless the flat again if you like, but it probably wouldn't do any good, because this isn't a presence or a ghost or anything.'

'If there's no point in that, what should I do?' It was a genuine question.

'Well, actually two things spring to mind. The first is that I think you need to patch things up with your mum. Do you think you might be able to do that?'

'Yes,' she answered, 'we've fallen out before, so I think I just need to apologise, and things will be all right there. What's the other thing?'

'Well, last time we were here, you said you had some anti-depressants from the doctor.' She nodded. 'When was the last time you had a medical review?'

'About a year ago,' she replied.

'OK,' I said, 'I think it would be a good idea if you get in touch, because maybe you need something a little bit stronger, just to get you through the next couple of months. How would you feel about that?'

Janet sobbed slightly. 'That sounds like a good idea, thanks.' And then she said in a very little voice, 'Can you bless me before you go?'

'Yes, of course, we'd be delighted to, and if you like we can anoint you with the oil for healing again.'

Janet nodded enthusiastically, so that's what we did.

Once we were back in the car, my colleague and I turned to one another. 'She took that very well,' he said.

'Yes, you just never know how people are going to react.'

'You're right,' he said, 'but I think she may be OK now.'

'Let's hope so,' I smiled.

Fast-forward eighteen months or so. It's a hot afternoon, in fact a very hot afternoon, and I am standing on a wide boule-vard in Paris, looking at an inadequate map that the city authorities assume will tell me how to work out where to catch the bus that appears to have had its route diverted. My family has just been to the French Army Museum, where we have passed an afternoon admiring suits of armour from various periods, before heading for a look at the interior of the church at Les Invalides where Napoleon is entombed. It has been a long day, and our holiday has just started. My mobile phone rings. It is a British number.

'Hello Jason. It's Janet. You remember, you and your friend came to see me last year to bless my flat. Anyway, I've moved to a new house, and it's all happening again. I've seen those shadows on the wall, and my necklace has been strangling me, and I think I've seen something like a ghostly figure. So, I'm wondering if you will come around again, if it's OK, and because it's the school holidays I'm not in work at the moment, so you can come around any time, really.' Janet paused for breath.

'I'm really sorry, I'm on holiday,' I said.

'I can't hear you; it sounds like there's loads of traffic your end,' she bellowed.

'I'm in Paris!' I shouted, trying not to draw attention to myself. 'What?!'

'I'm in Paris, but if it's urgent, I'll get someone to come out and see you.' A lady looked at me, and crossed to the other side of the pavement.

'Yes, I need to see someone soon,' yelled Janet.

'Leave it with me,' I screamed back, and lost the connection.

While we waited for what we suspected was a non-existent bus, I had an exchange of texts with the Parish Office back in Wrexham, explaining what was going on, and the wonderful Ann in the office said that she would talk to one of the other members of the deliverance team, and get them to sort out Janet's problems.

Ann knows that I am a relatively well known deliverance

minister, so she is adept at dealing with these things. Thanks, Ann!

Back in Paris, I relaxed, or at least relaxed sufficiently to realise that my wife had just flagged down a taxi, and that we were giving up on the whole idea of catching a bus anywhere, and the holiday continued undisturbed. As I said, the parishioners almost never contact me directly, bless them.

When I got back, I spoke to my colleagues in the team including her local vicar who said that they had been out, and that Janet was now all right, but they didn't go into any detail.

The year wound on to its end, with Christmas looming on the horizon at the end. Christmas in Wrexham Parish Church is amazingly manic, and climaxes with the famous Crib Service, a family celebration where I have to not only keep the story going while two toddlers dressed as angels wrestle one another to the ground at my feet, but where there is an expectation that I will don some sort of costume and provide some sort of theological message while dressed up as Rudolf, a lion, or indeed Superman!

And then there are all the other carol services for groups such as the Scouts (their motto is 'Be prepared' – if only that were a reality rather than an unachievable aspiration!), the local hospice, various charity organisations, and then a large number of schools, whose offerings range from professional through to so chaotic the whole thing takes on a life of its own.

And in the midst of all this, predictably, there was a phone call: 'Hi Jason, it's Janet, can you come around again?'

'Hi Janet. What's happening?'

'Well since we last spoke I've moved house again, and, well, it's all happening all over again.' Janet's voice broke off as she sobbed. 'I just can't cope.'

'It's OK, I'll come around. Is there a good time?'

'I'm not working at the moment,' she said, sounding glum, 'so any time would suit me well.'

I asked where she'd moved to, and it was in the same town. I told her I'd get back to her. A few moments later I had a brief conversation with my colleague, who said that the new address was still in his parish, but a glance at pre-Christmas diaries suggested the earliest date we could both make was sometime in January.

'Would you be happy to deal with it?' he asked.

'That's no problem.'

'Great,' he replied, 'see you on the other side!'

I laughed and wished him well with Christmas. I then glanced through my own diary, and realised that by some miracle, I could make both the following morning, and the one after that. After a hasty conversation across the office, I rang Janet back.

'Can you make tomorrow morning?'

'I need to take my little boy to school, but I'll be back by about 10am. Is that all right?' she asked.

One of the great benefits of having a large, busy church is that from time to time you get colleagues to train, and as part of their training, I will often take them if I can on deliverance calls. The colleague who came to see Mrs Jones with her electric ghost was someone I had once trained, as was the colleague I took on this occasion. He'd just dropped into the office at exactly the right time, and when I suggested he might like to come along, he agreed with alacrity.

If I think it will be a complex case, I will take another member of the deliverance team, but, given the fact that I knew the lie of the land with Janet, I was more than happy to use this as a training opportunity.

And so, the following morning, having left Wrexham at 9.15am, we found ourselves driving down yet another residential road, looking for the right street and the right house. The area was not nearly as nice, but this time at least Janet had a whole house, rather than a flat. I knew roughly where I was going, but it was one of the areas where the satnav signal tells you where to go about thirty seconds too late. My colleague had the grace not to comment.

When we arrived, the house looked like it had been recently spruced up, and the garden as if someone had taken a razor blade to it: it was totally bare, not a blade of grass, not a shrub, nothing. We had had time to talk through some of the background on the way so, as always, we sat for a few moments in the car, and said the Lord's Prayer and St Patrick's Breastplate, which, as always for me, felt almost like a physical attaching of armour.

'Ready?' I asked.

'Yes, when you are,' he replied, and then commented, 'There are no curtains open in the house, maybe she's not up.'

'Actually, you're right,' I responded. The blinds were still drawn in what looked like the living room, and the curtains upstairs were definitely closed.

'This is the time we agreed,' I said, 'so we'll see if she's in.'

The house was sporting a brand new uPVC door, sparking white in the winter sunshine, but, as so often with new doors, there was no knocker, and no doorbell. I knocked with my bare knuckles. No response. So, I tried harder, much harder.

'I think I've left enough skin on there for a sizeable DNA sample,' I commented.

'Yes,' said my colleague, 'they will have heard that.'

'I've got her number on my phone, I'll try that.' But again, there was no answer.

'We organised this yesterday,' I said, 'she can't have forgotten, but we'll leave her a note, and she can get back to us.'

A few moments later, we were pulling away again. 'I am really sorry,' I said.

'Please stop apologising,' he replied, in what was becoming a sort of ritual between us, although both sentiments were sincere. There was more apology as I lost my way back, weaving my way through a one-way system that seemed to have sprung up from nowhere.

About an hour later when we were back in the office, my phone rang, and it was Janet. 'My little boy was being sick and I had to collect him from school, so I was out when you called,' she explained. 'I'd still like to see you, though, what are you doing tomorrow morning?'

Miraculously, the diary was still clear until noon the following day, so, after a quick consultation with my colleague who was sitting across the office from me, we agreed to come, but I explained that we wouldn't have as much time.

'Would 9.30 work better for you?' she asked.

'That's great,' I said. 'I'll see you tomorrow.'

Obviously, having learnt from the previous day, we found our way to the house first time, but this time when we stopped outside it was obvious there was someone at home. All the curtains and blinds were open, and there was a light on in the hall. Once again, we stopped and prayed for a few moments, and when we got to the door, I was able to knock gently (just as well, as my knuckles were still sore from the previous day). Janet greeted us with a nervous smile. I noticed that she had lost some weight since I had last seen her, and seemed to have aged more than she might in that time. She welcomed us, and I introduced my colleague as she introduced her boyfriend Alex, a burly guy who just about managed to cover his embarrassment with a smile.

I hadn't really managed to have an in-depth conversation with

Janet over the phone, so as usual I invited her to tell us what had happened. 'You know, it's the same sort of stuff as last time,' she began. 'Again, my necklace has been moving on its own and has been trying to strangle me again. I did film it on my phone, but I was so frightened, I deleted it.'

I don't know whether my colleague was disappointed about not seeing the footage, but I felt a certain relief. I made a mental note to explain to him later.

But Janet continued, 'And those shadows I told you about, well they're back as well. Alex has seen them too, haven't you love?'

Alex just sat and looked terrified, but he did nod and gulp at the same time.

'Thanks for telling me,' I replied, 'is there anything else?'

'Well, I'm now off the drugs,' she said matter-of-factly.

'The medication?' I queried.

'No,' she explained, 'I have been feeling so low over the last few years that I've experimented a little bit with drugs, but I've stopped doing that now.' She smiled, and I wondered how long she had been drug-free for.

'It's not a good idea, you know,' I said, and she nodded understandingly. 'And if you're experiencing the sorts of things you've been experiencing, you know with things moving around and shadows on the walls, drugs can make it a whole lot worse.'

'I know,' she said sadly. There was silence for a few moments, and then she said, 'Because we're in a new house, will you bless it for me?'

'Yes, of course,' I replied.

'And will you bless us too?' Again she looked at Alex, who nodded nervously.

'Yes, that's no problem either,' I said. 'Can I just ask if you've been baptised or christened, Alex?'

Alex looked even more nervous, but spoke for the first time. 'No, my mother was chapel, so I was cradle-rolled. It's not the same thing is it?'

'No, but it's not a problem, I can still bless you.'

Just to explain, anointing with oil (which is what I was thinking about doing) is considered to be a 'sacrament'. Sacraments are the traditional way in which the Church channels God's grace (Grace is how God works in the world). In Roman Catholic and High Church Anglican theology there are seven sacraments: baptism (or 'christening' as people sometimes call it for babies), the Eucharist, ordination, confession, marriage, confirmation and anointing with oil (either for those who are dying, or by extension for those in need of healing). The oil, by the way, is blessed by the bishop once a year in the Cathedral on Maundy Thursday, the day before Good Friday, when the clergy also renew their ordination vows. The seven-sacrament system works on the principle that to receive any of them, you need to have been baptised first.

At the time of the Reformation, the Protestant reformers decided that there were only two sacraments (baptism and what they would call Communion) because these are the only two that were established by Jesus, and they also questioned a lot of the theory behind these two remaining sacraments, some of them arguing that it was contrary to the spirit of the thing to baptise babies because they are not able to express their faith, which is something the reformers considered necessary.

A huge number of books have been written on the subject of the sacraments, and the arguments still rage even among Anglicans – some of whom would follow the Catholic line (as I do), whereas others are happier with the reformers' line. Suffice it to say that in this case, Alex hadn't been baptised as a baby, but his mother felt she needed to mark his birth at the chapel, and so his name was written on something called the cradle roll: a list of children born to members of the chapel. In other words, he had unwittingly been caught in a five-hundred-year-old theological row, but now wasn't the time to explain!

So, we went ahead with the service of blessing the house: blessing the water and the salt, and then gently moving around the house, splashing small amounts of the holy water at the walls. As I moved around, I noted that the house was decorated in a very similar style to Janet's previous flat, and also that there were very few photographs around, but although I took some of it in, I didn't really register much. Finally, back in the living room, we said the Lord's Prayer together, and then I blessed Janet, touching her on the head as I did so, and then Alex, who also stood awkwardly to receive a formal blessing.

With a final: 'You know how to get in touch . . .' we left.

As is almost always the case after a training exercise, I did my usual 'Observations, questions, queries?' exercise with my colleague.

'Yes,' he said. 'First observation: they relaxed visibly when you blessed them, and the whole atmosphere seemed to change – you probably weren't aware of it, though.'

I was impressed, not only had he picked up the change in their bearing, but he'd also noticed that I was so 'into' the action that I wouldn't have noticed myself. We batted that round for a few moments, and then I asked, 'What was the second observation?'

'Well, she talked about her little boy, but there were no photos, and in the spare room, there wasn't even a bed.'

And, yes, I had sort of noticed, but sometimes it takes someone else to point it out before it really registers. However, that was one I couldn't answer.

The following day, once again, the phone rang, but this time of course, I recognised the number. 'Hi Janet, how are you doing?' I asked.

'I'm fine, thanks,' she replied on what sounded like autopilot. 'And thanks for coming around yesterday. But I was wondering if I could see you again, please.'

'Er, yes, I suppose so. Is it urgent?'

'Well, no, but I would like to see you soon,' she said.

'OK, not a problem. I've got a carol service this afternoon that finishes about 2.30, shall I come around after that?'

'Yes, that would be lovely. Is your friend coming too?' she asked.

'No, he's on the school run, I think.'

'It doesn't matter,' she said, 'it shouldn't take long, but I was just wondering if you would anoint me with the oil again.'

'No problem,' I said.

So, later that afternoon, I arrived once again at Janet's house. She greeted me at the door, and I asked if Alex was around. 'No, he doesn't live here, he still lives with his mother.'

I nodded an acknowledgement.

'You remember when you first came around, and you told me that you thought it might just be me triggering off all this stuff?'

She paused, and waited for me to answer. 'Yes, that's right,' I said carefully, remembering the 'poltergeist conversation'.

'Do you think it's happening again?'

'Yes, it sounds like it.'

And she crumpled slightly, clearly with relief. 'So, this isn't something that's following me around?' she asked quietly.

'No, it isn't. I'm pretty sure it's you.'

And she smiled, genuinely, possibly for the first time since I'd met her.

'Will you anoint me with the oil, then?'

'Yes, of course I will.'

That particular little sacramental service lasted almost no time, and was followed as always by the Lord's Prayer and a more general blessing. Once I'd done that, we had a brief conversation about what the next steps for her might be. Deliverance ministers act as consultants and I was mildly worried that she might be forming some sort of attachment to me, so I suggested that she might like to go along to her local church for continued pastoral support.

'There's a chapel around the corner, I've been there a couple of times and they seem very friendly', she said.

'That's great,' I replied, 'having a local support network is really good. Although you know how to get hold of me if you need to.'

She smiled and nodded. 'Have you got plans for this evening?' she asked.

'I've got another school carol service at 6.30 – I know how to live!' I smiled. 'How about you?'

Again, she smiled back. 'I'm off to see my little boy. He lives with my mother now.' Well, at least that was one mystery solved, although the fact that she was taking recreational drugs may or may not have been the cause of her sense of being oppressed, but I hope that somehow she is now able to live a more fulfilled life and that she finds the support at her local chapel.

It is very unusual to see people repeatedly in a deliverance context. In fact, most of the time, we never see them again. In many senses, this is not at all a satisfying conclusion, especially in a case like this when I had seen someone quite a few times, but these are the conditions under which we work. We do, however, hope that if things do go wrong, they will make contact with us again as Janet did, rather than going elsewhere. But I once came across someone who claimed he was suffering from spiritual oppression, for whom I was the latest in a long line of diocesan deliverance ministers he had been to see.

## 'I'm suffering from spiritual oppression'

For many years now, I have been a great fan of Phil Rickman. He writes novels about a fictional Anglican deliverance minister called Merrily Watkins who works in the Hereford Diocese. In fact, not long after I embarked on this ministry, Phil came to give a talk in Blaenavon, the village where I was the vicar, so I went along to hear what he was going to say. Actually, to be honest, he was sharing the stage with fellow author Barbara Erskine, whose novels I had also enjoyed, so I went primarily to hear her not him. At the end of the talk, I shuffled forwards, bought one novel from each author, and duly had them signed. And as there was no one else around, I commented that I was the vicar and was about to go on the official training for the ministry of deliverance. Phil was very keen to hear how it went, and so we started a sporadic correspondence. I once sent him the first chapter of a still-unpublished novel that he kindly featured on his 'Book Starter' series on BBC Radio Wales, where he has a regular slot as Phil the Shelf. The chapter, or actually the first sentence of the plot-summary, was mauled by the consultant they had got in, who didn't seem to have read very much more, although Phil himself was kinder about it. Occasionally, Phil will ask me questions about technical issues, more often about how the Church works than about the deliverance ministry, and I'm happy to help him out if he needs it.

On one occasion, for example, Phil's German publisher had organised for a group of journalists to come over to meet him, to have a tour of 'Merrily Watkins Country', and also to meet a real live deliverance minister. I was not, apparently, first choice, but when a big funeral came up for the priest Phil had lined up, he turned to me, and I was able to go and field questions in the Swan Hotel in Hay-on-Wye. Phil told me that he sold more copies in Germany than in the UK, and that these Germans would want to ask me about what I did and how it worked. In actual fact, most of the questions were asked by Phil himself, until someone started asking me a personal question about the state of my mental health, and whether I thought there must be something wrong with me. It really was remarkably disconcerting.

However, on the back of my relationship with Phil Rickman, I really did at one stage seem to enter a world that I knew nothing about, as he asked me to act as an adviser when ITV filmed his *Midwinter of the Spirit*. I had numerous conversations with the wardrobe department (but it was not my fault that in one scene Merrily wore her stole over her chasuble!), and sent them photos of myself in my vestments, and of the contents of my deliverance minister's bag. I also found myself recording St Patrick's Breastplate in ecclesiastical Latin so that one of the actors could practise saying it, and have wondered whether, in the final event, they used my recording.

On another occasion, I spent a whole evening Skyping method actor David Threlfall. It was an extraordinary conversation, because he wanted to get inside the character of Huw, Merrily Watkins' mentor. So I have never been asked so many odd questions like, 'What car do you drive, and how old is it?', but presumably if you are 'becoming' a character, the fact that you have a battered nine year old Citroën Berlingo may mean that you feel differently from someone who is walking back across the car park to collect a brand new convertible BMW. I had never thought about these things, but now began to wonder how my teenage son felt when he said, 'Please don't collect me in the Berlingo!' But that is exactly what happened when I was invited on set for filming one afternoon, and, because we had just moved to Wrexham and my wife and older son were doing a weekly commute from South Wales, I asked if I could bring him too.

They were filming on location somewhere near Manchester, and we were welcomed with open arms. The cast and crew were lovely, and were happy to chat, to share tea and to make us feel at home. Sadly, it was only for one evening, but it was a very special evening.

In fact it had been some years earlier that someone had contacted Phil through his website to ask whether he could recommend a deliverance minister. Phil, to be fair, was very careful indeed. He rang me up, and then passed on the email to me.

The person I spoke to on the phone was very well spoken, told me his name was Paul, and sounded as if he were in his thirties, although it is very difficult to tell someone's age for certain from a phone call.

'I wonder if you can help me,' he began.

I said my usual, 'I'll do my best.'

'I hope so,' he replied. 'I live in the Midlands, and I'm suffering from spiritual oppression, and I've been trying to find someone to help me. I've spoken to various Anglican deliverance ministers, and none of them seems to be able to do anything.'

He was laying down something of a challenge, which, call it pride, I was keen to take up. There was, however, a snag. A deliverance minister is only allowed to function under the jurisdiction of their bishop, which means effectively within their diocese. So, I explained that I would love to be able to help, but that I couldn't come to him. 'That's no problem, I can come to you,' he said.

I thought about how to play this, so I suggested he came to the Tuesday evening Eucharist, and then we could have a chat afterwards. 'Yes, by all means,' he said.

'Can I ask if you've been baptised?'

'Yes,' he said, 'and confirmed too.'

'In that case, you would be very welcome to receive communion at the service,' I replied.

'Yes, that would be really nice.' And so, we agreed that he should come the following Tuesday.

As I've implied, there are several different brands of Anglicans, and lots of different kinds of Anglican worship, and St Paul's in Blaenavon was at the High Church, Anglo-Catholic end – right at the very end, to be honest. The Mass, as it was called, on a Tuesday evening was celebrated with a good deal of ceremonial: vestments were always worn, and there would always be at least two altar servers, wearing lace-trimmed cottas (like white smocks that come down to just below the waist) over the long black cassocks (basically very long coats that should reach your shoes). In addition, there was always incense, a very ancient sign of the presence of God and of the prayers of his people and a sure-fire sign that this was High Church Anglican. There was also a very prominent statue of Our Lady, the Blessed Virgin Mary, and at each service we used the Hail Mary prayer. The building itself was late Victorian, and unmemorable other than for the fact that there was a fourteenth century stone altar that had once been used at an ancient church on the mountainside. This stone altar was the one we used on a Tuesday evening. The only other memorable thing about St Paul's was its astonishing atmosphere of holiness. You could tell that this was somewhere that people had prayed.

But this was a church where, if we were in double figures on a Tuesday evening, there must have been a religious revival. Paul was slightly older than I had thought from our conversation on the phone, around the forty mark I would have guessed. He was well-dressed, and gave every appearance of having been to church regularly, even if he seemed not entirely comfortable with the very High Church ritual, but then, that was understandable.

When the time came to receive Communion, he came forward with everyone else, and held his hands out in the approved fashion – right hand over left. After the service, I went as always to the back of the church, greeted him in a way I hadn't had chance to beforehand, and suggested he might like to come back to my house just up the road for a proper chat.

Unlike the other encounters I have loosely characterised in this chapter as being examples of people suffering from spiritual oppression, in this instance, of course, this was the issue that he had identified. He had clearly done his homework, which was not necessarily helpful.

As I have suggested a couple of times, being a deliverance minister is a bit like being a medical doctor; there is usually some sort of diagnosis and you hope you can also offer some sort of cure. But at the same time, the people you encounter are also sometimes a bit like patients who have read up online, and self-diagnosed. Most of us have done it at some stage, at least with medical complaints. We have looked up bubonic plague or something like that, and when we sneeze, we think we've got it.

Deliverance ministry works in a similar fashion. The minister then has to decide whether this is the right diagnosis, and if it isn't to suggest something else. None of the other cases in this chapter were of people who claimed they were suffering from spiritual oppression, which made dealing with them easier: Paul, however, was convinced this is what his problem was.

'It's having this sense that there is someone just behind you,' he explained, 'not inside you. I'm not possessed.' I think I probably winced. 'So, I don't want you to do a major exorcism' – he knew his stuff I'd give him that – 'I just want you to free me from this feeling.'

As always, I probed gently about his medical history, which to be honest he was happy to share.

'I've been to see my doctor about this,' he said, 'and the doctor just told me he thought I was making it up.'

'Did your doctor prescribe any medication?' I asked.

'No, she told me to go and find myself an all-consuming hobby.'

'And did you?'

'No,' he said, 'because I am suffering from spiritual oppression.'

'OK,' I ventured, 'have you spoken to your local vicar?'

'Yes,' he snorted contemptuously, 'he told me he thought I was making it up too. I wasn't impressed, so I asked at my local Diocesan Office about the ministry of deliverance, and they put me in touch with someone locally. But he wasn't much help either.'

'What did he suggest?' I enquired.

'He tried to psychoanalyse me, telling me it was probably something to do with my childhood. But of course, it's not, because I am suffering from spiritual oppression.'

The conversation wound on and on in this fashion, and I just got the impression that we were getting nowhere. In fact, I think we talked in circles for the best part of two hours, but his insistence that he was suffering from spiritual oppression was unshakable. I asked him about what it felt like to receive Communion that evening. He said that it had been a nice experience. He had been sent to church as a boy, and had sung in the church choir, so he'd been confirmed. Like many people, he said, he had drifted away, but not completely, although he tended to go to church only at Christmas. But as this was at his local church, whose vicar hadn't taken him seriously, he wasn't sure he wanted to go again. I suggested there might be lots of other churches he might try in his local area, and that in my opinion if he really was suffering from spiritual oppression, going to church and receiving Communion regularly was about the best thing I could suggest.

Finally, rather exhausted by conversation, I offered to anoint him with the sacramental oil. He readily agreed, so that's what we did, and about ten minutes later, he disappeared off apparently satisfied into the summer night.

As I have said before, we almost never find out whether what we have done has helped, and occasionally I wonder about Paul, and hope that somewhere he found the peace that seemed to be lacking in his life. The idea of spiritual oppression is something that really is rather nebulous, and seems to cover a whole range of issues. There is, of course, the more specific issue of demonic possession. But before we turn to possession, which you would have thought would be the stock in trade of the Christian exorcist, we'll just take a detour into the world of those who possess psychic gifts.

# Chapter 8

## 'Learning to live with it'

Most of us, including priests, live a world that is basically very highly ordered and rational. In fact, one of the things that human beings are best at is trying to explain the world around them. It's been said that the ancient Greek word for 'human being', *anthropos*, means something like 'one who looks up', and this is often seen as a reference to the way that human beings alone of animals try to make sense of their environment (even if they are not always that good at looking after it).

But very often we also use a lens to help us focus our thoughts about how to interpret the world around us more easily. Many people will call this a 'philosophy' after the ancient Greek schools which taught various ways of seeing the world and making sense of it. Sometimes these ideas have come into modern parlance: we talk about 'being philosophical' about it, referring to the Stoic ideas of acceptance that were taught by Zeno in the third century BC, which was for many years the dominant school of philosophy hence 'philosophical'. But there were others too.

Among the most influential were schools of thought devised by two very different students of Socrates. Socrates' ideas were developed by Plato. He encouraged people to see into the beyond, teaching that what you see around you is a mere shadow of true reality. Aristotle, on the other hand, taught his followers that the reality was found in the material objects around you, and not somewhere else. You might call him the father of empirical science, and from the modern-day perspective, you would have imagined that Aristotle wholly won the day. But this isn't quite how it has worked out. Plato had hit on the idea that human beings long for something we don't see, and this was developed into a whole school of what you might call spiritual practice, as people who followed this idea would spend some time in what they called contemplation, which sort of meant that they were trying to put themselves in touch with ultimate reality. It was a very easy step from this to the idea of calling ultimate reality 'God', and so this whole stream of ancient philosophy found its home more or less naturally in Christianity. For Christians God is ultimate reality who, despite being unknowable, chooses to reveal himself in Jesus.

Now this is not quite how *all* Christians see their own religion, and certainly not how lots of people who are not Christians see it. Atheists obviously tend to regard the whole God thing with a good deal of suspicion if not ridicule. When they describe what they think Christians believe it is a God who is a bit like the tooth fairy and Santa Claus rolled into one. But this is not at all how committed Christians view God (although it is possible that people who are 'culturally Christian' may be more inclined to this view, to be fair). But there are also people who would regard themselves as 'spiritual' who seem surprised that Christianity has a very deep spiritual and mystical tradition. These are the sorts of people who tend to see 'religion' as a series of rules that you have to follow, and that therefore should be rejected as rules are regarded as contrary to spirituality which ironically is exactly what the New Testament says, if only they took the trouble to read it, as it speaks about the way in which love of God and one's neighbour is at the very centre of religious experience. Christian spirituality can be said to be an exploration of what it is to encounter the God of love which then leads on naturally to the way in which Christians show that love to others.

Atheism and 'being spiritual' are both ways in which many people in today's world make sense of what is happening around them, and these sit alongside things like Christianity or Islam, or the other great faiths of the world.

Obviously, I am a committed Christian, but that term covers a multitude of sins (in more ways than one!). I am an Anglican, that is a member of a slightly odd Christian group whose foundation story tells us that it split off from the Universal Church (or at least the Western Church) because the King of England wanted to get divorced. Ironically, until very recently, the Anglican Church has taken a much harder line on divorce than most other Christian bodies, only really allowing people who are divorced to be remarried in church in the last twenty years or so, but unlike the Roman Catholic Church, it has never allowed marriages to be 'annulled' unless they have not been consummated. That said, despite its foundation story, it's probably best to see the Anglican Church simply as the continuing national church of England (and Wales), even though there was some attempt to change its basic doctrines, especially with regard to the Eucharist. Basically, the same people were going to church at the end of the Reformation as were at the beginning, in fact in some cases the same priests were still there. In Wrexham, for example, the same priest Hugh Puleston was vicar from 1520 to 1566, and so in those forty-six years would have seen all the attempts at reformation from one extreme to another. Of all my predecessors, he's the one I'd most like to meet!

Different Anglicans, as I have already suggested, will have different takes on what it means, and will have different ways of viewing the world. For my part, I would tend to emphasise the continuity rather than the disruption, but many of my colleagues would see things very differently. And one of the things that helps me to focus my life is a very traditional mediaeval tool: the sixth century *Rule of St Benedict*. Now, obviously, I am not a monk. I am married, I have children, and I do not live in a monastery (and there are Anglican monasteries), but I still take a lot of inspiration from the *Rule*, to the extent that I am something called an oblate, which is a sort of associate member of the Order of St Benedict. This came about because I once visited an Anglican Benedictine Abbey, and felt totally and completely at home there. There was a sense of calm about the place, and a sense that this was a very special place that had been touched somehow by God. So, I made enquiries, and after a few visits, I was allowed to become an oblate. Being an oblate means having a 'rule of life' which is a voluntary code that helps me live my life as a Christian.

Part of this requires me to read the *Rule of St Benedict* itself.

The *Rule* is a strange document. It is remarkably short for one thing, and talks a lot about the sorts of things that monks ought to be doing in church, prescribing the number of Psalms that they ought to say each evening and that sort of thing. But then it does something extraordinary. It says that if someone can come up with a better way of doing it, then that's OK, which really isn't what you think a 'rule' is all about, let alone the *Rule*! In fact, the *Rule* keeps doing things like this: suggesting that people need to be treated as individuals with individual needs and weaknesses rather than sticking to the principle of treating them all the same, which is what you might imagine it would suggest. In fact, what the *Rule* says about the leader whom it calls the abbot has often been cited by modern leadership gurus as a model for how to lead successful organisations in today's highly charged world.

Its basic ideas are found in three vows that the monks are expected to make – and, remember that this is a voluntary act! These are not the three monastic vows that people learn about in school, which are usually cited as poverty, chastity and obedience. These in fact derived from St Francis in the thirteenth century six hundred years later. No, Benedict's monks took vows of obedience, stability and something he calls *conversatio morum*, which appears to be Latin for converting the way you live your life. Obedience means obedience to the *Rule* itself, obviously, but also to the person in charge (the abbot). And stability means that once you join a monastery, you are stuck with the people around you, and you work out your Christian life as part of a community which may involve people you don't like. In addition to all this, the *Rule* talks a lot about humility, which really isn't a very fashionable idea in today's world where we are always being encouraged to 'sell ourselves'. But St Benedict's counter-cultural idea seems to be that we ought to be able to be realistic about ourselves, and maybe not take ourselves as seriously as we usually do. But possibly most radically of all, St Benedict himself suggests that obedience ought not just to be a top down thing, so he talks about mutual obedience. This is something that people in hierarchical organisations get really twitchy about, but it seems to mean that not only is the boss subject to the rules, but that if they agree to do something for one of their minions, then they are obliged to do it too. For Benedict, obedience appears to be a two-way street.

As I have said, for me, this is a helpful lens through which to see my life as a Christian, but also my life as a priest who has a place in a hierarchical structure. When I am in my own church, only the bishop outranks me, and that is quite a responsibility. So, having a guide not only for how I am in myself, and also how I am as other people's boss (and some of them do call me 'boss'!) is a really useful thing. It also helps that it is thoroughly plugged into the Christian tradition. It has got about fifteen hundred years of road-testing so the wheels are unlikely to come off! But the *Rule* itself is also a really important historical document and has influenced life in Western Europe in a way that you might never have thought possible.

The simple fact of the matter was that for most of the formative period of Western Europe, the only people who could read and write were priests. (We're still technically called 'clerks in holy orders', although no one is quite sure what that means, despite being the origin of the word 'clergy', and most of society's – not just the monastery's – administration was done by clergy. The most valuable among the clergy were monks, because more than any other priest they were taught to read and write properly, and they were also not dependent on the income from a parish and they didn't have a church to run. So for centuries, the people who drafted laws in Europe were men who had gathered every day, not only to pray, but to hear a reading from the *Rule of St Benedict*, a document which talked about taking care of the sick and the young, treating people as individuals, and kept banging on about obedience to a common good and this idea of humility. It even talked about the way in which leaders really ought to be people who can make decisions based on advice, sometimes from a whole community, sometimes from a group of wise counsellors. Now you may think these ideas are self-evident, but other societies not so very far away are very differently ordered. So they may be seen as being to some extent part of our Western cultural inheritance from the *Rule of St Benedict* whose monks were the ultimate infiltrators, subverting quietly the unruly passions of the newly baptised barbarians, and turning them at least in theory into good law-abiding Christian rulers. In most European countries, from about the eleventh century, the Benedictine monks were in retreat, as newer monastic movements came and went, but their influence is still felt to this day.

It was probably in England that the Benedictine influence was felt most strongly because England was the only country in Europe where monks ran some of the great cathedrals all the way to the Reformation. It all stemmed from the way that England became Christian. The foundation story goes that Pope Gregory sent the prior of the Benedictine Abbey of St Andrew in Rome to convert the Angles, having seen a pagan boy in the slave-market, and because of his blond hair the Pope commented that he was more like an angel than an Angle. The monk who was sent, a man called Augustine, really didn't want to go, and tried several ways to wriggle out of it, but, being a Benedictine, he was used to obedience, so he eventually arrived. Ignoring his instructions to set up the base of his mission in the old Roman capital at London, he established himself at Canterbury, where he was given a welcome by the local pagan king whose wife was already a Christian.

The king was baptised and Augustine became his adviser, and no doubt provided monks to help him with his administration. But the cathedral at Canterbury, instead of being run by canons as continental cathedrals were, was staffed by Benedictine monks, as was Augustine's next foundation at Rochester, and various other important cathedrals such as Winchester, Worcester, Norwich and Durham among others, not to mention Westminster Abbey itself, which has played a huge role in the life of the nation. In addition, there were other famous Benedictine abbeys such as those at St Albans, Gloucester, Chester and Peterborough, all of which are now Anglican cathedrals, plus very many that are not or have been lost. What it all means is that somewhere in the mixture that made Anglicans what they are is a good deal of the Benedictine spirit of the time before the Reformation and the Dissolution of the Monasteries that went along with it. In fact, the Reformation historian Diarmaid MacCulloch in his recent book on Thomas Cromwell comments that actually the English cathedrals are in effect still monasteries. It's just that, once again, no one seems to have noticed.

So, as an Anglican priest and a Benedictine oblate I am aware of this massive weight of tradition behind me. But I am also, of course, a deliverance minister, and for some reason a surprisingly large number of deliverance ministers are oblates or associate members of other religious orders (the Franciscans call them 'tertiaries', for example). In fact, going to a deliverance conference is a strange experience, because I am not normally aware that such people are out there, and then I discover that large numbers of the delegates belong in this category. St Benedict is, it has to be said, the patron saint of exorcists, and there is a St Benedict's medal which is often inserted into a crucifix which many exorcists (including me) carry. I'm not sure that I think it works, but it makes me feel a whole lot better if I know it's there.

I'm also not sure why so many deliverance ministers are associated with religious orders, but I do wonder whether it all has something to do with the idea of contemplation that I mentioned earlier: this idea of trying to see beyond what it is front of you to some sort of reality that lies beyond. But occasionally as we go about our business, we come across people who seem to have no problem seeing what is not apparent to others. In fact, as one of them once told me, it's just a matter of learning to live with it. We tend to call these people 'psychics' or less frequently 'clairvoyants'. On a bad day they could be called 'witches' and indeed, some people apparently think that having such attributes must be a sign of demonic possession.

There is some debate in the serious literature about whether being a psychic is a good thing for a deliverance minister. Some authors say it is essential, others that it's a hindrance and completely unnecessary. Given the fact that we tend to deal with other people's experiences rather than our own, I wouldn't personally see it as a useful thing at all, but then I am not a psychic, so I would say that! Maybe the best I can say is that not being psychic hasn't been a problem for me.

## 'She's over there, watching us'

Over the course of my time I have occasionally been aware that people have been sent to see me by psychics or mediums. There was one instance when I went to perform a blessing on a fish and chip shop because the people who owned it had consulted a medium, who told them that they needed to contact their vicar to sort out the ghost of a little boy who was haunting their child's bedroom. In most cases, we never get to meet the psychics themselves, but this one was different.

The voice on the phone was that of a lady who I realised instantly had the sort of confidence you get from being in a job where you get to tell people what to do. She explained that she was trying to sell a house that she had bought recently as an investment and had renovated, only to discover that it was haunted. And would I come out and remove the ghost for her, please.

'You sound very sure about that,' I commented.

Most of the time people arrive with a series of what one might call symptoms that require some sort of diagnosis and cure, to use the medical language we so often employ, so in this case I was interested in the fact that she was quite so matter of fact about it.

She sighed slightly in the manner of one who was fed up of telling people something. 'I'm psychic, you see. And before you ask any stupid questions, I'm not a fairground fortune teller. I don't do this for a living. I don't do crystal balls or anything like that. I'm not a spiritualist. In fact I go to church regularly. I just happen to see people who are dead. It's just one of those things I've had to learn to live with. So, when I tell you I have a ghost in my house, I have a ghost in my house.'

I was speechless, and I think I gulped something like, 'OK.'

'I'm pleased we've got that straight. Can you come and move her on, please?' I managed to mutter something I hoped was both affirmative and intelligent.

'Good. When can you make it?' she asked, and a few moments later I was staring at the now silent phone wondering what had hit me.

Nevertheless, a few days later I found myself on one of those anonymous post-war housing estates that you can find in almost any town in Britain. This one happened to be in the South Wales Valleys but, apart from the giveaway that there were lines of mountains either side of me, I really could have been anywhere.

The Valleys have come in for a bad press for many reasons, some of them justified, but many of them not. However, the fact that they are nestled between the foothills of the famously picturesque Brecon Beacons means that even in the worst cases of industrial devastation, you can find a rugged beauty. In this particular town, industrialisation had been and gone about a hundred years before so, despite the fact that it had a significant residual population, there was little to do in terms of employment locally. But newly opened main roads meant that what was once a back-water was probably a more attractive proposition to someone renovating a house and, pulling up outside the house, I could see that she had a good eye. All things considered, this was a nice part of the world: gardens were well kept, and there appeared to be a good deal of pride taken in the general appearance of the area.

The lady met me at the door, and introduced herself as Maggie. I wasn't sure that she had told me her name when we had spoken on the phone. The house was bright. It has clearly been recently painted, and looked like it was in the process of being 'dressed' for sale. It smelled of emulsion, but I could imagine that in a few weeks' time, it would probably smell of freshly ground coffee, or newly baked bread, or whatever it is that makes houses smell like home.

Maggie herself was in her late fifties or maybe early sixties. She was smartly dressed, but not overly smart, and she had a faint air of resignation about her: I think she suspected that

I was going to ask her a whole load of questions about herself and her abilities. I decided not to disappoint her.

'Do you mind if I ask you a few questions?'

'I would be very surprised if you didn't,' she replied with a faint sigh.

'You said you're a psychic,' I saw her face twitch, 'and you've seen something here . . .'

Maggie took over from me. 'Yes, I've spent the whole of my life seeing things or people, usually people who are dead and somehow have been left behind. It's something I inherited from my grandmother. These things seem to skip generations. In fact I've been wondering about my little granddaughter, who will occasionally look into a corner with surprise, but I hope it misses her.'

I smiled encouragingly.

'It's not something you would choose to have, really, but you learn how to live with it.' Maggie fell silent.

'And this house . . . ?' I ventured.

'Yes, there's an old lady who is still here. I can't see her all the time, but sometimes I know she's watching me and then, just occasionally she'll be there for a few seconds.'

'Do you know who she is?'

'I think she must be the lady who owned the house about ten years ago. I bought it from a family who had in turn bought it from the estate of an old lady who had lived here. I assume it's her.'

'Can you see her now?' I asked, mildly nervously.

'No,' she said, 'but I can feel that she's around.'

I nodded. 'OK.'

'If it makes you feel better, I can sort of sense a longing for peace from her, if that makes any sense to you,' she offered.

'I think it does,' I smiled nervously.

We looked at one another for a few moments. 'Do you want to do your thing, then?' she asked.

I began to explain what I was going to do, but she stopped me, 'I've been to quite a few of these before over the years. You're going to bless the house with holy water, but if you can say some prayers for her peace as well, that would be great.' Clearly Maggie was one of those people who liked to be in charge.

Fortunately, there was a glass-topped coffee table that I could use as my base of operations.

I was just about to begin the rite for the blessing of the house when Maggie gasped quietly. 'I can see her. She's over there, watching us.' And she gestured towards the wall next to the kitchen. I tried not to be put off.

One of the things that you might expect when saying prayers for the unquiet dead is that they might be present, but it's a whole different thing being told they are standing there watching you. It took a huge amount of concentration to get the words straight and then, of course, I had to walk almost literally through the place where I had been told the old lady was standing, so that I could bless the kitchen that opened off the open plan living room. I completed my circuit of the house, and returned to base, not greatly assisted by the fact that Maggie was still looking intently at the wall next to the kitchen door when I came back.

'She's still there,' she commented quietly, and not entirely helpfully.

I tried to ignore her, and concentrated on saying prayers for the repose of the souls of the departed (or at least in this case those who should be departed and aren't). I then invited Maggie to say the Lord's Prayer with me, and I finished with a blessing as I always do.

Maggie was smiling. 'She's gone,' she said. 'I didn't see her go, but before she went, I could see that she was happy. I think it was time for her to go.'

There were lots of questions I wanted to ask Maggie, but for some reason I couldn't. It was partly because I felt drained, and also because it simply didn't seem appropriate. She offered to pay my travel and I refused, as always, and suggested she made a donation to her local church. 'I already do that,' she said, 'take it for your own church, please.'

It was one of the very few occasions when I have actually taken a donation, which I dropped in the collection box when I next went to church.

'As I said, I have been to a few of these over the years, and you did it very well,' she said.

'Thank you, that's really kind of you.' And we smiled at one another.

In the car on the way home, I was still asking myself why I hadn't wanted to ask any questions about her being a psychic, but not long afterwards I got the opportunity to ask another psychic about his experiences and, unlike with Maggie, I was able to have a long conversation with him about it.

## Frank's story

We have already met Frank. He's the father of Lucy, whose house was haunted by the ghostly organist in the night-dress, and when he heard I was writing this book, he was keen for me to tell his story. In fact he pretty much insisted.

Frank has lived most of his life in South Wales, and spent most of that life as a commercial traveller in the ironmongery business. The world used to be full of people like Frank, men who would travel the length and breadth of Britain, visiting small independent shops, and acting as the agent for a manufacturing company in the days when there were shops like ironmongers, which have since been replaced by large warehouse type stores on the edges of towns.

This world of small businesses was one I knew well, because it was the world in which I grew up. My family owned a small sweet factory in Merthyr Tydfil, and a series of sweet shops both in Merthyr itself and in neighbouring Aberdare. But they also acted as wholesalers for other small enterprises, and these would be visited by people like Frank. In fact, there was a family joke about having met the man from Mars: Mars, of course, being the chocolate manufacturer based then in Slough. Strangely, meeting the man from Cadbury never quite had the same level of excitement. As a child I only had the haziest idea about these people, but Frank was one of this now dying breed whose patch was Wales and the South West of England. If you wanted a recommendation for a hotel in, say, Dorchester, then Frank was your man.

Frank is now long retired but still enjoys a pint in a hotel, which is where we met one lunchtime, although because we were both driving it was a pint of soda water and lime!

'It all started when I was a boy,' he began without very much prompting, 'the first time I saw something like that. We used to live in a terraced house, which in those days meant that people were in and out of one another's houses.'

This was a standard feature of life in South Wales not so long ago. Some older people still think it's faintly scandalous that you have to lock your door when you're at home, because in the 'good old days' they not only would leave their houses unlocked, but with the doors pretty much wide open most of the time, so that friends, relations and neighbours could simply drop in.

'Our next door neighbour was called Mrs Davies. We weren't belonging, but we were told to call her Aunty Gladys,' Frank chuckled. 'In my generation, one of the things that bound all Welsh people together was the fact that they had someone they could call Aunty Gladys. Anyway, I was a bit afraid of *my* Aunty Gladys, because she was what we used to call an invalid, which meant that she'd taken to her bed at some stage, and never really left it. It was a different world,' he mused.

'Belonging', by the way, is the Valleys way of saying 'related', often very distantly and by marriage or some other means. I remember being told by someone I'd never met before that we were 'belonging', and my father still laughs about someone who was involved in some sort of scandal but was said to be 'belonging to the Brays' almost as a miti-gation. In close-knit traditional societies like those of the Valleys of yesteryear, these things were important. So what Frank was saying was that Gladys Davies was in no way shape or form related to his family but being her next-door neighbour, his mother felt some sort of moral obligation to help her. 'She was always in and out with some broth or something like that,' he explained.

'Anyway,' he continued, 'one day I was playing in my bedroom, and the strangest thing happened. I saw Aunty Gladys come through the wall. I must have been about four or five at the time, and I'd never seen anything like this before. She just came through the wall, wearing her dressing gown, and just sort of disappeared. So, I went downstairs and I told my mother, "Aunty Gladys has just come into my bedroom through the wall." She was really cross, gave me a clip across the ear, and told me not to make things up.' Frank paused ruefully. 'And just then one of the other neighbours walked in to tell us that Mrs Davies next door had just "passed on" as she put it. I started to speak, and my mother silenced me with a raised hand, so I shut up, not wanting to risk another clip. And then when the neighbour left, my mother just sat down at the table and looked at me in amazement. "What does passed on mean?" I asked. "It means she's just died," she said. We looked at one another, and we never mentioned it again.'

Frank took a long sip of his drink wishing, I suspect, that it was something stronger. 'And that was how it started,' he said. 'Over the years I keep seeing stuff. I used to see my grandfather for a while after he died, until I asked him to go away, and he did.

'And I get these, like, premonitions. Lucy tells me that she used to get really fed up when she was a girl and the phone would ring, because I'd know it was for her. In fact, some of the time she tells me I would call her to answer the phone *before* it had started ringing.'

I laughed slightly. This amazing seeming ability of Frank's was something that Lucy had told me about.

'Do you think Lucy's inherited this?' I asked, thinking about the ghost at her house.

'She's got a vivid imagination,' was all Frank would say on the subject.

'Is there anyone else in the family who might have been psychic?' I asked.

'I think my great-grandmother might have been,' he replied, 'and one of my great-aunts was as well, not that she made anything of it. The rest of them weren't, but they were interested in that sort of thing. One night apparently my grandmother and her sister went to see Sir Arthur Conan Doyle who, as well as writing the Sherlock Holmes books, was a famous touring medium. Anyway, the story goes that he came to town, so they decided to go and see him, and they were chatting on the way about what to do about the house they both lived in. It was a big house, bigger than either of them needed. Anyway, Conan Doyle said something like, 'I have a message for someone in the audience. You must divide the property', which they thought must have referred to them.'

'So, what did they do?' I asked, as Frank occasionally looked for some participation from his audience, and this was obviously a story he enjoyed.

'What did they do?' he repeated his eyes sparkling, 'well, they built a bloody great wall down the middle of the dining room!' Frank sat back in his chair and laughed, repeated what was quite clearly the punchline, and then continued laughing until the tears were streaming down his face. I was not quite sure why this was funny, but decided not to pursue it.

I waited for Frank to finish laughing, and he took another great gulp of his drink, muttering darkly about it not being beer. I waited for a suitable moment, and then said, 'Lucy said that you had some sort of experience at Aberfan that you wanted to tell me about.' Frank's merriment disappeared at once. The Aberfan Disaster has that effect on people.

As a boy growing up in Merthyr Tydfil in the 1970s, I lived under the shadow of the Aberfan Disaster. We all did. Merthyr Tydfil is a large town that came to prominence in the late 1700s as a centre of iron making, and was at one stage the largest producer of iron in the world. It's had its ups and downs, but is currently reinventing itself as a commercial centre for the northern Valleys and the surrounding areas, and is more prosperous than most people would ever imagine, although there are still significant areas of severe social deprivation.

As I said, Merthyr was founded on iron, which comes as a surprise to people who associate the Valleys with coal, and although there was some minor coal mining in Merthyr itself, most of the major mining activity took place lower down in the Valleys. Until 1958 Aberfan had been simply another one of the pit villages that had sprung up in the Valleys since the 1860s, decorating the sides of the valleys themselves like strings of fairy lights. The valley floor was littered with the mines, and, of course, with that other essential of Welsh life, rugby pitches.

The story of Aberfan is very well known. For many years, the spoil from the nearby coal mine was piled up in a series of massive tips on the mountainside above the village. This was not so unusual. Most villages in the Valleys were surrounded with such tips and some of them still are, although over the years many of them have been taken away. In fact, by the late 1960s this process of tip removal was already underway, and the tip at Aberfan was apparently scheduled to be removed. Unfortunately, one of the tips had been created over a series of springs, so the base of the tip had become unstable and waterlogged. October 1966 proved to be a particularly wet month which meant that the already unstable coal spoil became liquefied.

At 9.15am on 21 October, the tip slid down the mountainside towards the village, and engulfed Pantglas School, the local junior school, killing one hundred and sixteen children and twenty-eight adults. As a child, I heard stories of heroism from the day of the disaster. I can remember my own primary school teacher ten years after the event telling the class about the way in which teachers tried to shelter their pupils as they realised something awful was going to happen.

The accounts are horrific. Many of the bodies would not be identifiable, and the official response was dismal. But still many men from the area travelled to help in the rescue efforts, which quickly turned into an effort to recover the bodies of the dead. My father has always carried the burden of not having been able to as he was laid up with pneumonia, although his mother, my sweet old Grandma who had trained as a nurse before the war, volunteered to help, and spent her time working in the mortuary, helping in the attempt to identify the bodies. My father's sister was still living with her parents at the time, and has vivid memories of my grandmother coming home from Aberfan and hugging herself in distress. On my mother's side, her brother – my uncle Nick – was in London at the time, and came back to see if he could help. He was photographed by David Hurn from the *Daily Telegraph* with his arm round my aunt Jane, looking in desolation at the sight. It is one of the classic images of the Disaster.

The effects of the Aberfan Disaster are still felt to this day, ensuring that disaster relief is targeted at those who need it. At Aberfan, scandalously, some of the money raised for the community was spent by the government on clearing the remaining tips. The establishment, too, was shaken to its core. In fact, it has been said that the Queen's greatest regret has been not going to Aberfan sooner.

Back in the pub, it was almost as if a shadow had fallen over the table, and Frank took another drag from his drink. 'One of the really awful things about this thing that I have is that I will have a premonition or whatever you call it, but sometimes it is so vague, I can't do anything about it. Sometimes it feels like a curse more than anything else.

'And that's what sort of happened with Aberfan. I can't remember when it was exactly, but I was travelling up the valley and I turned into Aberfan. Wait a minute,' he said, 'I can remember seeing political posters for the general election. When was that?'

A quick check on the smartphone told us that it was held on 31 March 1966. 'That'll be it, then. It was spring 1966.' Frank took another sip.

'As I said, I turned off the main road, down over the bridge, past the Merthyr Vale Colliery, and then up that hill into Aberfan. You know where I am.'

I nodded in recognition: I had travelled that way every day on a bus to work in Cardiff. The colliery closed in the mid-1980s, but the road remained pretty much the same.

'Anyway,' he continued, 'I went up the hill, and then you turn right onto the main road. And there in front of me was an AA motorcyclist, flagging me down. I couldn't work out what was happening, but the road was blocked. So, I got out of the car to see what was going on. And there in front of me was a long line of black cars, and I realised they were hearses – a whole line of them! I couldn't believe my eyes! I'd never seen anything like that before or since.

'Anyway, I don't know how long I stood there, and remember I was standing in the main road, but a man came up to me and asked me if I was all right. And I said, "Look!", and I pointed. And he gave me a really strange look, and said, "What is it?" and I said, "Look, there's a line of hearses there!" And he just stood there and stared at me. And when I looked again, it was all gone. It was a bright, sunny day, not the dark, gloomy day it had been a couple of seconds ago. "Are you all right?" he asked again. "Something terrible is going to happen here!" I said. And, do you know what he said?' Frank looked at me with wonderment in his eyes. 'He said, "That'll be the tip. You can hear it groaning."

'I couldn't believe it! He *knew* it was a problem! They *all* knew! Anyhow, we stood there and looked at one another, and he said, "What's your name?" And I realised I'd made a bloody fool of myself, so I said, "Don't worry about my name, just do something about the tip." And I got into the car and drove off as fast as I could. I didn't even bother to make my call at the ironmongery.

'When I got home, I told my wife, and she said that it was probably the medication I was on for my chest, and to be honest, I didn't think very much more about it. I thought maybe she's right, and after all I did try to tell them.

'I was in Dorset when it happened. I remember watching it on the little black and white TV in the hotel. I just couldn't believe it. I was stunned. We all were in the hotel.'

Frank took another sip of his drink, now nearly finished. 'I've never stopped feeling guilty,' he said, 'but there really was nothing I could do, nothing at all.'

We sat in silence for a few moments.

'Fancy another one?' I asked, gesturing at his now empty glass. The shadow passed.

'Just a half this time. If I have another pint of that, I'll be anyone's,' he joked.

We chatted for a while longer, but although I knew that Frank had had other experiences of the paranormal, he refused to be drawn on them. As we eventually left the pub, Frank stopped me and fixed me with his intelligent grey eyes. 'I'm glad I've told you the story. Make sure it goes in the book!' So here it is.

Psychics are ordinary people with attributes that many of us will find strange, but quite a few people have what you might call premonitions at some stage or other. Some writers have suggested that this is simply part of what it means to be an animal. People who live with pets will know that their animals can often seem to 'read their minds' in a way you get used to, but can be slightly uncanny.

We live with three cats in my family – Hector, Noel and Frank (no relation). Hector is the classic black cat that you associate with witchcraft, and that people have all sorts of superstitions about. Most pet owners are worried at those times when people let off fireworks, Guy Fawkes Night or New Year, but we worry about Hector at Halloween as, on more than one occasion, he has come in covered in flour, or obviously having been persecuted in some way. This is particularly distressing as he is the most affectionate of the three. But Hector is a cheese lover, and will know not only that I am helping myself to cheese from the fridge, but seemingly *when* I am going to. He doesn't appear when I am after the fruit juice, for example. Is this super cat hearing, does he know my snacking habits that well, or is he reading my mind? One of the others, Frank, seems to know that I'm coming home before I walk up to the house. There are other examples of seemingly 'psychic' behaviour in the animal world.

But when it comes to people, such attributes are sometimes seen as problematic, or, in some cases, downright evil or even demonic. There are, therefore, some religious groups, which I sadly suspect includes some Anglicans, who would regard such attributes as a sign of demonic possession and would be more than happy to proceed with a full exorcism of such people. However, the fact that both of the 'psychics' I have described are both committed Christians and regular church-goers might give them pause for thought. As we shall see, being psychic might not be a guarantee that someone is a good person but, certainly in the case of Frank, I know this to be the case. Neither of them asked for this attribute, or has sought to develop it in any way: for them both, it is something that you learn to live with, a bit like being left-handed, and certainly not an indication of demonic possession, to which we will now turn.

# Chapter 9

## 'Help! I'm possessed'

People are fascinating on all sorts of levels: they can be very kind indeed, giving of their time and resources in a way that can be quite astonishing, but also at the same time capable of acts of callous cruelty and even pure evil. The strange thing is that very often you can find both extremes in the same people. I have heard stories from my colleagues that the same people who will go out of their way to help their neighbours, will spend hours doing voluntary work for local charities, and will be pillars of the church in so many ways can also turn very nasty indeed. One colleague was nearly broken by the fact that some of the leading lights in her church had taken against her. They apparently organised a classic poison pen letter writing campaign against her and would ring her at two o'clock in the morning, but withhold their number. But at church on Sunday, she said, they would be there greeting people and welcoming them, as if nothing had happened!

Most priests are astonished by the generosity and kindness of their parishioners, and the amount of voluntary time they put in.

In my present church, for example, there are around a hundred volunteers who basically run everything from the office and the website to the bell tower and the flower stand. In fact some of my ministerial colleagues are themselves volunteers who do what I do part-time and for no financial reward. I take my hat off to them all, particularly as they are also funding the whole operation as well. The same goes for people who run hospices and all sorts of other charities across the country. We are a society of volunteers.

At the same time, of course, there are always rewards for volunteering. Most of the time, the reward will be the feeling the people are contributing to a cause in which they believe (in the case of the church, this belief is quite literal). Just occasionally, however, the reward is power, and power, as we know, corrupts, and if it doesn't corrupt absolutely, it can be used for good or ill, depending on personal inclination or circumstances. There is often a tension between people who are paid to do a job and volunteers, who in some cases may have some power over them. A paid officer answering to a board of volunteer trustees will know this tension very well. But while tension and the abuse of power may be uncomfortable or difficult, rarely do these things spill over into absolute evil.

## The nature of evil

You would have thought that 'evil' would be relatively easy to define. According to one way of thinking about it, evil is the opposite of 'good', but it's also obviously true that what constitutes good and evil can be culturally conditioned. A classic example might be our attitudes to homosexuality.

The Western world has been on something of a journey in its attitudes to this issue over the last sixty or so years. Until 1967, homosexual practices were illegal in England and Wales, so therefore homosexuality must somehow have been considered bad before then, but not afterwards. Since 2013 it has been possible for homosexual couples to get married in the same jurisdiction, so homosexuality must now be considered to be good, and this change has occurred in the space of less than fifty years! At the same time, in some parts of the world, homosexual acts are punishable by death, whereas other traditional societies have been remarkably tolerant of such practices.

Similarly, in the West we're pretty much convinced that polygamy (the practice of having more than one wife or husband at the same time) is quite a bad thing, whereas in some parts of the world where homosexuality is seen to be a problem, polygamy is regarded as a generally good thing. In other words, defining good and bad or evil can be difficult.

Christians, of course, tend to look at the Bible for guidance, although any Christian thinker worth their salt will also know that if you look hard enough at the Bible, you can justify pretty much any course of action from its pages! It does, however, have some helpful things to say about good and evil. In fact, the very first story in the Bible in the Book of Genesis, once you start to read it as theology (not as history or science, neither of which it is!), can help quite a lot. The Bible describes a world that is created by God, and at the end of each act of creation, God declares that what he has made is good. And it's almost as if, for this story, creation isn't so much about making things, but about ensuring that what is made is in its right place, and is balanced: light and darkness, water and dry land, and so on. And then, right at the end, God looks at the ordered world that he has made, and he announces that it is very good. In other words, for the Christian foundation texts, there is something about good that is creative, but also that brings order. If evil is the opposite of good, it is something that brings both destruction and disorder.

There are lots of things in today's world that may be said to bring disorder and destruction, but the Bible is careful to distinguish between bad things that happen (like an earthquake or a volcano erupting), which it sees sort of as the flip side of creation, and moral evil which is deliberately destructive or disorderly, and because it is deliberate, it is caused by someone who can therefore be described as evil.

The classic example people like to use is Hitler, whose actions were deliberately destructive in that he caused the Holocaust in which so many millions of people including (but not exclusively) Jews were destroyed.

But Stalin might be a better example, because not only was he responsible for the deaths of more people than Hitler, but he also ensured that his legacy would include pretty much permanent disorder. Have you ever wondered, for example, why so many of the new countries in what was the Soviet Union or indeed the Eastern Bloc have sizeable populations of the 'wrong' people within their borders, and are therefore inherently unstable? Well, it was because Uncle Joe, as he was known, drew the lines in what he knew to be the wrong place thus ensuring, for example, that there are lots of ethnic Russians within the borders of Ukraine.

Now that's what you call evil! And, of course, all it takes is for someone – let's call him Putin – to come along and take advantage of all that, and have a good go at spreading disorder in the West in various ways. Is that evil? Well, it certainly looks like it. (Oh and by the way, Putin's régime has the active support of the Russian Orthodox Church, but then, before fingers are pointed too much, the history of my own Anglican Church isn't exactly free of taint either.)

But, of course, there is a reason for all this evil. It's to do with power more than anything else; evil people bring disorder and destruction because it gives them power. And this can manifest itself either in the power they have over other people, or in their sense of absolute power.

You might think such evil exists only rarely, but in actual fact it is around us all the time. Pretty much anywhere there is power, there are people willing to exploit it. Just going back to that story in the Bible again, Genesis describes God creating an ordered world, and then it describes him handing over responsibility for that world to human beings. For Christians, then, God gives away power. So, it follows that where power is amassed or concentrated on one person, there is likely to be some sort of abuse going on – as the Bible would say, 'sin is crouching at the door.'

As I say, this evil can be found wherever there is power which can be used to spread disorder and destruction, and unfortunately I have encountered this evil personally in my life and ministry. I have genuinely met people that I am convinced are, for want of a better word, evil.

In one case, I was able to observe the destructive force at first hand, because it was aimed at me. I had had a series of conversations with this person, who had sought to undermine me whilst appearing to help me. It's very difficult under these circumstances to know what is going on, especially in an institution such as the Church, where you assume that people are acting out of the best of intentions. I have to admit that, although I was initially taken in, I didn't quite react in the way the person was expecting, and was able to mitigate some of the effects.

However, one occasion is etched on my memory – when I became aware that the person who had been trying to 'help' me was in fact using the information to destroy me, or at least to destroy part of my ministry. It was an extraordinary moment, and there was nothing I could do, but I remembered the way that my flesh crawled when I had spoken to them, and my sense of unease. It was a defining moment for me, the realisation that such an evil person was actually at work. Of course, I wasn't the only target. It became evident that, over the years, this person had destroyed other people too, and that maybe I had come off lightly.

But this is a book about the ministry of deliverance, so how does all this fit? Well, deliverance ministers are quite good, it seems, at spotting when this sort of thing is going on – they are, after all, the people that the Church trusts to deal with issues of spiritual evil. But they are also the people the Church entrusts to deal with those who are possessed by evil spirits. So, is it possible that such evil people are 'possessed'?

## What is possession?

It is possible to see the origin of the idea of possession in the Bible again, but this time in the life and ministry of Jesus. The New Testament contains four Gospels which can be seen as theological biographies of Jesus (with the emphasis again more or less on the theology), usually ascribed to Matthew, Mark, Luke and John, of which the earliest is almost certainly Mark. Mark's Gospel has a sort of rough and ready feel about it, and an ancient tradition links it all the way back to Jesus' best friend Peter. In this book, Jesus is seen again and again as an exorcist, casting out demon after demon. The theological point is that Jesus is the Son of God, and therefore has power over the forces of evil wherever they may be found.

In fact, the very first miracle story that Mark chooses to relate is an exorcism. The first thing Jesus does is to begin to call people to follow him, starting off with fishermen Simon (later called Peter) and Andrew, and James and John, and, then, the following day, because it's the Jewish Sabbath, they all go to the Synagogue, where Jesus takes the lead in teaching them. Suddenly, there is a man with what Mark calls 'an unclean spirit' shouting, 'What are you doing here Jesus of Nazareth? Have you come to destroy us? I know who you are: you're the Holy One of God.' Jesus just yells at the spirit, telling it to shut up and to come out of the man. The people around are amazed especially at Jesus' authority, and then they tell everyone about him. The story focuses on Jesus' authority based on his divine nature (Holy One of God), but this is still a classic exorcism.

There are numerous exorcism stories, but one in particular stands out. It is in Mark chapter five. The story features another man with an 'unclean spirit', in this case a gentile (a non-Jew) living in a gentile world, who spends most of his life stark naked, living among the tombs – both characteristics would have been horrifying to a Jewish audience. But when he sees Jesus, he calls, 'What have you to do with us, Jesus Son of the Most High God?' Jesus asks him his name, and he answers that his name is Legion, because there are a lot of demons possessing him. But Jesus silences him, and casts the demons out into a herd of pigs. They run down into the sea where they drown. It's one of those stories where people get hung up on the details, in fact I have seen people cry when they think about the fate of the pigs (not a joke).

There have been many studies of the exorcisms of Jesus' ministry, but two features seem to emerge: the first is that the stories are there to point to who Jesus is (for the Gospel writers he is, of course, the Son of God), and secondly, that a lot of the stories seem to feature things that we might interpret as evidence of mental illnesses or diseases, such as epilepsy. A good example of this might be in Mark chapter nine, when we are told that a little boy has another unclean spirit that means that he can't speak or hear, and which makes him froth at the mouth. Jesus' disciples try to heal him but they can't, and when they ask Jesus what they are doing wrong, he answers, no doubt with a smile, 'This kind can only come out through prayer.'

The world of the Gospels is very different from the world that we live in, and there are very different cultural assumptions, but the stories go on to tell how Jesus gave his followers authority to cast out demons, and to some extent that is what we are still doing.

*Except we almost never do.*

There are very occasional documented cases of deliverance ministers carrying out a major exorcism, but in most cases, they are not entirely sure they can *categorically* say that the person was possessed.

Among those who I have met and spoken to, if you were to ask them, hand on heart, whether a person was actually possessed – in other words, not just inspired by evil, or given completely to evil, but actually wholly consumed and controlled by an evil spirit which is not themselves – then they almost always hedge their bets.

There are documented cases, as I've said. It is difficult to describe them at first hand because I have not been involved, however here is one that was outlined at a conference. The priest in question is considered to be one of the greatest deliverance ministers of his time and, although now retired from a very distinguished ministry, was consulted widely on a range of cases. But for him, one in particular stood out.

A young lady had been attending an evangelical church, but her family became concerned about her mental health. It deteriorated rapidly, and she was admitted to a psychiatric hospital.

While she was there, her condition continued to baffle the psychiatrists. Of particular concern was the fact that she seemed to be possessed by a series of male demons which manifested themselves as Lust, Greed and Death and spoke with distinct voices. Because the psychiatrists were very concerned, they called in the people they considered to be the experts in this field, and the Anglican deliverance ministry team sent out two trained exorcists, one of whom was the priest whose story this is.

'I can remember walking into the psychiatric hospital,' he said. 'These places are always very strange and, of course, you never know what to expect, but this time there was an extra frisson of anticipation from both of us. We were shown into the ward, and we encountered the patient for the first time. But what was really strange, and should have got us moving much faster, was that she recognised immediately that we were the exorcists. And we were so dumbfounded that we nearly got it horribly wrong.'

He took a sip of water, possibly for dramatic effect I thought, and then took up the story. 'You see, what we should have done was to silence her straightaway, but instead what happened was that "they" started to address us. I remember that they had very coarse voices,' at which point his voice changed to imitate the sort of voice you associate with a villain on *EastEnders*. '"I'm Lust", said the first voice, and started to describe some of the things that my colleague had got up to as a young man.' The priest smiled slightly at the memory, but there were clearly things he wasn't going to tell us about the case. 'The wind was taken completely out of his sails, I can tell you,' he continued, 'but then the voice of Greed started to get going. And again, that was another very different male voice coming out of this small woman. But at this stage we realized very quickly that we had to do something before the third demon, the voice of Death, started to speak, and we were very worried about what he would come up with! So, we finally silenced the demons in the name of the Lord Jesus which is, of course, what we should have done when we walked in. And then we used the formula for major exorcism on each of the three demons in turn.' Again, he paused slightly and shuddered from the memory – this time it didn't appear to be a storyteller's technique, the recollection was obviously painful.

'She had, of course, been restrained, but still it was an amazingly tough thing to do. The medics were there on hand too, but we felt very vulnerable.' He nodded, and his mouth twisted slightly. 'But it worked,' he said. 'After we had said the words of exorcism, she shrieked. And then she crumpled and lost consciousness for a few moments. Obviously, the medics rushed forward, and we stepped back, but she wasn't out for very long at all. And then when she did regain consciousness after a minute or two, she was fine, although she was very tired and couldn't really remember anything about it, which is just as well, really. But you could tell that she was normally a very bubbly sort of person.'

He paused again and took a sip of water. It was obvious that telling the story had cost him some effort. 'We had a short debrief with the medics. They were thrilled and were absolutely convinced that the young woman had been possessed, and that we had expelled those three demons from her.

'But as my fellow priest and I walked back to the car we were able to have a conversation.

'"Do you think she was possessed?" I asked.

'"Not completely convinced," he said. "You?"

'"No, I'm not convinced either."'

The priest smiled and shrugged slightly. 'So, the medics thought that this was a spiritual thing, a demon that we had exorcised. But the priests? Well, we had our doubts – we thought she was mentally ill.'

When the Christian Deliverance Study Group published the textbook *Deliverance: Psychic Disturbance and Occult Involvement* (SPCK 1987 and revised edition 1996) which was edited by Michael Perry, then Archdeacon of Durham, they detailed three such cases. One was this case.

Two other cases were outlined. A young woman who had been a committed satanist for many years was looking to leave her group with the help of a Christian friend. When she encountered a priest, she fell into a trance, hissed and curled up like a snake. But when the words of exorcism were pronounced, she felt free, and with the help of Christian friends, she eventually cut links with the satanist group.

The third was a middle-aged woman who was a witch, and had lived in the same isolated village for the whole of her life. She encountered two priests, and immediately she knew that one of them had led a wild youth from which she was able to call out details. The other was an Arabic scholar who was able to talk to her in an Arabic dialect, which would have been unknown to her. On being exorcised, she lost both these powers.

So, given the fact that this is a real, although very rare, phenomenon, what are we looking for? Well, there are three basic signs that someone is possessed. The first is that they have preternatural strength and are able to physically do things they shouldn't be able to do. The second is that they should have preternatural knowledge of the world around them, not just the future, but the people around them, as in the cases above where the person who was being exorcised knew details of the priests' personal lives. And the third is that they will have knowledge of languages that they cannot possibly have picked up by some other means. So if you encounter a little old lady who is swinging an armchair round her head, can tell you what you had for breakfast and in whose bed, and is singing a Roman legionary song in her best dog Latin (or, like the witch, is able to speak colloquial Arabic), this is a good indication of the presence of something other than someone having a good time. Classically you will need all three, although I suspect an exorcist worth his or her salt is not going to hang around too long with a tick list, especially if they 'accidentally' woke up in the wrong bed this morning!

So, assuming you have finally found someone who you believe is genuinely possessed, what do you now do? Well, you will need to proceed to an exorcism.

There are two types of exorcism. What we call minor exorcisms are basically prayers to God for deliverance, so the words, 'deliver us from evil' in the Lord's Prayer constitute a minor exorcism. The other place we tend to come across them, although we almost never refer to it as a minor exorcism for obvious reasons, is at baptisms, when we ask God to set the 'candidate' free from all evil. I have heard second hand stories about mainly Roman Catholic priests who have drawn people's attention to the fact that this constitutes an exorcism, but I suspect it doesn't go down well. In the Middle Ages, however, they were much less squeamish about these things, using salt as part of the ritual, and opening the North door of the church so that the devil could escape – in the case of my church in Wrexham, this would mean straight into the town centre, although if you had ever seen the centre of your average market town at 1.30 on a Saturday morning, you might think that this is a natural habitat for your average demon!

However, if you find that you are dealing with someone whom you believe is suffering from genuine demonic possession as defined above, you will need something stronger than a minor exorcism: you will need a major exorcism. This has to be done, incidentally, under medical supervision, although to be fair, anyone exhibiting the classic signs of demonic possession is almost certainly going to find themselves in the local psychiatric hospital, with professionals standing round wondering what on earth is going on, as in the case of the young woman with the three demons.

So, being a good Anglican, and under the authority of the bishop, that bishop is the person the deliverance minister needs to speak to first if they think they are likely to have to perform a major exorcism, and must get the bishop's agreement. All bishops should, at least in theory, provide the words prescribed to be used for the major exorcism (although if the bishop doesn't have the words to hand, most deliverance ministers will know where to find them, often in a slightly battered booklet at the bottom of the deliverance bag). The words procured, the bishop gives the deliverance minister permission to use them on that occasion and on no other.

· Occasionally, I have come across Anglican priests who claim that they have been given blanket permission to conduct as many major exorcisms as they like and as often as they like. I wouldn't like to say they are flouting the rules, but suffice it to say that if it all goes wrong (which, of course, it might) the Ecclesiastical Insurance Group might not cover them, especially as all deliverance ministry is covered by the bishop's insurance, which is why, as the deliverance team, we meet with the bishop once a year to report back and to have our general commission renewed.

Once you have your permission, the first thing you are supposed to do is to silence the spirit (working on the assumption that you don't want to be put off by having the entire contents of your private browsing history or your gambling addiction made public), and then command it in the name of Jesus to leave the sufferer, and to go to the place assigned for it. Presumably the person, if they are genuinely possessed, will have to be restrained as the demon, once it has found a nice comfortable home, is unlikely to want to go of its own volition, but I can't really understand the whole idea of crosses being placed into orifices that is the stock in trade of the Hollywood exorcism. The demon may not want to go quietly, but the idea behind the major exorcism is that the words themselves work, although having a cross can provide a useful focus, and give you a sense of reassurance. Presumably, if the patient has been baptised, you would also want to anoint them with the oil for healing, and also to give them Holy Communion as soon as possible.

As you may have gathered, the whole idea of people being possessed is very much in vogue at the moment. But as I have said, if your entire will has been taken over by an evil spiritual entity, then the chances of it allowing you to go and tell a priest that you are possessed, and that you want to be exorcised, is remote. It is, however, one of the things that deliverance ministers come across most often, and like all these things, isn't greatly helped by the Internet.

The Internet is, of course, the great wonder of our age: all the knowledge of the ages is there, as are some of the stupidest things you will ever read. For example, one of my colleagues gave me a calendar of church-based cartoons for Christmas by Dave Walker whose 'Guide to the Church' is one of the great highlights of the *Church Times*, which is basically the weekly Anglican trade magazine. One particular cartoon featured in the wonderful calendar, alongside the utterly hilarious 'Guide to the Church Fridge', was what to do with a helium-filled balloon that is bumping along the ceiling in the church – any vicar has been there. There were drawings of various suggestions for getting it down: air gun; 'elderly parishioner on makeshift platform' (we've all been there too); prayer; calling the bishop; and 'sending up another balloon (as recommended on the Internet)'. We all had a good laugh, until someone said, 'That's genuine you know, I read that on the Internet myself!' Fortunately, they didn't think it was a good idea, but the fact that if you ask Google how to get a helium-filled balloon down from a high ceiling, someone has suggested sending up another one, gives you some sort of idea of what you can find! But if you think that no one would ever believe that, just remember the equally baffling idea that the recent Coronavirus epidemic was caused by 5G technology. Enough people believed this in the UK to burn down at least five telephone masts. And if you search for any of the phenomena that deliverance ministers come across on a regular basis, you will discover that someone has suggested demonic possession as a cause.

This really does make our lives difficult. In fact, in some parts of the Internet, pretty much anything that you might call 'sin' is caused by some sort of possession. You may have thought that the phrase 'the demon drink' is just a manner of speaking, and for the majority of people who have used it, that's what it is, a figure of speech. But let me assure you (and I mean assure not reassure!) that where there is a demon there is an exorcist, or at least someone who claims to be an exorcist, who will cast the said demon from your soul and body, often for a small or indeed large consideration – although, as I have said several times, reputable Anglican deliverance ministers do not charge. Not only does this apply to alcoholism, but it also applies to the 'sin of homosexuality' which is quite clearly (according to some) a form of possession, and therefore a major exorcism is prescribed. It doesn't work, of course, because exorcism only works on genuine demons, but it presumably makes the exorcist feel better!

And if that is what some religious professionals are coming up with, imagine the damage that can be inflicted by those who are not. For the deliverance minister, Internet-induced self-diagnosis is a problem. Increasingly large numbers of people come to us claiming that they or a member of the family is possessed. This is despite the fact that, as I have said, while demonic possession is a theoretical possibility, it is so rare as to be almost non-existent. But this doesn't stop people trying.

## 'I want to be baptised'

It was a Saturday afternoon and the sun was shining. It was the sort of day that every bride hopes for when she plans her wedding day, whether or not she has anyone to get married to. The bridegroom often seems to be something of an accessory on these occasions! But it was a perfect day, and I found myself in church filling in the marriage registers in preparation for the impending wedding.

Anglican clergy in England and Wales act as registrars when people want to get married in church. This means that we have to work our way through the sometimes complicated laws about who can marry whom and (more importantly) where. In the old days, this used to be fairly clear cut: you needed to be resident in a particular place to be married there. If you didn't live there, but had a connection of some description, you might apply for an Archbishop of Canterbury's licence, an amazing (and expensive) piece of parchment which would mean that you didn't have to spend three weeks in a guest house in a village with a pretty church in order to get married there. These days there is something called a 'qualifying connection' to a place which allows you to bypass all of this, but interpreting this is complicated, and different vicars clearly interpret the rules differently. These days we also marry people who have been divorced, not because the law changed but because some eager lawyer noticed that it had been illegal for the Church *not* to marry them. The law changed in 1949, the Church cottoned on in about 1999.

Once you have worked out whether people can be married in your church, you then have to call banns, which is an archaic way of publishing the fact that these two people are getting married, and if anyone thinks there is a legal reason why they should not, they are obliged to divulge this. There are two basic reasons why you might not be permitted to be married in church (or indeed anywhere else). One is that you are too closely related, such as being long-lost brother and sister, or son-in-law and mother-in-law. The second is that you are already and still married to someone else. This is part of our cultural inheritance from Ancient Rome. In our society, which abhors polygamy, you can still have as many husbands or wives as you like, but only if you have them one at a time. The banns are a way of establishing that both halves of the couple are free from either of these 'legal impediments' as they are known. There is, however, a major flaw in the system, and that is that while in a small village people may well know the couple, in a large urban centre with a population of tens of thousands, the chance of anyone who comes to church on a Sunday actually knowing the couple, let alone the ins and outs of their and their families' personal lives, is remote. But we still have to go through with it, and very often the couple will come to church, which is a bonus as far as we're concerned.

Once all that is done, the wedding can go ahead. This means that the marriage registers need to be filled in. This, for many clergy, is a nightmare. There are two originals, one copy and one internal document that need to be handwritten, but not just handwritten, they need to be produced without making a mistake using a fountain pen in the dreaded registrars' ink. Mistakes can be corrected up until the time when they are signed off at the wedding service, but registrars' ink is more of a problem. It is pretty much indelible, having been invented so that if there is a flood in the church, and the registers get wet, they will remain legible, and all that legal information will not be lost forever. This is proper ink. It only comes in bottles, so when you run out you can't just put a cartridge in, you have to manipulate the pen into the bottle, and then wipe it clean, trying all the while not to get it on yourself, or your clothes, because it is, after all, indelible. Oh, sorry, did I mention? It also clogs up your fountain pen, so not only do you need a constant supply of new fountain pens, but even the new pens need cleaning.

But on this particular Saturday morning, things were going well: the initial paperwork was nearly done, I had managed to refill the fountain pen without too much in the way of ink explosion, and I had also managed not to make a mistake that needed cumbersome correction. In addition to all this, I had completed most of what I had to do by way of preparation in good time and still had nearly an hour before the wedding service was due to take place. What could possibly go wrong?

Just in my line of vision, a face appeared. I held up a minimally ink-stained right hand in the universally understood gesture of, 'I'm just writing out the bridegroom's father's name for the third time, can you hang on for a second, please?' The face stopped where it was. I finished the line, having only the bride's details to fill in (for the third time).

'I'm really sorry to bother you, Jason,' said my verger very apologetically, 'but there's a young man downstairs who says he wants to be baptised. I've told him you're busy, but he seems fairly insistent.'

I looked at my watch, trying to ignore the blue-black stains between the fingers of my left hand. 'Does he know we've got a wedding at 12?' I asked.

'Yes, but he said he'd wait.'

I sighed. 'Give me two minutes, and I'll be down.' I returned to the wedding certificate I was filling in, gave it my total concentration, and managed to get to the end without any noticeable mistakes.

Stopping to wash my hands, in a few minutes, I was back in the church and ready for action. The man who wanted to see me was, I guessed, in his early twenties, small of stature, but relatively big of frame, and he looked exceedingly nervous. My verger looked at me to see whether I was happy to deal with it, and when I nodded, she left me to it. 'Hi, I'm Jason,' I said, holding out my hand.

He just looked at my hand and muttered, 'I want to be baptised.'

Now we've encountered baptism before but, although this is something the church does all the time, it's not quite as simple as it might appear, especially for adults.

Each church has its own policies regarding children who are being brought to be christened, as we tend to call the baptism of infants.

Many churches have a restrictive policy which may mean that the parents have to attend church regularly for a specified period of time before the vicar will even talk to them. They may have to go on some sort of baptism preparation course, which may simply involve watching a short film one evening, or it may involve a course that lasts a week. There won't be a test at the end, but you will certainly have a very good idea of what

Christianity is about and what is expected of you as you bring up your child. I am reliably informed that some such churches experience growth as a result of this policy, so this must be the right thing to do, or so the argument goes.

Other churches have what they call open baptism policies which means, in effect, that they put as few barriers in the way as possible. This particular church had an open baptism policy for children. There was only one condition, and that was that you had to come to church for one service, after which the baptism would be booked with few questions asked. Given the fact that this church was also growing numerically, sometimes at the expense of churches with restrictive policies, this was felt to be the right course as well.

But adults are a different matter entirely. Children are baptised on a promise that they will be brought up as Christians (whatever that means), whereas adults need to make some sort of commitment both in attendance and in terms of what they believe. One of the great joys of being a parish priest is baptising an adult, but it really is something that we don't do every week, and it works on the principle that they intend to be confirmed by the bishop. Confirmation, one of the seven traditional sacraments, is a bit nebulous, but always involves the bishop laying hands on your head, and praying for you. It is usually regarded as the way that people who were baptised as infants make a public declaration of their faith, which is then confirmed by the bishop.

So to the demand, 'I want to be baptised' that was posed one sunny Saturday afternoon, the answer was something along the lines of, 'I don't think we've ever met. Before we think about baptising you, you'll need to come to church for a couple of months . . .'

My spiel was cut short. 'No, I want to be baptised now!' The young man seemed very anxious. I began to explain, in my usual polite fashion, why this was an unusual course of action when he interrupted me again. 'I want to be baptised now because I'm possessed.'

Deliverance minister that I am, I have to admit that the wind was completely taken out of my sails. 'What?!' I spluttered.

'I'm possessed,' he said again, 'and I know that baptism involves an exorcism.'

I hope I didn't groan out loud. 'I'm really sorry, I can't do it now, you really do need to show some sort of commitment to the Christian faith.'

He looked very grumpy at this point, so I tried a different tack. 'What makes you think you're possessed, anyway?'

He just glared at me from under his eyelids. I suspect this was supposed to look 'evil', but unfortunately, the effect was more comic than anything else.

I felt desperately sorry for him. 'Look, shall we just pray together now?'

'No, I want to be baptised!' he glowered.

There were voices behind me: the wedding party had begun to arrive. The ushers were gathering at the back of the church and, in the time-honoured fashion of all ushers, wondering what they were supposed to be doing.

'I really do have to go,' I explained, 'but please let me say a prayer for you before I do.'

'No, I just wanted to be baptised,' he grunted and hung his head while giving me another of his best 'evil' looks before shuffling off towards the other side of the church. There really didn't seem to be anything I could do, so I left him to it, and shrugged at the verger who nodded sagely.

It would, however, have been the easiest thing in the world to take him at his word. In fact the path of least resistance would have been to offer to baptise him if not there and then, then after the wedding was over. The other possibility might have been to offer him some sort of exorcism, and I suspect if he had found himself in a church of a different stripe, this may have happened. It would, however, not have been the right thing to do.

I did encounter the young man again a couple of times, but every time he saw me, he would mutter, give me his best 'evil' look, and shuffle off quickly. The final time I came across him was as I was passing the local mental health unit at the hospital. He was walking towards it, not shuffling, but walking purposefully, with someone I knew to be a mental health worker. Judging from the way he was interacting, it was clear that he had found what he was looking for, and for the first time since I had seen him, I didn't feel sorry for him any more. They approached the door together, the health worker held the door for him, there was obviously an exchange of friendly banter, and they disappeared from sight.

### 'My mother-in-law is possessed: can you do something?'

This case was one that a friend of mine, Pat, was involved in at a different church. Like my church in Wrexham, it was one of those churches which kept its doors open all day, and had lots of people dropping in and out. One day, Pat encountered a woman who was very distressed. She had been lighting candles and leaving prayer requests. Pat is a very sympathetic and pastorally minded woman. She asked the lady in question whether she could help. The reply when it came flummoxed her completely: 'I think my mother-in-law is possessed. Can you do something?'

Pat tells me that she was reminded of the mother-in-law jokes told so memorably by Les Dawson, and was about to say something like, 'You think you've got problems, you ought to meet mine,' when she realised that the lady was in deadly earnest. So, being a kind person, she listened to the story about family breakdown, and about the way in which the lady felt that her husband had been driven away from her by his mother. He had eventually gone off with another woman. The more the story came out, the more distressed she appeared, and the more Pat began to wonder whether everything was not right with her state of mental health.

So, she talked her down. She asked about her medical history and whether she was on any medication.

'My doctor gave me these tablets to calm me down,' she said, 'but I don't need them, and I've thrown them away. There's nothing wrong with me, it's all my mother-in- law's fault. As I said, she's possessed.'

The conversation apparently went around and around for several minutes, until eventually Pat got the lady to agree to go back to the GP, and to explain what had happened. The fact that she was deeply disturbed herself was revealed a little while later. One of the parishioners was looking through the prayer requests, and discovered that there were a series of notes left clearly by the lady (she had signed them), asking for prayers for her and her ex-husband. The notes said her ex-husband was now living in sin with Sandra Jones (not her real name) and a real address and postcode was given. Not only had the lady herself signed them, but she had also left her own address and contact numbers!

It was pretty much at this point that I became involved, more than anything else because Pat needed someone to talk these things through with, and I was the person who came to mind.

I reassured her that she had done exactly the right thing, but it was evident that the lady was in quite a lot of distress. It is one thing claiming to be possessed yourself, something completely different telling all and sundry that you think your mother-in-law is possessed!

This wasn't quite the end of the story, however. Not only did Pat have the lady's phone number, but the lady had picked up Pat's phone number from the weekly news-sheet in the church. Most of my parishioners treat my mobile number as a sort of emergency number, but this lady treated Pat's number in the way she would treat, well, a friend.

She would ring her up at all sorts of inopportune moments: Christmas Day was a classic one! She would also leave endless messages on the voicemail. 'To be honest,' Pat commented, 'she doesn't really need someone to listen, she just needs someone to tell.' But slowly over the course of about a year, the situation slowly eased, and the last time I asked, they were sending one another Christmas cards, and that was about it.

So, not quite a classic deliverance case, but one where it would be entirely possible to jump to the wrong conclusions, even if the likelihood of the mother-in-law being exorcised was very remote!

## The incubus

As I have already implied, I think the Internet is a double-edged sword. There are amazing benefits and amazing dangers all mixed up together, but this case was one of the most bizarre cases illustrating the dangers of the Internet.

Quite some time ago, one of my colleagues asked me about a woman called Betty who had started coming to church. He was a bit worried about her. It seemed to be quite a sensitive case on all sorts of levels, and there were lots of things he was unable to divulge for what he said were pastoral reasons.

Clergy are quite used to this sort of thing, to be honest. But other people are frequently surprised at what Anglican priests do. When my name first appeared in *The Sunday Times*, for example, I am reliably informed that the discussion on the BBC Radio 4 Press Preview centred on the fact that they were surprised that there were deliverance ministers in the Anglican Church at all. It was also said that everyone knows that this is something that Roman Catholic priests do. The fact is, of course, that each diocese in the Church of England and the Church in Wales has at least one deliverance minister, if not a whole designated team. But this was a ministry which has hitherto been completely below the radar. There are other things that Anglican priests do which come as a surprise to most people, including many churchgoing Anglicans, and one of these is that we hear confessions.

As I have said, there are seven traditional sacraments in the Church, one of which is confession, or the ministry of reconciliation as it is often called in Roman Catholic (and some Anglo-Catholic) circles. It was one of the things that the Protestant Reformers set their face against, and some Anglican Evangelicals are also very worried by the idea, but it is still part of the Anglican tradition, even if you have to look quite hard for it.

Historically, the idea of a special confession and the receiving of a categorical absolution, when the priest claims the authority of Jesus himself to wipe away the sins confessed, can be found in something called 'The Visitation of the Sick' in all versions of the *Book of Common Prayer*, even the very Protestant version of 1552. However, whereas for Anglicans it has always been regarded as something that you might do if you feel you need to – the classic formulation is 'All may, some should, none must'

– a private confession was not a requirement before receiving Holy Communion. In the Roman Catholic Church, however, it still is, at least technically, although some Roman Catholic priests are less fussy about it than others.

So, occasionally, Anglican priests find themselves hearing confessions, although very, very few Anglican churches will have confessionals for the purpose, preferring to find a quiet corner of the church, or indeed the vicarage study, depending on circumstances. Sometimes, confessions take place in the context of spiritual direction. This is an idea where people can have someone to talk about their spiritual lives, and as part of that, what is troubling them will frequently come up as an issue. Sacramental confession and absolution is the natural way of dealing with that.

The other occasion when we tend to hear confessions is in an emergency. This is most likely to happen when someone comes to the church during the day if it's open, and just spills the beans. The opportunity to confess is one of the most important things to be able to offer someone, and as a priest some of the most important encounters of my life have been when I have heard someone's confession when they have been particularly down.

So, when my colleague muttered something about not being able to talk about some of the issues for pastoral reasons, I assumed that it was in the context of sacramental confession. Just as Roman Catholic priests are bound by the 'seal of the confessional' never to divulge what is said, so are Anglican priests, although in the case of child abuse we do have a duty to report it which overrides. In this case, however, my colleague said that it was not in the context of confession, and the more he thought about it, the more he felt that it was something I should know about, and possibly deal with as well as he was pretty much convinced it was a deliverance case.

Having dealt with whatever qualms he might have felt, my colleague fleshed out some of the details. As I said Betty had started attending his church. Apparently she had been married there, but was now widowed, and when she decided she needed to start attending church services, this was the one she immediately thought about. The vicar noticed straightaway that things 'were not quite right' as he put it, and she seemed agitated. So, at the end of the service, he approached her, and offered her a coffee and the opportunity for a chat. 'She didn't really want to talk to me at first,' he explained. 'But there was obviously something going badly wrong in her life, so I gave her as much time as I thought she needed. But she wasn't very forthcoming. The next Sunday, there she was again, but this time she didn't even wait until the service was finished before she went. I was really frustrated. The following Sunday, I looked out for her again, but she wasn't there, and I assumed that she was just another one of those people who just drifts through, and then drifts off. And then, lo and behold, there she was the Sunday after that. And this time, she stayed. I didn't approach her quite as directly as I had the first time, but I noticed that when I had finished chatting to someone else, she was still around, so we found a quiet corner, and she began to talk to me. It's a really strange story, but she is pretty much convinced that she is physically possessed by an evil presence of some description.' He paused for a few moments. 'It's not something I've ever come across before, to be honest. What should I do?'

'Did she tell you what sort of thing was happening?' I asked.

'No, not really, just that there was something that was physically inside her. Is this something you've come across in your deliverance ministry job?'

I thought for a moment. 'I don't think I have.'

'What do you think I should do?' he asked earnestly.

'You might ask if she's happy to meet us together and to tell us what the problem is. And find out whether she'd be more comfortable in church or at home.'

For many people this is a realistic choice. Most of the time, we tend to see people in their own homes, more, I suspect by force of habit than anything else – visiting is what vicars do because it's become sort of ingrained in our collective DNA.

However, some people are more comfortable in a church building. My colleague was more than happy with this as a suggestion, so he agreed to get hold of her, as he now had her phone number and contact details. A day or so later, he rang me and told me that she would very much like to meet us both, and that she would prefer it to be in her own home. A range of dates and times was on offer, and so we agreed to meet there.

This proved to be more difficult to find than at first it appeared, which is of course the story of my life. But I did eventually find it, and it was yet another block of flats in the heart of suburbia, although this one had open views of the sea in the distance. Like many of these new blocks of flats, there were multiple front doors with seemingly random numbers on them. Presumably if you knew your way round there was some sort of pattern, but given that I don't have a PhD in Applied Mathematics, it took quite a lot of wandering round to find the right doorbell at the right front door. It helped that my colleague was already there, and waiting for me. 'Not the easiest place to find,' he commented apologetically.

'You're telling me.' I smiled.

'Ready?' he asked eagerly.

'Ready,' I agreed, and he rang the bell. After some time in the building wishing that I had studied Applied Geography at university instead of endless rounds of Theology, we were rescued on the stairwell by a small lady with dark curly hair and a wizened face from a long time in the sun.

'I'm Betty,' she said, 'no one can find this place. Even the postmen get lost.' It was clearly meant as a sort of joke, but Betty didn't smile, she just looked worried.

She led us up a flight of stairs to her flat, which proved to be full of light and which did have a wonderful view of the sea.

'Stunning,' grunted my colleague appreciatively. Betty nodded, obviously she wasn't terribly interested.

My colleague introduced me, and I held out my hand, and this time she took it. 'It's nice to meet you,' she said formally. Betty then turned to my colleague. 'Since I saw you last, I've found out what it is that is bothering me.'

'Oh, good,' he answered, obviously hoping that there was a rational explanation for what was happening.

'It's called an incubus,' she said almost proudly.

Now, to be honest, I have to admit that this was a new one on me. I remembered the whole idea of the incubus as a male demon who has sexual intercourse with women, but this was buried somewhere deep within my mind, and I remembered too that there was something called a succubus which, from what I could recall, was the female equivalent of an incubus, but that was about it. It may possibly surprise people that my knowledge of such things is so scanty, but from the point of view of the Christian deliverance minister, we simply take care of paranormal phenomena in the way a Mafia godfather takes care of people who get in the way. However, at this point I rather wished I had paid slightly more attention at college.

'It's an incubus,' she repeated. 'Have you ever come across one of those before?'

My colleague looked stunned and even more confused than me. Clearly, he had spent even less time studying demonology than me.

'I've been doing this a long time,' I said, 'and to be honest, I've never come across an incubus before.' I looked at my colleague who gulped and shook his head.

'I thought not,' said Betty with more than a hint of pride. Clearly for her being possessed by an ancient sexual demon was something not to be sniffed at.

'Can I just ask why you think you have an incubus?' I asked.

And I then heard the answer I had been half expecting and dreading. 'My daughter looked it up on the Internet.'

'You can't believe everything you read on the Internet,' suggested my colleague.

'But it was in the *New York Times*,' Betty responded, 'it must be true.'

There was really no answer, other than to suggest that in this instance President Trump was right when he spoke about fake news. (In fact I believe the *New York Times* is one of the news outlets he most often accused of this.)

Despite the faintly comic nature of the situation, this was a real person who was calling for help, so I knew we needed to go back to basics.

'Can you tell us what exactly the problem is, and how it started?' I asked.

'It started a couple of months ago,' Betty began, and then backtracked. 'Maybe I'd better start at the very beginning. I've been living here since my husband died. We used to live just up the road, but I decided that when he died, five years ago, I didn't need to live in a big house all on my own, so I found this place, and I fell in love with the views, and it helps that my daughter and her family live at this end of town. My husband had been very ill for quite a few years before he died – cancer,' she explained, 'but since that time I haven't been interested in, you know, men,' and she glanced down, the fingers on her hand twisting slightly as she rubbed the thick gold band of her wedding ring. She looked up and her eyes filled with a fierceness. 'When you have had champagne, you don't want watery beer, and my husband, he was champagne.' She looked over at a photo of a man in late middle age.

My colleague nodded, 'No, of course not.'

'Do you understand? I haven't been with a man from that day to this.'

We both nodded solemnly, feeling slightly uncomfortable. But it was to get worse. 'A couple of months ago, as I said, things started to go wrong down below if you know what I mean.' She didn't stop to find out, but I suspect that the expression of pained embarrassment on my colleague's face was mirrored on my own. 'I had this rash, you see. So, I went to the doctor, and she examined me and then gave me a prescription for some cream to put on it. I asked her what was causing it, and she laughed and said, "Relations".' The woman snorted with indignation despite the slightly bizarre euphemism. For me 'relations' usually refers to members of the family, but quite clearly the meaning this time was sex.

It was at this point that I wished that we had known a bit more about what was happening in Betty's life before arranging the visit, because it seemed highly inappropriate to have a woman discussing the intimate details of her health with two men. Strangely, Betty quite clearly didn't seem to mind at all.

She continued. '"Relations!" I said to her, "That's impossible!" But the doctor just laughed,' she said with a degree of scorn.

'Did the cream work?' I asked weakly.

'I've no idea, I just threw it away. Quite clearly, I didn't have anything that was caused by doing *that*! I've never been near a man from the day my husband died to this.'

And I believed her. 'So, what happened then?' I asked.

'Well, the more I thought about it, the more I realised that there is this thing – this incubus – which is sort of attached to me. I can feel it now, like it's sitting up here between my shoulder blades,' she gestured towards the afflicted area. 'You can't see anything. You can't feel anything. But I know it's there: I can feel its weight.'

Naturally my colleague and I looked towards her back, and yes, she was right, there really was nothing at all to see.

'And then, at night, when I am in bed, I can feel it climbing down my back, and then it enters me, and it stays there until morning when it climbs back up my back.'

There was a stunned silence for a few moments, at least I hope it was for a few moments, because it felt like hours.

'Thank you for telling us,' I croaked eventually, 'it must be very difficult to live with.'

'Yes, it is. I don't get very much in the way of rest, to be honest.'

'Does it happen absolutely every night?' I asked, getting back into my stride.

Betty thought for a moment. 'Yes, it does,' she said eventually, as if she had to convince herself. 'Yes, definitely.'

'OK, thanks,' I said.

'So, your daughter thinks it's an incubus?' ventured my colleague.

Betty nodded enthusiastically. 'Yes, that's right, but she also found out how to deal with it too.'

We both looked blankly at her. Betty's certainty started to evaporate. 'Well, she told me what the *New York Times* said, anyway.'

There was a further lull in the conversation. One of us was going to have to ask her what it was. Eventually I broke the silence. 'And what did it recommend?'

'Well, it said first of all to get some dried sage, and to set fire to it so that you could smoke all the rooms of the house,' – Betty's eyes drifted around the mushroom-coloured walls with their tasteful watercolours – 'and,' she continued, 'to get some dark rum, not any of that Bacardi, mind, but real dark rum, and then to hold it in your mouth and to spit it in all the corners of the rooms.'

There was a further stunned silence. We weren't doing very well on the conversation front. Again, I felt that someone needed to speak. 'I wouldn't do that,' I said, looking at the ceiling, 'you would get all the neighbours out if you did that, because it would set all the smoke alarms off.'

Betty looked worried. 'Is the smoke that bad?'

'Yes, I'm afraid it is,' I answered, 'I was called to a shop not so long back where they had got in a pagan practitioner just before me who had smoked the building with sage. The smoke was really thick and acrid. I can see why they thought it might work, I can't imagine anyone wanting to stay with all that smoke around,' I heard myself say, trying to make light of the situation.

'So, it worked?!' exclaimed Betty eagerly.

'No, it didn't, which is why they got me round to bless it afterwards.'

'And did that work?' she asked.

'I think so, at least they never complained about it again.'

'Can you do that for me here?'

'What, bless the house for you? Of course, we can,' I responded.

'And the rum . . . ?' she asked hesitantly.

'I have to admit that's a completely new one on me,' I said, shrugging. 'As far as I'm concerned, the only good thing to do with rum is to drown it in Coke.'

Betty relaxed a bit. 'Would blessing the house help with the incubus?'

I thought for a moment. 'I don't think it would, to be honest. In fact, I think the best thing you can do is to go back to the doctor, or maybe see another doctor if you can for a second opinion. Do you think that might be a possibility?'

It was Betty's turn to think. 'Yes,' she said eventually, 'the doctor I saw was a locum. In fact they are all locums at that practice.'

'So, it shouldn't be too difficult, then.'

'No,' she said. 'Will it help?'

'Yes, I think it will. But we can bless the house and also pray for you too for God to heal you. Do you know whether you'd been baptised or christened?' I asked.

'Yes, and confirmed too.'

'That's great,' I said, and offered to anoint her with the oil for healing, which she agreed to readily.

It is one of the great privileges of ministry being allowed into someone's home, and Betty's home was, like so many I had seen over the years, almost spartan: there were a few ornaments on the fireplace, a few watercolours, and one or two family pictures, but almost nothing else in the living room. The kitchen was new and spotlessly clean, and the rest of the house was immaculate, but there were very few personal touches. As always, when we are blessing a house, we spend the most time in the room where the perceived paranormal activity has taken place. In this case, this was obviously Betty's bedroom. There was a large pink teddy bear on the bed, and some fitted wardrobes, but, again, very little else. We offered to bless one of the olivewood crosses I often carry round with me, and, again she agreed. Finally, we anointed her with the oil, and we stood back.

'It moved when you were saying the prayer,' she commented,

'but it's still there on my back.' And then she relaxed again. 'Do you really think I need to go to the doctors again?' she asked with a degree of reluctance.

'Definitely,' I said, and meant it.

'OK, I'll do that,' she said, sounding as if she had come to some sort of resolution: 'Yes, I will.'

'Good,' I smiled, and we took our leave as she promised her vicar she would be back in church on Sunday.

We walked back to the car park together. 'What did you make of that?' asked my colleague.

'Strange, really, because I've never come across an incubus before, even if I think that wasn't the problem at all. You?'

'Hmm,' said my colleague, 'I know what you mean. I started off thinking that it might be a genuine possession,' – I think he saw me wince – 'but like you,' he continued hastily, 'I'm not so sure now.'

'Yes,' I said, 'it reminds me of a case I had a while ago, where someone had somehow managed to convince themselves that they were being eaten by giant rats,' – my colleague looked genuinely shocked – 'but it turned out to be cancer.'

'Does that happen often?' he asked, sounding as shocked as he looked.

'Not too often, but the mind does all sorts of strange things,' I mused. 'In this case, I think the most important thing is that Betty gets to see a doctor as soon as possible, because she may have some sort of gynaecological problem that she doesn't want to admit to.'

My colleague thought for a few moments as we stood by the cars. 'Perhaps I'll ask one of the friendly women churchwardens to take Betty under her wing, without telling her, of course, what the problem is. Do you think that would be a good idea?'

'I think that sounds like a splendid idea, to be honest.'

'OK, I'll do that.' Sadly, like so many deliverance cases, I never did find out what had happened.

I did, however, ask a friend who knows about these sorts of things about the whole idea of the incubus.

'Is this one of your deliverance cases?' she asked. I admitted that it was.

'Was the woman in question of childbearing age?'

'No, would that make a difference?' I asked.

My friend laughed. 'Of course it would,' she explained, as if I were about five years old. 'The point of an incubus is that they get women pregnant. And he's quite clearly barking up the wrong tree if she's never going to have his baby.'

I thought it best not to pursue this line of thought.

'You're going to tell me next you don't know anything about what a succubus is,' she continued. I muttered something, and allowed her to enlighten me. I also looked up burning sage on the Internet, apparently known as 'smudging'.

It appears to be a common practice in the West Indies and has been adopted by Wiccans – followers of what they would see as white witchcraft. Only one article I found mentioned it in common with rum, but that was Jamaican white rum, so even the type of rum was wrong, and it didn't even appear to have come from the *New York Times*!

## But I really am possessed!

Up and down the Welsh Marches are a series of market towns, many of them with a large church. In the centuries before the Norman Conquest, the Anglo-Saxon Kingdom of Mercia established not only its border with Wales in the form of the famous Offa's Dyke, named after the eighth century King, but also established a series of trading posts just to the Mercian side, where the Welsh could come to trade valuable commodities such as the sheep for which they have always been famous. So, pretty much in a straight line from Chester on the Dee not far from the sea to Gloucester there is a series of these places, spaced roughly fifteen miles apart. Fifteen miles was not a random number, of course, because it was considered the furthest distance which someone could be reasonably expected to travel to market; if you lived an equal distance between two markets, you would have to travel just over seven miles to get to one, and seven miles to get home. Most people, of course, lived closer to one or another.

And this ancient border is still there, and the towns and cities still dominate the border regions: Chester, Wrexham, Oswestry, Shrewsbury, Church Stretton, Ludlow, Leominster, Hereford, Ross-on-Wye and Gloucester. They are all just to the east of Offa's Dyke or on the River Wye, and they are all in England, other than Wrexham where, in the years immediately before the Norman Conquest, the local Welsh kings of the Kingdom of Powys Fadog pushed past the traditional barrier, and took over a large amount of the fertile Cheshire Plain as far as the River Dee itself.

So, Wrexham is on the English side of Offa's Dyke, but is very definitely a Welsh town, proud of its position as North Wales's largest town. But there is a difference between it and most of the other settlements in North Wales, because Offa's Dyke not only marks the place where English place names give way to Welsh, but even to this day Wrexham remains what it always has been: an English-speaking town.

As I said, each of these places has a rather splendid church. For the whole of the Middle Ages, the only cathedral in this line was at Hereford, although under Henry VIII the great

Abbeys at Chester and Gloucester became the cathedrals of newly founded dioceses, and the Abbey Church of Shrewsbury narrowly missed out on becoming a cathedral under the Victorians. Each of the main churches on the list are worth visiting in their own right, although the parish churches at Ludlow, which was at one stage *de facto* capital of Wales, and Wrexham itself are particularly splendid, both having massive mediaeval towers which dominate their towns, visible for miles around. These churches have a grand civic feel about them, and seem to have ridden out the storms that have surrounded them, because storms there were.

The Mercians seemed to have reached some sort of accommodation with the Welsh, and along the border close to Offa's Dyke, they seem to have created their own mutually dependent culture. But the Normans saw things differently, partly maybe as a result of incursions such as the one that created that Welsh-governed enclave on the Cheshire Plain. So, they set up what they called the Marches, which were run by the Marcher Lords. The idea was that these Marchers were given licence to conquer as much territory as they liked as they pushed into Wales along this ancient line, and in the process a blind eye was turned to their methods. There are still stories told about their atrocities.

One story concerns what is now the sleepy market town of Abergavenny where, over Christmas 1175, a group of Welsh princes and lords led by Seisyll ap Dyfnwal were invited to banquet and to share their grievances by the Norman baron William de Braose. In supposed revenge for the killing of an ally, however, de Braose had Seisyll and his followers massacred. It was one of the causes of mistrust between the English and the Welsh in that part of the world, and some people reckon that the massacre has affected the town ever since, including even its church where de Braose was probably buried, although his tomb does not survive. (Strangely enough though Seisyll, whose name seems so amazingly Welsh, may have been the ancestor of a much more significant family even than de Braose, as an anglicisation of Seisyll produces that most English-looking of names Cecil. The name was made famous by Sir William Cecil, Lord Burghley, famous courtier of Elizabeth I, whose ancient ancestral home is found just north of Abergavenny right on the border.)

But Abergavenny was typical of the sort of town that was being built by the Marcher Lords. It was a walled garrison town, with a castle and a Benedictine priory church staffed by foreign monks, where the souls of the Lords could be remembered for eternity. There are many such towns dotted around the Marches – Monmouth, Brecon and Chepstow are fairly typical – and in many senses, Cardiff probably would have been before the great flood of 1607 swept so much of it away. These and others served as centres of Anglo-Norman influence for many years, and are still, to some extent, very often seen as 'posh' places by both their inhabitants and the less privileged folk who live around them. Each of the places I have named have rather lovely churches, but there are also other, smaller places in the Marches whose churches are, not to put too fine a point on it, positively creepy.

It is one of the strange things about buildings that they do seem to absorb events, which may well explain the idea of the place memory that we looked at earlier on. But churches seem somehow to amplify this sort of thing, and some churches really do have what one might call 'bad vibes'. And they are not all ancient churches by any means; more modern churches can be just as weird. In fact, there are some churches and parishes that seem to afflict people and clergy in particular. I have heard of at least one parish where *all* of the clergy over a fifty-year period have had breakdowns of some description or other, the worst resulting in the suicide of the vicar. This particular church was closed and demolished, but even then, the locals reported ghost lights in its grounds afterwards. There are other churches where clergy seem not to last very long and whose health is affected in other ways, for example by suffering multiple heart attacks, and although clergy are not always the healthiest or fittest of people they do tend enjoy long and happy retirements.

The suicide was that of a vicar of a modern church, but as I said, there are several ancient churches in the Marches I could name that people frequently cite as creepy. I visited one with my friend Pete whose house, you will recall, was once haunted by an old flame.

As we were wandering around, looking at the monuments, suddenly he appeared at my side. 'What's wrong with you?' I asked.

'I know it's stupid, but I just don't want to be left alone in this place,' Pete replied with a shudder, looking around.

'I know what you mean,' I said in a small voice, 'there is something really odd about this place.' We didn't stay long.

On another occasion I was with a different friend, this time, coincidentally, a fellow deliverance minister from a different diocese whom I'd met in a mutually convenient place for lunch. We walked into the church, and he stopped and cringed. 'What's wrong with this place?'

'I've got no idea,' I responded, 'but it gets me every time as well.'

'Do we have to stay?' he asked, looking around.

Another that we visited as a family seemed to be the most neglected and unloved building I had even seen in my life, complete with a jumble of mismatched chairs, and a pull-down projector screen attached to the mediaeval wooden rood screen.

It felt almost as if the spirit of the Marcher Lord who had lived just up the road had seeped into its very fabric, turning what should have been a very beautiful church into one that made one feel sad and scared at the same time.

There is another ancient border church that a fellow priest once described to me. 'We've got a really good congregation on a Sunday morning and it feels full of light and joy. But once they've gone, it's like someone had turned the lights off, and it becomes mysteriously dark and gloomy,' they said, 'and then you can't wait to get out. In fact, I once had to go in there on my own at night to collect something from the vestry. I managed to make it most of the way down the nave, but then about three-quarters of the way down, it suddenly felt cold, like, very cold, and I couldn't cope any longer. I'm ashamed to say I just ran the rest of the way, and if someone told me I was screaming, I wouldn't disbelieve them.'

It was in one of these churches on the Marches that we gathered to meet someone who was convinced she was possessed.

I was initially contacted by Sarah's local vicar, who said he had permission to pass on her emails to me. To be honest, this was a young woman who had done her research. She had clearly found a website that told her what Christian exorcists look for in someone they deem to be possessed, and told her vicar that she was being afflicted with them: she had been on a train home from London where she had been working as a waitress, and started to speak in Classical Arabic which, she said, she had never studied.

On another occasion Sarah said she had correctly predicted that a friend's father would die and was terrified when it actually happened. These, together with other things that she didn't mention in the emails, meant that she was quite clearly possessed, and therefore needed to be exorcised. In fact the phrase she used was major exorcism – she really had done her research.

The emails had been shared with me, but the vicar was really just asking for advice, rather than for me to do anything about them. Quite clearly the vicar didn't believe her. And I had my doubts, especially about the ability to speak Classical Arabic.

The ability to speak foreign or alien languages has an interesting history in Christianity. One of the strangest phenomena that is sometimes experienced in some Christian circles is technically known as glossolalia, or more often 'speaking in tongues' – 'tongues' being what the older translations of the Bible called 'languages'. It is sometimes linked with the incident that kick-started the Christian Church. This is described in the New Testament book of Acts, where in chapter two we learn that, after the death, resurrection and ascension of Jesus, the remaining disciples were gathered in a room together during the Jewish festival of Pentecost. While they were there, the Holy Spirit descended on them, looking like tongues of fire, and gave them the ability to speak in foreign languages so that they could communicate the good news about Jesus to the people around them in a way that they could understand. There is a spectacular list of names of places in the Bible at this point, which people who are asked to read this reading in church either know off by heart or struggle with. The point of the reading is that the Holy Spirit gives to the Church the means by which to communicate the good news about Jesus, but the languages mentioned were real living languages at the time.

There is, however, another possibly related phenomenon which is also mentioned in the Bible, and which is probably closer to modern-day 'speaking in tongues'. It, or something like it, is mentioned in St Paul's New Testament Letters where, particularly in Corinth, it was 'a thing'. What seems to have happened is that the early Christians were filled with enthusiasm and started to speak in languages that no one could understand, a sort of ecstatic babble. Paul is unimpressed, partly because the people who could do this thought that they were the spiritual elite, looking down on the people around them who couldn't do it. Paul's take on the whole thing seems to be that it is all right in its place, but not a huge amount of good if no one understands what you're talking about. In any event, the whole thing seems to have died out in the first century, and although Christians still read about it, no one seemed to know what 'speaking in tongues' was. In fact, some writers suggested that it was still to be found in the context of the singing of the Mass by the priest.

However, the whole idea of 'speaking in tongues' has come back into the Christian Church with a vengeance in the last century and a half, where this sort of spiritual phenomenon was characteristic of the revivals of the late nineteenth and early twentieth centuries, and is very often found in the Pentecostal Churches (named after the festival when the first Christians began to experience such things). At one of these church services, there will usually be a time when all of the congregation will sing gently in this ecstatic babble, starting off quietly and then usually rising to a gentle crescendo before tailing off into silence. In these churches, being able to participate in this singing in tongues as it is called is associated with something called the 'baptism of the spirit' and is something that parents earnestly want their children to experience. I remember once hearing a radio interview with someone who had been brought up in one of these churches who said that pretty much the first thing you learned to do was to fake it, such was the pressure to conform.

It also found its way into more mainstream churches through

the Charismatic Renewal movement of the 1960s, and now occurs in some form or other in most Western Christian organisations, including the Roman Catholic Church. It is also found in Anglicanism too and is usually associated with 'charismatic evangelical' congregations, although it is not restricted to them, by any means. So, for example, Justin Welby, the Archbishop of Canterbury, is open that he prays in tongues every day.

It is not something that I personally wish to dismiss, because on occasion it's happened even to me. The first time was one day when I was praying with a technique known as 'imaginative contemplation' where you imagine yourself standing in front of Jesus. I realised that I was praying quietly, but aloud, and that eventually I ran out of words, and found that the sounds were still coming. They really did appear to be words, but I didn't know what they meant, other than the fact that somehow they were words of prayer and praise. The whole thing probably didn't last more than about five minutes, and as I had heard at Charismatic Renewal meetings (but had never participated), the 'words' gradually subsided into silence, a quite deep, God-filled silence. Once I had come out of that I was, if not exactly angry with God, then a little bit miffed: good liberal catholic Anglicans do not habitually speak in tongues!

Given all this background I didn't dismiss it completely when Sarah claimed to have been speaking in Classical Arabic on a train from London. But I was still a little sceptical about some aspects of it, to say the least. I am pretty good on languages, ancient and otherwise, and to be honest, although I have a good idea of what modern Arabic sounds like, I wouldn't know if I were speaking Classical Arabic on a train, other than the fact that if I were doing it properly I'd feel ill, as, apparently, there are sounds in Arabic that are produced by a part of the throat that Europeans only use when they are vomiting. I have heard charismatic Christians claim that someone who was speaking in tongues was quite clearly speaking in Hebrew, despite the fact that no one present understood a word. So, given the ease with which one can fake such speech, and the fact that there was no one around who could verify that this was Arabic, Classical or otherwise, I found this unlikely as an indicator that this person was possessed.

The other suggestion about the prediction of a friend's father's death was maybe more interesting. There are, as we have already seen, psychics who are quite clearly not possessed, but who do have the ability to know things about the future. But as I looked at the details I had been given, that didn't seem to be what was going on with Sarah. I remember a friend of mine in school, for example, feeling really guilty because someone they knew had died unexpectedly. People always feel guilty when someone they know dies – it is one of the facts of human nature. What made this one different was that they had imagined the death the week before.

It is possible that this person had had a premonition, but it is just as likely that in the randomness of thoughts that we all have, one of them the previous week was about the death of this person. I can, however, guarantee that my friend was not possessed, and I wasn't convinced about Sarah either. And at the end of the day, once again, I only had her word for it.

The final 'test' of possession, that of preternatural strength, is the most difficult to fake, and I was interested that Sarah didn't seem to have demonstrated that one, although given the fact that with the others there didn't seem to have been any other witnesses, she might have gone for that one too.

You may think I'm being hard on poor Sarah, but I did feel very sorry for her. At the same time, I couldn't collude with her, because that may have done untold harm. In any case, I just had a series of emails to go on. So my advice to her vicar was that she was almost certainly not possessed, as much as anything else because if she had been possessed she would not have been seeking to be exorcised; as I have said before, if your entire body and will has been taken over by an alien entity it would not allow you to try to get rid of it.

The email was sent and the whole thing went quiet, until about six months later, when I was approached by the Bishop's Office to ask me to deal with Sarah, who didn't seem to be getting anywhere. Complaining to the bishop is the sort of thing that tends to get results (at least from rank and file clergy like myself) but doesn't exactly help you to win friends! So it was, I have to admit, a rather grumpy me who put the wheels in motion to meet Sarah. I spoke to her vicar, who said that he had known that she was getting in touch with the bishop, and he made the arrangements for me to meet Sarah in his church. I also called a friend who is a retired medic to come along with me, and she readily agreed. Given the sensitivities, I was particularly grateful to have a woman with me.

It was one of those winter afternoons where the sun never seems to come out and there is an oppressive grey sky above you, and you feel cold just being out and about. As I said, we were heading towards one of those ancient churches on the Marches that was famous for being, if not haunted, then creepy, and we were going there to meet someone who was absolutely convinced she was possessed by a demon – or so we thought. It was the sort of thing that you might think I'm making up, but it really was that bad. When we arrived, the light looked as if it was already fading, although, given the fact that it was only two o'clock in the afternoon, it was probably just a result of the clouds looming above us. We parked in a side street and then approached the church. It was a fine and in fact remarkable piece of architecture, although we were approaching it via what seemed to be a cutting through the mounded-up churchyard. We looked at one another. We knew without saying that we were walking through what were almost certainly piles of human remains which had mounted up over the centuries during which the churchyard was the only place to be buried. Such things don't usually bother clergy – they bother other people a lot more – but they did at the time.

Anyone who has been a priest for any length of time gets used to the fact that at some stage you will come into contact with the dead. Occasionally, we will be asked to see the body of a newly deceased loved one. This has happened to me once or twice in my ministry, although I understand that it was much more common in days gone by. On a couple of occasions, I have actually had the privilege to be called in where someone is dying to say prayers for them and for the family gathered around, even though the first time it happened I hadn't met the family before, and had been called in by the hospital because all the other clergy had better things to do on a Saturday evening. Actually so did I, but I went anyway, and it was a deeply moving occasion.

Clergy, of course, perform funerals, and so we come into contact with the dead, although they are always in coffins of various descriptions. Only once have I been asked to do an 'open coffin' funeral of the type that was common once in the South Wales Valleys, but which is now, I suspect, very rare indeed (and, yes, the coffin was in the front room). We also are involved with the burial of ashes, and in the case of my own mother and my wife's aunt, I became responsible for bringing the ashes to the place of burial: mum's ashes were in a casket, but the others were to be poured into the ground, a task I found myself doing, surrounded by the rest of the family who kept a safe distance.

But then there are the remains of those long-dead, and these are to be found both in the churchyard and, in the case of an older church, within the building. In fact, in any church older than about 1800, the chances are that you are walking over the remains of past parishioners. When people move things around in old churches, or take up floors, they will frequently find jumbled-up human bone, which will then be reburied with great reverence in a more convenient place. Just occasionally, human bone will surface in churchyards too, although this is not as common an occurrence, you will probably be pleased to know.

The whole idea of burying the dead inside churches goes back apparently to the fact that the early Christians worshipped sometimes in the catacombs in Rome, and in other cities in the ancient world, partly because they were safe from persecution there, but also because they were comforted by the physical presence of at least the bones of the apostles, or of others who had been great examples of holiness.

On this occasion, however, walking through the grave mounds on a bleak winter's afternoon, the presence of the Christian dead was not in any way comforting. In fact, I think I would say it had quite the opposite effect. So, making it as far as the door of the church itself, we pushed it open, and yes, it did open with a satisfying creak. We then had to fight with the thick velvet curtain that someone had fixed to the inside of the door in an attempt to keep out the draft.

We walked in, and looked around.

The church had a singular air of being unloved and just being sad. It wasn't sinister in the way that I had remembered from previous visits, but it didn't feel friendly either. At that point, we heard a clatter from the other end of the building, so we went to investigate. As we walked towards the far end near the altar, we heard the unmistakable sound of a photocopier springing into life.

'Hello,' said a bright and friendly voice, 'have you come to see the vicar? He said he'd be in later on, so I thought I'd come in and do the news-sheets for Sunday. Would you like a coffee while you wait?' The voice came from a blonde woman in her early sixties, dressed in the classic attire of a country lady – not uncommon in the nicer parts of the Marches. She explained that she was the parish secretary. 'I love spending time in the church,' she breezed happily, 'it's got such a lovely, peaceful atmosphere.'

My friend and I looked at one another. Neither of us felt the need to say anything at all.

The lady handed us both a cup of instant coffee with some powered milk floating in the top. 'It's the best I can do,' she smiled. My friend liked freshly made real coffee. She stared at the cup, and then clearly decided that it was the best that was available, and was better than nothing. I was one step ahead: it tasted like it looked, but then, as I have said before, clergy get used to drinking what they are given.

The secretary buzzed around, her printing finished, as she looked for something else to do while she was waiting for the vicar. She didn't have to wait long, because from the back of the church, we heard a muffled creak as the door was opened, and the faintly reassuring sound of someone else fighting with the velvet curtain.

I knew the vicar slightly, but given the nature of the diocese and the geographical spread, this was the first time we had worked together on anything. He was also relatively new to the area. 'Thank you very much for coming over,' he said, as he held out his hand. 'I know it's a long way, but I really appreciate it.'

We both shook his hand, and he muttered something before disappearing into the office where the parish secretary was still at work. We heard him explain that he had a private meeting, but he accepted the offer of a coffee. Very soon, the secretary had breezed out, all smiles.

'I've asked Sarah to come a bit later,' he explained, 'so that we could have a quick chat before she arrives. You both know some of the background?'

We both nodded. 'Well, I'm going to leave it to you as much as possible, although obviously I'll stay around if you like.'

We agreed that it would probably be a good idea if he did. 'That's no problem. I'm here to help,' he responded.

'The church seems different from the last time I came,' I commented.

'Thank you for noticing,' he smiled. 'I've been here a couple of years, now. When I came there were all sorts of stories around about the church being haunted by the lords of the manor,' he gestured to a huge tomb in the corner of the church, where clearly they were buried. 'I've spent a lot of time here praying, so I'm pleased you think it's better.'

'Yes,' I said, 'it feels like a good place to meet Sarah. And if you're happy, *I'll* take the lead on this.' He nodded.

At this stage there was a clatter and the creaking sound of the door, but because the secretary had had the sense to tie the velvet curtain back, at least Sarah did not have the indignity of arriving with a face full of slightly damp smelling drapery. You never know what to expect when you meet people in deliverance work, but Sarah was small, dark haired, and had bright intelligent eyes, although they had red rims as if she hadn't slept well recently. She did, however, have a commanding presence about her, and if she was daunted by our presence, she hid it very well indeed.

'Thanks for coming, Sarah,' I began, once we had made the necessary introductions. 'Can you tell us in your own words what's been happening?'

And so, she began. 'It started a few years ago when I was a student. I was going through a bit of a bad patch at the time, in fact, I had just split up with my boyfriend, who was also one of my housemates. I was just sitting in my room when my shoes started moving on their own, just like someone was moving them around, but there was no one there. So, I looked it up on the Internet,' I hope that at this stage I didn't groan out loud, 'and it said that if this happened, then you are possessed.'

It was one of those moments when I wanted to scream, but I didn't. I managed to stay calm, and said, 'OK, thank you. What else has been going on?'

'Well, since then, I realised that I have been afflicted with a series of demons. In fact the number changes every day. So, if you ask them how many there are, they will answer.'

We just looked at her.

'Look, I'll demonstrate. How many are you today?' And a voice that was very much like Sarah's answered, 'Forty-two thousand, seven hundred and six.' Sarah smiled triumphantly. 'You see, it doesn't even sound like me.'

'OK,' I said, trying to keep the scepticism out of my voice.

'No, you try, see. How many are you now?' she said, and replied in the same voice, 'Thirty-seven thousand, eight hundred and twenty-seven. You see, they change all the time, but they always tell me their name is Legion.'

'Well,' I thought, 'at least someone knows their Bible!' But aloud I said, 'Yes, thank you for that. Is there anything else?'

Sarah looked startled. 'Isn't that enough!? How much more proof do you need that I am in need of a major exorcism?'

I looked at her and said, 'I'm really sorry about this, Sarah, but I don't think anything you've told me so far has led me to believe that you are in any way possessed, and so I can't possibly perform a major exorcism on you.'

'But I spoke in Classical Arabic on the train,' she said desperately, and in minute detail she told us the story.

'But how do you know it was Arabic?' I asked as gently as I could.

'Er . . . It sounded like it,' she almost pleaded. And then she sat up. 'But if I'm not possessed, how can I know stuff that I shouldn't?'

'People sometime pick things up from what's going on around them,' I explained, 'or, maybe you're psychic, as some people are,' and I told her a little bit about Frank's story.

'But, my shoes moved. Don't you believe me?'

'Yes, I believe your shoes moved.'

She looked puzzled.

I continued, 'It happens to all sorts of people all the time, but it doesn't mean they are possessed.' It was her turn to look sceptical. So, I told her a little bit about my experience of dealing with poltergeists.

'But this voice, that's not mine. See! You're a bad girl, Sarah. That's not my voice.' But, of course, it was – in fact it sounded exactly like her normal voice.

All told it was one of the longest conversations I have ever had as a deliverance minister, and it went around in circles over and over again. There were different details every time, but nothing that would make me change my mind: whatever else was going on in this poor girl's life, it was psychiatric, not spiritual.

We talked about the fact that she was on anti-psychotic medication which, she claimed, made very little difference, because she was, of course, possessed. Sarah was increasingly desperate to try to convince us of this, until after about an hour of patient explanation she said, 'So you're not going to conduct a major exorcism, are you?'

'No, I'm really sorry, we're not,' I said, 'but we can bless you, and give you Holy Communion if you like.'

'And, of course, you're going to splash me with holy water to see if I react, because if I'm really possessed I will react,' she said enthusiastically. 'I know all the things you exorcists use to find out if people are possessed.'

I had not intended to splash her with holy water. In fact, other than my own congregation on the occasions when we renew our baptismal vows (usually at Candlemas and Easter), I don't tend to splash people with holy water – I'm not Van Helsing after all!

This, however, resulted in about twenty minutes more discussion about the fact that she thought she was possessed, with me pointing out just as firmly that I was pretty much convinced she wasn't.

Eventually we agreed the way forward. I had brought the holy oil that you will all be familiar with by now, and also I had brought consecrated bread and wine, the Holy Communion, although I had come prepared to celebrate a full Eucharist if necessary. So, we got up.

It was only at this point that we realised that sitting in the same position in a very cold church for an hour and a half is not a good idea. My legs felt numb, and I desperately hoped I would not fall over, because Sarah would no doubt have seen that as a sign of the demons at work. I successfully staggered to the altar with my bag, and started to fish out the things that I needed.

'Ah, holy water, I knew it. You *are* going to splash me with it.' Sarah was almost exultant.

'No,' I said, 'it's just fresh water for cleaning the vessels after we've used them.'

I placed the bottle to one side of the altar, and then laid the square linen corporal on it and with it the small silver oil stock with the holy oil. I then took the silver box with the hosts, the consecrated bread – the Body of Christ – and counted out four onto the paten, the small gold plate set aside to hold them. The consecrated wine – the Blood of Christ – was in a small glass bottle, so I poured a small amount into the small gold chalice. The candles had already been lit, and a crucifix was placed on the altar.

Sarah muttered, 'This is really bad,' under her breath, and then said, 'That was them not me.'

I just nodded and handed her one of the cards with the order of service on it, and then handed another to my colleagues, who had remained very quiet during the whole thing.

Sarah barely flinched during the service. She was an occasional churchgoer, so the whole thing would have been very familiar to her, and only when she was presented with the chalice did she react at all, but it was more of a twitch than anything else. I anointed her with the holy oil on her hands and on her forehead, and then I allowed a few moments of silence before clearing the altar. It was only at that stage, when I was rinsing the chalice with what I thought was fresh water, that I realised from the salty taste that I had grabbed the wrong water, and that this was in fact holy water, but I still resisted the temptation to splash some at Sarah, not, of course, because I was worried that she would react, but because I *knew* she would, and would use it as a demonstration that she really was possessed after all.

Sarah and the others went back to their chairs, although I noticed that my friend didn't sit down. I walked over to them.

'Thanks, Sarah. I am very pleased to tell you that I am absolutely convinced you are not possessed,' I announced.

'Really?' she seemed surprised, 'why?'

'If you were possessed, the demons really would have reacted to what we've just done, and because they didn't, we can say categorically that whatever else is happening, you're not possessed.'

Sarah looked puzzled, but then sort of pleased. 'Er, thanks,' she said, but before we could begin the conversation again, the vicar made it clear that he needed to be somewhere else, so we made our way to the door.

'These voices?' asked Sarah.

'Have you thought about investigating Tourette's syndrome?' I suggested.

'I haven't got Tourette's,' she said indignantly.

'Maybe not, but worth looking at how people with Tourette's cope with their problems.'

'OK,' she said grudgingly. 'Anyway, thanks for this afternoon.'

'You're welcome,' I said and went back down the path with my friend, although this time the mounds seemed a good deal less threatening.

'What did you make of that?' I asked as we got to the car.

'Poor soul,' she said, 'she *did* so want to be possessed.'

'It takes all sorts,' I sighed, and then looked up. 'Hey, the sun is coming out,' and just for a few moments, we finally saw the sun.

Like so often with these cases, I'm not sure whether Sarah was satisfied, but I haven't heard from her (or indeed, the bishop at least on this matter) since, so I assume that things have settled down for her.

# Chapter 10

## *In which we say goodbye*

The BBC is one of the great national institutions that was set up 'to inform, educate and entertain', an ideal I hope I have managed to achieve in this book.

The whole subject of deliverance ministry in the Anglican Church has been long under wraps for good pastoral reasons. No one wants everyone to know that they have had a visit from the deliverance team to bless their house – well, almost no one anyway. It has by and large been treated almost in the same way as hearing confessions; people are frequently amazed that Anglican priests do such things. The difficulty, of course, is that if people don't know you are offering a service, then they can't access it, and if this book has in any way demystified the Church's response to the ministry of deliverance for you, and told you that help if you need it is at hand and free of charge, then it will have served a useful purpose.

It may also have given you some sort of insight into the life and work of a priest – maybe you'll never look at your vicar in quite the same light again! And if you have also gleaned some idea of what we believe and why, that's good too.

Most importantly it is worth saying that the experience of paranormal activity is no respecter of persons. The people whose stories I have told come from a range of socio-economic backgrounds, and although some of them were experiencing some sort of psychiatric disorder, we know that this is also a well known feature of contemporary life.

And finally, if you are experiencing some sort of paranormal activity of any description, please do not immediately look it up on the Internet, because someone out there will tell you that you're possessed. Instead please get in touch with the local deliverance minister, either through your vicar or through your local diocese, and they will be able to offer you all the support you need. Because there are a lot more of us deliverance ministers out there than you might ever have imagined!

# Acknowledgements

For years, parishioners and friends have been saying, 'You could write a book', so here it is, even though I needed a lot of persuading that it was a good idea. Firstly, thanks to Luigi Bomoni at LBA for seeing the potential; to Hannah Schofield and all the others there, as well as to Ben Dirs who pointed me in the right direction. I am also very grateful to Mark Booth from Coronet for rescuing me from being fed to the tabloids one week at a time, and for his light-touch editing; to Erika Koljonen, Becca Mundy and everyone at Hodder for taking more care of the book than I did; to Sadie Robinson in particular who spotted a whole host of ghastly mistakes, as well as to Nicola Thatcher for her guidance, and Jonathon Price for his sharp proofreading. Thanks also to Max Miechowski for taking such wonderful pictures (sadly they were of me), and to Libby Earland and Natalie Chen at Hodder for the artwork. Thanks, too, to Dominic Gribben for organising the audiobook and to Liam Wheatley for his infinite patience while I was recording it, and also to Steve Jones at ROC2 Studio in Wrexham for making it possible. Phil Rickman took time out from Merrily to read the manuscript, and to make some very kind comments, so my thanks to him too.

Various friends and members of my family have encouraged me and made sure I have all the details correct, so thanks to my father – Fred Bray, to Gaynor, Tiffeny and Fiona; to Steve and Helen; to Trish who read an early draft; to James who didn't, and to Ann in the St Giles' office who offered to proofread, as well as all those who told me their spooky stories – you know who you are! A particular word of thanks goes to Anna Morrell in the Church in Wales office for encouragement and a huge amount of help; also to the Rt Revd Gregory Cameron, the Bishop of St. Asaph for his generous support; and to Bishop Dominic Walker for some technical advice and early encouragement in this ministry.

My colleagues in the deliverance world have unwittingly contributed a huge amount to this book, including the St Asaph Team past and present: Robert, Lynette, Rex, Trish, Neil and Daniel, as have some of my more immediate colleagues in various parish settings, so thanks also to David, Cheryl, Rob, Rufus, Phil, Heather and James, most of whom appear in various guises in these pages. My parishioners in Wrexham have been an astonishing source of support too.

It's worth saying that, although each story is basically true, in every case, details have been changed, so to them, and to all the others whose names are now lost in my memory, my thanks.

Finally, I would like to say that my immediate family have helped keep me sane during the process of writing these memoirs, but maybe 'grounded' is a better word, so my love and heartfelt thanks to Laura, Thomas and Benedict Bray to whom I dedicate this book.